Confessions of a

Rebel Debutante

Confessions of a

Rebel Debutante

A Cordial Invitation

ANNA FIELDS

G. P. PUTNAM'S SONS
New York

G. P. PUTNAM'S SONS
Publishers Since 1838
Published by the Penguin Group
Penguin Group (USA) Inc., 375 Hudson Street, New York, New York 10014, USA •
Penguin Group (Canada), 90 Eglinton Avenue East, Suite 700, Toronto, Ontario M4P 2Y3,
Canada (a division of Pearson Penguin Canada Inc.) • Penguin Books Ltd, 80 Strand,
London WC2R 0RL, England • Penguin Ireland, 25 St Stephen's Green, Dublin 2,
Ireland (a division of Penguin Books Ltd) • Penguin Group (Australia), 250 Camberwell Road,
Camberwell, Victoria 3124, Australia (a division of Pearson Australia Group Pty Ltd) •
Penguin Books India Pvt Ltd, 11 Community Centre, Panchsheel Park, New Delhi–110 017,
India • Penguin Group (NZ), 67 Apollo Drive, Rosedale, North Shore 0632,
New Zealand (a division of Pearson New Zealand Ltd) • Penguin Books (South Africa) (Pty) Ltd,
24 Sturdee Avenue, Rosebank, Johannesburg 2196, South Africa

Penguin Books Ltd, Registered Offices:
80 Strand, London WC2R 0RL, England

Library of Congress Cataloging-in-Publication Data

Fields, Anna.
Confessions of a rebel debutante: a cordial invitation / Anna Fields.
p.   cm.
ISBN 978-0-399-15631-1
1. Fields, Anna—Childhood and youth.   2. Young women—United States—Biography.
3. Teenage girls—North Carolina—Burlington—Biography.   4. High school students—
North Carolina—Burlington—Biography.   5. Debutantes—North Carolina—Burlington—
Biography.   6. Burlington (N.C.)—Biography.   7. Burlington (N.C.)—Social life and
customs.   8. Los Angeles (Calif.)—Biography.   9. New York (N.Y.)—Biography.   I. Title.
CT275.F5516A3   2010   2009036950
975.6'58043092—dc22
[B]

Printed in the United States of America
1   3   5   7   9   10   8   6   4   2

BOOK DESIGN BY NICOLE LAROCHE

While the author has made every effort to provide accurate telephone numbers and Internet addresses at
the time of publication, neither the publisher nor the author assumes any responsibility for errors, or for
changes that occur after publication. Further, the publisher does not have any control over and does not
assume any responsibility for author or third-party websites or their content.

Penguin is committed to publishing works of quality and integrity.
In that spirit, we are proud to offer this book to our readers;
however, the story, the experiences, and the words
are the author's alone.

For Momma, Daddy, Sangy, Granny Blanche, Granny Ruth and all my fellow Rebel Debutantes out there . . . and for my wonderful Justin, who keeps me from gettin' too big for my britches . . .

Contents

Confessions of a

Rebel Debutante

Introduction

"How do you do?"
"How do you do what?"

—MAE WEST

I've only got one good story: how I became a Rebel Debutante.

Folks ask me to tell it whenever I'm at parties. They're always interested in my upbringing because they envision "the South" as one of two stereotypes: either *Gone With the Wind* or Jerry Springer. They can't imagine that the truth lies somewhere in between . . . buried deep within an old-fashioned tradition known as "finishing" school.

"What is that?" these folks always ask. "What does it mean to be 'finished'?"

Two words: Wellingham Academy. A premier boarding school cultivating and educating many of the Southeast's most prized Debutantes.

A *Debutante* (or *Deb*)—a fancy-sounding French word that means "female beginner"—is basically a young lady from an aristocratic or upper-class family who has gone through *Cotillion*—the preparation years, usually from age eleven to nineteen. Once she's reached the age of maturity, her family introduces her to society at a formal presentation known as her "debut," "coming out" or "Debutante Ball."

Traditionally, a gal's Debutante Ball remained the kind of event only royalty and true blue bloods enjoyed. Nowadays . . . well, it's more just an excuse to get liquored up and dance.

Oh, listen to me. I'm getting ahead of myself, aren't I? Some rules of thumb to get you folks started.

To be a Debutante, your family (1) was generally loaded; (2) had lived in the area for several generations; and most important (3) everybody knew it. Like my Aunt Sandy always says, it helps to have roots . . . or better yet, somebody to vouch for them to the Deb Ball committee in charge of planning the whole dang thing. Southerners are all about lineage. Tracing it, talking about it and defending it. So to be chosen to Deb, your Great-Granddaddy Something-or-Other had better have sailed from England and landed somewhere around Charleston or Atlanta or New Orleans. And somebody in your family had better have saved his shipping records or birth certificate or lock of hair to prove it. Also:

♡ You were in all likelihood the product of a two-parent home.
♡ Neither you—nor anyone in your entire family, for that matter—had any history of divorce, drug addiction, illegitimate children or any kind of police history. Even

parking tickets could be considered marks against your ladylike reputation.

♥ As far as you knew, you were straight, and . . .

♥ Unless you were already married at eighteen, you were a virgin. Lesbians count as "virgins," but need not apply.

♥ For the most part, you had some kind of vague notion of going to college in the fall, but . . .

♥ You wouldn't study anything uppity-sounding like Neuroscience or Women's Studies that might turn you into a frigid bookworm or a man-hater (aka lesbian). And furthermore . . .

♥ You were sure to avoid winning any kind of academic awards that might intimidate the local bachelors and prevent you from getting married right after graduation. Or, at least, before the age of twenty-four, after which folks might start to question your fertility, your sexual orientation or your sanity. If all of these seemed to be normal by their standards and you still weren't married, you'd be quickly deemed an "old maid."

Most important, you promised to show up to all the pre–Deb Ball events. These were usually organized into a schedule that looked something like this . . .

Informational Meeting: April 15
Debutante Announcement Dinner: May 15
Mothers' Meeting: May 30

Parent-Sponsored Parties: August 18, October 13,
   November 9 and December 8
Photography Session: August 25
Dance Rehearsals: Sundays, October 28 through
   December 28
The Art Ball: November 9
Mother-Daughter Luncheon: December 27

And culminating with the big finale . . .

   The (insert city/town name here) Debutante Society Ball:
      December 28

For the Ball itself, as a soon-to-be Deb, you needed a poufy white dress big enough to swim in, matching kid-leather gloves, a bunch of big-ass flowers you could pin to your shoulder or strap around your wrist and call a "corsage," a willing date and a dutiful father.

His only job (notice how there aren't any "father-daughter"–designated events on the calendar?) was to escort you onstage, hold your arm as you bowed to the crowd and then waltz with you as gracefully as possible. That way, everybody would be convinced that you were now a grown-up and full-fledged member of society.

Meanwhile, your date was supposed to stand around looking chivalrous and eager to compete for your affections. That also meant completing an intricate "cutting in" ceremony where he whisked you out of your father's arms and into his own. This sounds romantic, but could end tragically. If he was a little clumsy, couldn't remember all the dance steps to an evening of songs like "My Girl" and (my Momma's all-time favorite) "Crazy," by Patsy Cline, or couldn't keep a straight face while older ladies remarked on what a handsome married couple you two would make someday, the whole night could be ruined.

The Deb Balls in Charleston, New Orleans and Charlotte were the oldest and most prestigious. These included the St. Cecilia Ball held in Charleston on the third Thursday of January every year and the Mardi Gras Balls (Rex and Comus) held in the winter.

The St. Cecilia Society of Charleston is so exclusive that no membership list exists and divorce or social disgrace results in automatic expulsion. Membership in this society is reserved for the eldest male child of a long-standing Charleston family.

In North Carolina, things are a little different. Debutantes are led by the "Terpsichorean Society." This is a Debutante committee in Raleigh composed of older women devoted to charitable work. Together, they decide who will be invited to Deb each year by sorting through various rounds of nominations by local-officials-slash-persons-of-high-standing in each Deb location, running background and financial checks on each nominee, and finally selecting a handful of girls—usually around twenty. The Society then issues invitations, usually in December/January, to those chosen.

That said, let me be clear: I wasn't. Chosen, I mean. And that means I'm not a Debutante—not officially, anyway.

Sure, I qualified for all of the above. And, sure, I went through Cotillion classes and riding lessons and even graduated at the top of my class at Wellingham . . . but I was never officially chosen to come out. And that meant I never had a Debutante Ball.

Even after all those years of learning how to dance and curtsy and sing real purdy in public, I wasn't even invited to the Ball. I was labeled too "rebellious" and, thus, completely and utterly rejected.

Long story short, I'm no Scarlett O'Hara, folks.

Oh, no.

She was way, way, *way* out of my league. Or so I—and the Deb Ball committee—thought at the time.

Still, a girl could dream. And like most Southern girls, I clung to the Scarlett O'Hara fairy tale. I wanted to walk before a crowd of people in a beautiful white dress. I wanted Rhett Butler to kiss me just so I could slap him across the face and call him a "scalawag"! I imagined him falling madly in love with me after that. Then I'd enjoy a perfect Debutante Ball with him by my side followed by a perfect *Gone With the Wind* wedding with Melanie Wilkes crying nearby. Afterward, Rhett and I would ride off into the sunset like a happily-ever-after movie ending.

And so I entered Cotillion classes at age eleven with stars in my eyes. Finally, a romantic little tomboy got to escape her sheltered adolescence! For a time, it was heaven. Boys, punch, cookies and new dresses . . . all set to quaint, old-fashioned parlor music our parents had preselected as "appropriate." I felt like I was finally, maybe, possibly on my way to becoming Scarlett, after all. I was becoming a real Lady.

What else could a girl need?

Right?

Wrong. As much as I'd tried to convince myself that becoming a Debutante was just another stupid, sexist and totally conformist goal . . . when I wasn't ultimately chosen to "come out," I'll admit: I was crushed.

Every time that I went home, surrounded by other girls chosen in my place, hearing their stories, attending their dress fittings, even attending their Balls as an "especially invited guest" . . . I got nostalgic for my Cinderella days. At first, I tried to deny my attachment to all those years playing princess, learning to waltz and curtsy and care for the finer, forgotten pleasantries of Southern life. But in the end, I wanted them back. For all my rebelling against my Southern roots, I ultimately regretted leaving home and giving up on Scarlett so soon.

I've covered the globe—from the red clay of the South, to Brown University, to L.A., New York and back home. I've worked for Diana Ross, a slew of "screamer" agents, one of the fakest "real" housewives of New York City and ended up one of the luckiest interns in soap opera history. Long story short: I've got more than a few wacky, crazy tales from my travels . . . and this book reveals them all.

Chapter One

Sugar and Spice and . . . Well, Mostly Just Sugar:

• A (Wannabe) Scarlett Is Born •

I wasn't always such a slick-slender-sexy-cool Rebel Deb, people. Oh, no.

Just like many of you reading this right now: I used to be the Fat Kid. That's right. Until I was fourteen, my blond, blue-eyed American Girl body was covered in many inches of seemingly unnecessary "baby fat." *And* I was taller than all the other girls at Hillcrest Elementary School, which made the whole thing worse. I was a tall, puffy white marshmallow with thick glasses, bad skin and—till my Momma abandoned perms for body waves—a "white girl" 'fro. I was no man-catching, car-stealing, trouble-causing Rebel Deb. Not yet.

But all that was about to change. . . .

Oh, would you look at me! I'm getting ahead of myself again.

Anna Lee Fields was born at exactly 8:25 p.m. on August 13 in

Alamance County Hospital, Burlington, North Carolina. That made me a dead-set Leo from the outset, in case anybody's into what my Momma calls "that star-readin' hooey." Dr. John Robert Kernodle, the same fella who delivered my Aunt Sandy in 1949, Momma in 1953 and me in 1981, took one look at my marshmallow tush and said, "Whooo boy, that's one helluva lady!" But he was overjoyed nonetheless. See, old John Robert was out playing a round of golf when he got word that Little Miss Marshmallow tush was coming. A superstitious man, JR believed the third time would be a good-luck charm for his upcoming "Master Putters" tournament. So he left the round, rushed to the hospital—full golfing gear and all—washed his hands and promptly moved the other doctor away from my Momma's now-exposed "fanny parts."

"That baby's mine!" he said.

Two hours later, a wannabe Scarlett O'Hara was born.

And John Robert, good ol' boy that he was, promptly finished his round of golf.

Because of my Daddy's job, we moved around a lot. Town-hoppin', Momma called it. Never outside Carolina, mind you, but all in all, we lived in four different cities: Burlington, Wilmington, Elon and Gibsonville. We started out where my whole family had lived for generations. Where my parents met—in high school—and later married at the same United Church of Christ altar as my aunt, uncle and grandparents. Burlington was a tiny, insular world of old "true South" families. As time passed, I learned that my Granddaddy's first mill, Anne Dean Hosiery, became Jefferies Socks and then Hole-in-None. But when the hosiery business started going downhill, the mill was sold . . . and resold . . . until, eventually, it ended up in the hands of so many different folks in so many different places that we all lost track.

Most folks in Burlington could trace their family trees back to King George II and thought Democrats "just needed a little time to grow up." In places like this, old folks got together to talk about their cemetery plots. They'd put together picnic baskets full of salmon cakes, cornbread and sweet tea and make their grandkids take trips to "visit Poppa" at the local boneyard. They'd actually lay blankets down on the ground and talk to the dead as they ate their lunch. It was a grassy, red clay throwback to Tennessee Williams, with local general stores selling peanuts and pigs' feet. There's still a Piggly Wiggly on Church Street and a farmers' market selling "pick 'em yerself" strawberries down the road. But my favorite all-time Fat Kid hangout was Woolworth's.

They sold just about everything a young'un could want at the Woolworth's in downtown Burlington. I even bought my first pet there. A fat-bellied hamster I named Sugar Foot, who was tragically mauled to death when I let him loose in the backyard to roam and some stupid kid's cat hadn't been fed in a week.

Inside Woolworth's, there were linoleum floors, an electric fly-swatter and lots of mosquitoes buzzing around, waiting to bite the creamy baby-fat-covered arm of a future Rebel Deb as she reached into the icebox.

They even had a lunch counter where folks used to order boiled weenies and country-style steak with gravy, poured all over a couple slices of Merita bread. Daddy used to order toast and an egg sunny-side up so he could rip the bread into pieces and dip them into the broken yolk. Back then, folks made sure to eat the gristle on their steak for extra protein. They also considered a couple pieces of iceberg lettuce slathered in ranch dressing part of "gettin' yer daily veggie-tables."

My Aunt Sandy's first real job was behind that lunch counter.

In Burlington in 1966, there weren't too many places for seventeen-year-olds to earn spending money—especially girls. They were pretty much stuck doing laundry, babysitting, typing up letters for businessmen or cleaning house for a neighbor. If they lived in a part of town where neighbors had the money for that sort of thing, of course. And, if that were the case, their Daddies probably wouldn't appreciate them working at all. 'Cause, in 1966, a white girl from an upper-class neighborhood working a lunch shift just didn't look right. Woolworth's was different. It was considered a higher class establishment during a time when folks took a bit more pride in their work. When gas stations were well-lit, well-attended and shined your Chevy or Ford till it gleamed like a new penny. When TV dinners were new and exciting after centuries of wood-fired stoves and non-self-cleaning ovens that left char all in your mashed potatoes. Back in Aunt Sandy's day, people came to the Woolworth's lunch counter for a four-course meal. So Caroll and Blanche didn't mind her picking up extra milk money there.

Her first day on the job, Aunt Sandy had a local farmer sit down and order a ham sandwich. Not exactly a full meal, so she thought this one would be an easy start. Except, the farmer insisted, his sandwich had to be on whole wheat (which nobody ate in those days), with the crusts cut off and the meat placed underneath the cheese, which had to be under the tomato, which had to be underneath the lettuce. Oh, and he wanted buttermilk—not whole—warmed in a glass to exactly room temperature. My Aunt Sandy, doting soul that she was, spent the next twenty minutes cutting crusts and placing tomato slices and warming buttermilk in a saucepan because in 1966 microwaves hadn't been invented yet. All for one measly little ham sandwich. And he didn't even tip. Nobody did in those days, much. It still takes some cajoling to get Granny Blanche to leave more than a dollar—in change—on her table at any restaurant. Back in 1966, even without the tip, you could get waitresses at Woolworth's to do all that. By the time I came along, things had changed.

In the '90s, everybody tipped—good service or no service. The waitresses barely looked at you before throwing down the check with your plate. And beneath it, the Woolworth's counter was nothing more than a worn-down slab of tiled plastic with four grubby stools in front—all of which, if you gave 'em a good spin, would fall right out of their screws and land on the linoleum floor.

Don't get me wrong—not every Woolworth's waitress was bad. One of them even became a role model to me, and sticks out in my memory to this day. She was an elderly lady with pink hair who wore the kind of horn-rimmed reading glasses nobody buys any-more, and even back then, you could only find in the back aisles of Asher-Mcadams drugstore on the seedy side of town.

That lady told me a lot of things during my hours spent slurping chocolate milk shakes at Woolworth's:

♡ The farther away you move, the more you'll want to come home.
♡ Be kind. Everybody you know is fighting her own silent battle.
♡ Things can't make you happy.
♡ People who say that don't know where to shop.
♡ If you stop accepting "no" in life, you might start get-ting a different answer.
♡ Some boys will tell you they love you when they don't mean it.
♡ You won't find any answers in a bar, but if you stay

a while and drink enough, you might just forget the questions.

~~~~~~

And my personal favorite . . .

~~~~~~

♡ Someday, you'll be a real Lady, Anna Lee. And the Panthers will win the Super Bowl.

~~~~~~

This lady was a dear soul to me, and very instrumental in my early girlhood. Last time I saw her, she lay sick on her deathbed. We had a good chat, wherein she reminded me to,

"Eat well. And wear clean underdrawers every day."

"Yes, ma'am."

"You got enough clean underdrawers?"

"Eight pair. Fruit of the Loom, size 12. That okay?"

"That'll be just fine."

Then she paused to take a drag off her Virginia Slim. How she bought cigarettes in her condition, I'll never know. But I suspect folks will sell you just about anything when you're dying.

"And—most of all—be sure to stay away from your Momma's cooking. It's bad for your fanny. Never catch a husband with a big fanny. Remember that."

"I'll remember."

Another pause for another drag off her Virginia Slim, and then . . .

"You sure you got enough clean underdrawers?"

She promised to send me a coconut cake she'd bought at the

church fellowship meeting, but it never arrived. She died a few days later. She'd caught "the cancer," and I didn't go back to Woolworth's ever again.

A few years later, Daddy picked us up and we moved to Wilmington, a beach town several hours away near the South Carolina border. Here, I discovered the joys of hunting fireflies at night, hanging upside down from dogwood trees and building forts in our backyard "crick" with local boys who didn't call me "fatty pants" like their bratty, future-Deb sisters. These kinds of girls weren't Rebels like me. They didn't get dirty or save up quarters to buy crickets as bait for catfishing. They didn't know what a catfish even looked like. And they sure as hell wouldn't have faced the local bully, Ricky Stevenson.

Ricky Stevenson lived near me with a broke-down–looking dog named Spud. In the early-'90s South, before (as my Momma would say) "we got invaded by Catholics, Mexicans and carpetbaggers looking for cheap living and better weather," four children to one household was almost unheard of. We were good Protestants, mind you. And good Protestants, as Momma would say, just "didn't go around having that many babies."

Little Ricky liked to hit. And chase. And cut his own switches from a dogwood tree—*my* dogwood tree, mind you—so he could make the hit-slash-chase game more interesting. So, one day, with the other boys watching, I decided to bet Ricky Stevenson he couldn't catch me and switch me if his life depended on it.

So he cut a switch and off we went.

Two of my closest "boyfriends," Brent Nelms and Greg Porterfield, sat waiting in the woods, as planned. Ricky had terrorized Brent and Greg and released a few coons into our stash of catfish—leaving us with buckets of fish heads floating in water instead of hard-earned prizes—so they were eager to help. As I spotted the prearranged spot up ahead and slowed my progress, Ricky caught up. After a few seconds, he'd almost overrun me. And boy was he happier than a pig in shit! As he neared my stopping point, he reached out, switch in hand, and laughed.

"Gotcha!" he screamed, and took a flying leap toward the special spot. . . .

Where he landed feetfirst inside a sinkhole of sand and clay, covered in leaves. He was instantly trapped, buried up to his waist in Southern soil, and that's where Brent and Greg came in. Together, we tied a hog rope around Ricky's wrists and strung him up, switch in hand. I think he finally chewed his way through the rope and made his way home well after bedtime. . . .

Where he was switched with his own dogwood branch.

Brent, Greg and I laughed our way into the next week. Our fourth-grade neighborhood bully was reduced to a shamefaced, welt-covered laughingstock. Life was good.

But our childhood bliss was short-lived. A few weeks later, in the middle of Christmas vacation, my parents moved us back to Burlington. . . .

And into my Granny Blanche's Big House.

Situated on the corner of Rockwood and Woodland Avenue, Granny Blanche lived in Burlington's version of *Peyton Place*. She'd had the same cook and housekeeper for forty years. Two ladies named June and Hattie, who took care of everything from ironing to gutting a chicken for Sunday dinner. Hattie even potty-trained my Momma when she was little.

Hattie wore a hat and was the feistier of the two. She also used to mix up her reactions to things. Every conversation we ever had went something like this:

"Hey, Hattie."

"Just *fine*, thankya!"

". . . Well, good, I guess. How are you?"

"Well, *Lawd*, if it ain't Miss Anna *Lee*! How you doin', Miss Anna Lee?"

"Just fine. And you?"

"Well, thankya for stoppin' by! You come back now, ya hear?"

And then she'd walk off to finish vacuuming. I always wondered if that machine did funny things to her hearing.

With Hattie and June's help, Granny Blanche kept the kind of house most Southern ladies only dreamt of: pink tile and monogram linens in the bathroom. Dainty tea sets in glass cases in the parlor. Chandeliers hanging above East India china on the mahogany dining room table. She was the best cook this side of Texas, mostly due to her seasoning vegetables with just the right mixture of salt, pepper and fat meat, so her kitchen always smelled delicious. She'd invite her whole bridge club over for dinner every week, and that's when she'd bring out the crystal cake plates and good silver from her mother, Great-Granny Sommers.

Most folks outside the immediate family called her Aunt Blanche. She was known for entertaining in that soothing, comfortable, refined manner practiced only by the most graceful of ladies. Always humble. Always caring. Never one to bring up religion or politics amongst polite company, Aunt Blanche—Granny, to me—was part of a generation that spoke few words but said volumes and set a greater example through their strength of character.

This strength of character is why, I suspect, for the past eighty or so years, almost everybody in my family got baptized, married and buried all at the First Christian United Church of Christ off Church Street in downtown Burlington.

Back then, almost everybody got married. It was pretty much expected. And they made sure to do so in church, in front of God, their peers and their families. That part was supposed to show off their character. So I was surprised to hear different from Blanche. She and my Granddaddy tied the knot on a military base in Tampa, Florida, in 1946.

Some girls, she told me, who got married on those bases were "in trouble." In those days, that meant they were already in the family way. Others didn't have Daddies who were willing to pay for the ceremony. And still others couldn't afford wedding dresses made out of anything but leftover parachute material.

This seemed to contrast the perfect household my grandparents eventually moved into. When I asked her why they chose to marry so far away from everyone and everything they knew, Granny Blanche's answer was simple: They were anxious and tired of waiting.

See, back then, most folks (or at least the women) waited till marriage to do, you know, the deed. Besides, when your sweetheart's been away in World War II for the last four years, I don't suppose it much matters where you say "I do." You're just ready to go ahead and say "I did." Even a ten-year-old could understand that.

Blanche's newlywed husband was a self-made man. Caroll (who used to be "Carol," but Granny Blanche added an *l* on their marriage license because it looked more manly that way) Jefferies came from Gaffney, South Carolina. When he was seventeen and his dead Daddy's second wife couldn't feed them anymore, he left home for the army. About a year later, he wound up locked in an abandoned barn all night, trapped on one end of an old-fashioned shoot-out with a German soldier, and was later poisoned by Axis-power sympathizers. Apparently, cyanide makes your whole body swell up, and can give you elephantiasis of the nuts. Caroll was pretty sure he'd never father children, and back then, that also meant he was unlikely to marry. So he set out to make his fortune.

If you can't have love, why not try money?

He made his fortune by teaching himself how to make socks. He spent almost every afternoon watching a local weaver at his loom and then went to work in North Carolina's second biggest postwar industry: hosiery milling. A child of the Great Depression, he'd already met Blanche a while back at her Daddy's office. She'd been a secretary back then with a box full of envelopes to seal. The minute he saw her, Caroll sat down and started licking. One weenie roast and a little hand-holding in his truck later and he'd wooed his future wife.

After the war and their wedding, he took advantage of the GI Bill and started a sock mill that quickly branched into a national conglomerate. A onetime farm boy became one of the richest men in town, and Blanche got herself a town house to raise their two daughters closer to "society folk." Having grown up on a big farm that the bank repossessed in 1929, Caroll was determined to make up for his childhood loss and bought his own plot of land in the early '60s. He died the same year a huge, freak snowstorm hit Wilmington, so I couldn't go to his funeral. All I remember of the man was a set of hairy ears, a big nose and his love for overalls (which we had in common), animals, hard work and handkerchiefs. He had allergies at a time before antihistamines, and so developed a habit of carrying handkerchiefs around to blow his big, sweaty nose. Granny Blanche used to gross me out with stories of weeding through Granddaddy's overalls every night and finding hard, crumpled handkerchiefs full of dirt and man-snot. Eww.

She also told me how, when he lay dying of lung cancer, the only thing he regretted was not being able to watch his Anna Lee grow up and become a Lady.

Blanche was a perfect lady who knew a good man when she saw him. Her eldest daughter, Sandy, was the dutiful one who headed up the UCC Youth Group and eventually took over as president of the church. My mother, Carolyn, however . . . was the wild one. The kid sister with a 'tude. And super-duper hot, which both Blanche and Sandy had to admit. When she married Alan "Stinger" Fields in 1977, a football player from the other side of the tracks, Granny Blanche smiled. And kept her mouth shut. But inside, she knew the end of an era was soon to follow. She feared no "real ladies" would come out of such a rambunctious union. . . .

And she was right.

See, this perfect lady's only grandchild was kind of a nerd. A geeky outsider who didn't quite fit in with her peers. Or, as some of the girls who eventually *were* invited to Deb put it: "totally queer."

This also meant that, besides Brent and Greg back in Wilmington, I didn't have many real friends growing up—and absolutely zero girlfriends. I always said the wrong thing or wore the wrong clothes or read thick books about gross stuff like Egyptian burial rites. Stuff that "only boys read," and other girls thought was the pits. I'd morphed from unwanted boil on the red neck of Wilmington to unpopular pariah of the wealthy, Southern elite of Burlington.

Naturally, I wanted to change all this. Somewhere deep down inside, once you scraped the catfish guts off my overalls, I had to admit: I still wanted to be Scarlett someday. And I thought, in order to do this, I had to think, act and look like all the other girls.

First, I tried Brownies.

Momma dressed me in my uniform and kneesocks and we trotted down to the school cafeteria for weekly meetings every Wednesday. At first, it was okay. We crocheted pillowcases and ate big cinnamon buns and sang "Kumbaya" a lot. But then a girl named Patty Hagan, who acted like a princess just because her Momma always bought the latest JCPenney fashions, started giving me a rough time. I tried fighting back. I even called her "fatty Patty" once, but that got me in trouble with our troop leader, so I quit.

Then there was sleepaway camp.

John's River Valley was the kind of place "outdoorsy" folks went. There were lakes and rivers and hiking trails and tire swings tied to humongous oaks, and even a watering hole where you could swim. So long as you didn't cross the yellow rope they used to separate the shallow from the deep ends, of course. If you were an extra good camper, they'd let you and a college-age chaperone borrow a canoe and paddle a few hundred yards downstream.

The first night I arrived, I hardly slept a wink. But by the next day, I was so tired from hiking all the way up Grandfather Mountain that I passed out before dark.

The biggest honor of all, however, was being chosen to ring Big Ben.

Big Ben was the huge cast-iron bell set way up on a hill in the middle of camp. At about six a.m., the lucky kid would have to climb to the top and ring Big Ben back and forth till the whole camp was awake and ready to go.

Why this was such a big honor, I'll never know. As a confirmed "night person," I'd have rather swallowed an entire inchworm alive than climb up some big hill at six a.m. Leave that early-riser stuff to fishermen, I say. This Rebel Deb needed her beauty sleep.

Anywho.

Everything at John's River was hunky-dory, at least for a few days.

Then a whole bunch of kids from Elon Home for Children joined the camp. Next thing I knew, a group of orphans were stealing my shoes and shoving dirty socks under my nose while I slept. A few days of that, and I became a sleepaway camp quitter, too.

At this point, Momma was about at the end of her rope. There wasn't much else for a preteen girl to do to make friends outside of school in those days, and I'd already quit all the "classy" stuff. There was only one avenue of social acceptance left. . . .

Dance classes.

Joining the local jazz/tap class at Amber's World of Dance meant I'd have to don a tutu, fake a smile and participate in every choreographed chorus line of stuff-strutting a small Southern town could offer.

After struggling through a five-girl dance routine set to Madonna's "Holiday," I "accidentally" peed on one of my fellow princess monsters while we stood in line for the talent display. That got her—and everybody else's—attention. To Momma's credit, she passed it off as a symptomatic bladder control problem. The girl's mother was convinced. She let it go. I, however, was to compete in no more dance competitions, Momma and I agreed.

Years later, I'm now certain that any more of my parading around in a tutu singing "Glory!" would've resulted in Momma's personal version of hell: embarrassment in front of the neighbors.

I was nine years old, a fatty, and covered in bug bites and catfish guts. Oh, yeah: And I was a total nerd who could spend hours reading Anne Rice books or watching Mr. Wizard explain basic physics by throwing a Ping-Pong ball into a box of mousetraps. By this point, I loathed girls and loved boys . . . but only because they didn't care that I bit my nails and had no clue what "frenching" was. I wasn't cool or cute or ladylike. I wasn't what any "normal" Southern Belle-to-Be was . . . well . . . *supposed* to be. I was rebellious and threw rocks and collected lizards from the backyard. Worst of all . . . I had no idea what a Debutante Ball entailed.

What kind of "society" was Granny Blanche expecting?

Still, she was a loving grandmother to her only grandbaby. The day I was born, Blanche and Caroll were out at the farm, up to their eyeballs in corn. When they showed up for my arrival, Granny Blanche was the first to say my name, followed by what would become a secret code between us. "We've been waitin' for you a mighty long time . . ." meant "I love you . . ." and when followed by "little girl," meant "more than you'll ever know. . . ."

Still, I wasn't ever gonna be as sweet and ladylike as my Granny Blanche. I couldn't keep my mouth shut. I couldn't smile sweetly at boys who preferred a pretty girl to a smart one. What was a "Debutante," anyway?

At the time, the only girl I knew who "Debbed" was Kimmy Lee Linklater's older sister. Originally from Atlanta, Kimmy Lee was another New Kid on the Block—like me—except she was skinny and perky and didn't wear glasses and boys laughed at her jokes for altogether different reasons. When Kimmy Lee first came to Burlington, before she got popular in middle school and turned into a mega-bitch, she and I made friends. Future Debs are good at making friends. Popular is a way of life. But before all that, Kimmy Lee told me all about something called the annual Terpsichorean Ball.

They held the Ball every year, and Kimmy Lee's big sister had just come out in style. After all the girls finished bowing and their Daddies finished beaming, everybody ate red velvet cake and danced the Hustle. Toward the end of the night, some of the baby boomers switched to shagging to "Son of a Preacher Man" while the older folks swayed back and forth to Perry Como.

Until we moved back to Burlington, the closest I ever came to a Debutante Ball was the annual Farmers Market dance in downtown Wilmington. Every year, the same live band played "Yankee Go Home" over and over again. Momma always covered my ears during this part because the song had dirty lyrics I wasn't supposed to know and the band didn't play so well anyway.

As best I could understand it, what happened at the dance was, gals looking to get married showed up in their best dresses to shake a tail feather and, if all went well, catch a husband. The "catching" part involved each gal swinging a pitchfork over several bales of hay. Whoever swung the farthest got the honor of straddling the tallest bale and wiggling back and forth to a scratchy recording of "What's New, Pussycat?"

Don't get me wrong: Some real ladies—none of the Linklaters, I imagine—wiggled and giggled at those dances. They were more easygoing than the hoity-toity kiddie cheerleaders Momma wanted me to hang out with, but still, they made fun of my tomboyish behavior. Not a one was Rebel Deb material or knew her pitchfork from a pocketknife.

First, there was Inez Boggs. Inez was crowned Queen of the Squash Festival three times in a row and carried her prize butternut in a sling wherever she went. Then there was Callie Louise Magilacutty, whose Daddy was once mayor of all Glen Raven County and owned a prized pig farm. The Magilacuttys also ran the best political machine since the Clintons, Tammany Hall and Julius Caesar. One time, to celebrate his ascension to the mayorship, Mr. Magilacutty went out and bought a set of fifteen guinea hens for his farm. Eventually, the hawks and snakes got to most of them and he got down to two—a male and a female. The male would chase the female all over three hundred acres of land, and then the pair of them would scream all night as they made guinea hen love in the moonlight. Callie Louise loved those hens and brought them with her to every town hall dance, where they made more noise than the folks shacking up at Skid's Drive-In.

And so, as you can see, I was as yet naive to the world of Debutantes.

I was used to the fun, carefree world where Momma would yank off my training wheels and push me down a hill to teach me to ride a bike. Where I'd dress up in fake ballgowns and play Cinderella in the backyard—flinging my "glass slipper" in every direction and waiting patiently for Daddy to dig it out of the azalea bushes. Where I'd get my fingers stuck in pencil holders and make mud pies in dirty creeks. Where Rochelle Dunlop, my first babysitter, fed me chocolate pudding till I was like to burst. Where Momma indulged my early Rebel Deb tastes and let me wear crazy clothes to school, including my all-time favorite neon-pink skirt with black polka dots cinched by a red elastic belt. Where I could obsess over Jill Sobule and Cyndi Lauper till Momma gave me my first perm, turning me into the stringy-haired love child of both. Where I was rough-and-tumble and ready to take on any more Ricky Stevensons that crossed my path.

But Granny Blanche and Burlington's high society had bigger plans for their wannabe Scarlett.

It's too bad Granny Blanche and Caroll couldn't have waited to get married at the First Christian UCC. That building was one of the prettiest and most historical places in the South.

First of all, the sanctuary alone took up almost an entire city block. With its huge white dome and stained-glass windows dating back to World War I, it was breathtaking to behold. Especially on a bride's wedding day.

I remember the day Momma and I gathered in one of the back-rooms so she could slip Aunt Sandy's garter belt on before she married Uncle Stu. I remember I wasn't too happy with my bowl cut or the bright pink lipstick I was supposed to wear that kept rubbing off on my sleeve. Momma finally had to order me "Hush!" so she could secure the bit of lace around Sandy's thigh before the opening beats of "Here Comes the Bride."

When things finally started, I got to staring at all the Jesus figurines on the ceiling.

The sanctuary itself was like stepping into another world or a scene from the past. The windows were colorful and massive, and when the sunlight shone through, it looked like the whole town was on fire. Granny Blanche kept pictures from the 1930s of her Daddy, Earl Sommers, sitting with some of the old-timers on the steps outside. That was when folks wore hats and gloves to church and shined their shoes every morning. And since then, every person in my family has been proud to be a member.

As flower girl, I was supposed to make them even more proud. My job was to follow a few basic rules: Look pretty, smile a lot and walk a straight line down the center of everybody while throwing handfuls of rose petals every which way.

Clearly, I've never been too good with rules. I got so nervous and preoccupied with the ceiling that I forgot to throw a single petal. I don't know what Momma was thinking, making me flower girl. I'd already quit dance classes and Brownies. And now I was supposed to kick off a whole wedding?

After that, I spent most Sundays in that sanctuary dressed up in angel wings or running around during all-night lock-ins. But my favorite was when we'd hold fellowship lunch there.

Those Sundays, folks would bring in fried chicken, slaw and

green beans cooked with bacon bits. Service always started at eleven and ended at noon, when everybody would head downstairs for buffet-style eating. Our preacher at the time was the same one who'd married Momma and Daddy and, later, Uncle Stu and Sandy. He was soft-spoken and had the kindest eyes you've ever seen. Even when he got Alzheimer's, he was one of my favorites to talk to while chewing my chicken. Second to the old Reverend, there was Charlie "the Tuna" Vitou, who worked at the local occupational rehab center trying to help folks find work. He gave big hugs and big kisses and always told me how much he loved me, no matter what.

These were the days of kindness and charity. Of ten-cent long-distance phone calls that were free on holidays and weekends, and big analog "car phones" that folks mounted to the floor of their Cadillacs. Of getting your news from the newspaper and setting a freshly baked pie out on the windowsill to encourage folks to visit.

Every Christmas, Mommas and Daddies gathered their children around the single box-set TV they kept downstairs in the den and turned to Channel 3 for the local Santa Watch. A male reporter would appear on-screen in front of a red and green map of the whole state and point to where sleigh tracks had been spotted heading this way. So you'd better get your cookies and milk ready before bed. Otherwise, switches and coal might show up in your stocking before sunrise.

It was a simpler, easier time. Or at least it was for those gathered down at the UCC for Sunday fellowship lunch.

Sometimes, when the chicken-and-cole-slaw folks got tired, we'd have spaghetti or beans and weenies instead. On rare occasions, we'd dine to live music by the Cotton-Pickers, who Granny Blanche loved. Even at eighty-eight years old, she'd sing along, clapping her hands and tapping her feet the whole time. She was a grand Southern

Lady of the old tradition, and as the saying goes, they don't make 'em like that anymore.

My Granny Ruth, on the other hand, was a younger, hipper, more rock 'n' roll kinda gal.

She'd grown up in Burlington, married by eighteen, birthed two boys (one my Daddy) by twenty and been divorced by thirty. She spent the next thirty to forty years marrying and divorcing rich men across the country, from Burlington to Tennessee to Orange County, California. She even got herself a construction company in one settlement. And though Granny Ruth and my Daddy were estranged during most of my early years, when we returned to Burlington I spent a lot of time at her house. A one-level pile of wood sitting atop a half-acre of rose gardens and run-down tobacco barns, with a whole creek running through the middle.

To me, it was a magical palace. And her backyard was the stuff of dreams.

This was no surprise, considering Granny Ruth was a singer, actress and model in her day, and the most beautiful woman I'd ever seen. The first time she took off her shirt to give me a bath, I was amazed. Until I was thirteen, I planned on growing her same natural endowments.

Then one day, I realized Granny Ruth was ahead of her time in more ways than one. She'd also been the first woman in Alamance County with silicone breast implants.

Granny Ruth wasn't too welcomed by most of my Granny Blanche's friends but she sure did like singing in the choir. And she made sure I did, too. She had me in piano lessons by the fourth grade and standing up on her coffee table, singing tunes from *My Fair Lady* and *The Sound of Music* by the fifth.

The first time she made me do it in public was right there in the sanctuary of the First Christian UCC. I was supposed to sing "Amazing Grace." Granny Ruth had put my name down right there on the church bulletin: "Miss Anna Lee Fields to present a solo to the congregation this morning," which I'm sure she found flattering but gave me the shakes.

When the preacher called my name and I walked up the carpeted steps, I almost passed out. I finally steadied myself behind his podium and Rector Pringleton, the organist, started the first opening measures. I squinted into the crowd and prayed—begged—the Lord to help me remember all the words . . .

> *"Amazing grace, how sweet the sound that*
> *saved a wretch like meeeeee!"*

Ain't it the truth?

Thank goodness, everything went uphill from there. I remembered all the words, finished the song and made it back to my pew without throwing up on a soul. Granny Ruth was thrilled and insisted I try again. I was just happy my underdrawers was still dry.

A few weeks later, I stood up to repeat this nerve-wracking process at Hillcrest Elementary's fifth grade talent show. I was a sweaty, nervous mess of ten-year-old Jell-O pinned into a full-grown woman's party dress and ready to show her stuff. Granny Ruth had pin-curled my hair with plastic rollers and hosed it down with enough Aqua Net to choke a horse. Plus, I was wearing about a pound of rouge, lipstick and bright blue eye shadow to "give me some color" under the hot lights of Hillcrest's auditorium.

The floor creaked as I walked across the auditorium boards. Granny

Blanche had been in the very first class to attend Hillcrest, and I would be the last. The building was so old and creaky, we weren't allowed to jump during gym because the floor might cave in. The following year, when the city put Hillcrest up for sale, I took up a community petition to turn it into a homeless shelter. While mighty impressed by the mini-politico they had on their hands, the town fathers sold it to a private school instead, and it became Burlington's first Catholic . . . well, *anything*.

But for now I was still a shaky ten-year-old wearing too much makeup about to sing "My Favorite Things" to a giggling horde of fifth-graders. And their parents. And their grandparents. And friends and neighbors and babysitters and dog walkers and everybody else in the whole damn world, or so it seemed.

The lights were blinding. I remember floating above myself, just watching this little blond girl about to prostrate herself to the gods of Southern social failure. Then, the music started. And I opened my mouth. And, suddenly, this big sound came out, *whoosh*ing me back into my body with the first couple of lyrics . . . "Raindrops on roses and whiskers on kittens." The notes and sounds and words kept coming out of me and somehow, some way, *I was doing it*. I was succeeding. I was making noises that everybody in the room seemed to like and, as soon as I was done, clapped till Momma started to cry.

For the first time, I was special all on my own. People looked at me not because of my weight or my skin or my glasses, but because they wondered how such a big voice could come out of such a little girl. For the first time, I was proud to be me.

Once I started sixth grade at Turrentine Middle School, my life became a living hell.

All the other kids were sick and tired of hearing my "bee-u-ti-ful!" singing voice and started giving me stink-eyes after class. I was back to square one. Big-butted, albino white and the only kid sitting alone at lunch.

Momma's eating habits didn't help.

She'd fix creamed chipped beef on toast or chicken and dumplings for dinner. Don't get me wrong—Southern folks do eat lots of fresh vegetables, but we also slather them with gravy and mix fatback in with our beans. Mix all that with a pair of big glasses, and you've got yourself a big steamin' pile of middle school hell. Thank you, Jesus, and my big-butted German ancestry. . . . Well, and enough chicken 'n' dumplings, red velvet cake, sweet potato casserole and ambrosia—green Jell-O filled with nuts and cottage cheese—to push an already bulbous behind exploded into full-fledged Fat Kid territory.

I tried not to let my lunchtime loneliness get me down. I tried to ignore the preppy girls in their matching *Clueless* inspired outfits, with their perfect French braids and tiny cheerleading shorts rolled up at the top to hide the "muffin tops" they constantly complained about.

Muffin tops, huh? I could've showed 'em a whole bakery.

So, one day, I did.

Second, in a giant leap of faith, I got up the nerve to sign up for cheerleading tryouts. I was tired of lonely potato days and girls like Heather Poovey, who used to spit the juice from her Skoal chewing tobacco into a jar during homeroom and sang the same rap song every time she and her JV basketball team made a goal.

Go, Heather! It's your birthday! Not for real,
though! Just for play, play!

She and the Johnson twins were the snobbiest girls in school. But the boys were worse. They'd attack anyone within fifty feet of their lockers. I once overheard them call little Minnie Linklater a "chubby dump truck."

Minnie was no dump truck. In fact, Minnie was named "Minnie" because she could've hula-hooped with a Cheerio.

Point is, I was tired of it all. I was sick of being picked on and labeled uppity just because I could sing.

For once, I wanted to belong. I wanted to be popular. I wanted to be the glamorous, coveted Scarlett O'Hara in the room. And that meant I'd have to become a Turrentine Trojan: a jumping, leaping ball of school spirit. That also meant I'd have to jump around in the short skirt and tight-fitting vestlike thingy all middle school cheerleaders wore at the time.

There were two days of cheer camp before tryouts.

Cheering in the South is a religion, just like Debbing. And cheer camp is just like Bible school before Confirmation. Girls start as early as three and four, tumbling around in little leotards, putting their knees up on their elbows trying to manage a headstand. These babies are busy perfecting their cartwheels and ponytails before they're old enough to read and write. It's enough to make anybody's soft spot cave in.

I showed up the first day dressed in my P.E. uniform and a pair of white Velcro Reeboks Momma had written my name in.

The whole gym was full of wannabe cheerleaders.

Worst of all, Heather Poovey was there, too. She and her giggly friends stood in a circle in their matching, monogrammed booty shorts, shaking their not-so-thunderous thighs as they danced to Heather's latest rhapsody. Meghan Littlejohn's booty was the fastest shaker of all.

Alvie Littlejohn, Meghan's Daddy, graduated from Williams High School along with my Momma and every other member of Burlington high society. He'd married Meghan's Momma, a stern woman who preached Creationism to anyone who'd listen. The Littlejohns earned their living making stained-glass windows for churches—just like the ones at the First Christian UCC—and were regulars every Sunday. But, just between us, I never have and probably never will see another sixth grader shake her fanny in public with quite so much natural gusto as Meghan.

Each cheerleader intimidated me to the core. Their perfect bangs shimmering with Aqua Net and body glitter. Their flawless skin covered in spray-on tanner that left rings around their eyes. The Vaseline on their teeth reflected the overhead gym lights.

It was amazing. And very, very scary.

See, I was never all that competitive. At twelve, I'd rather catfish or read or fantasize about Scarlett than face her head-on.

They, on the other hand, were seasoned competitors. They had older sisters who'd taught them every cheer, stunt, move and routine before tryouts even started. I was an only child without a prayer.

Like a call to the wild, Heather, Meghan and every other wannabe cheerleader appeared in the gym that afternoon to obey the cardinal rule of the South:

Cheerleading is your ticket to popularity.

They started practicing in groups of a dozen or so. First we did crunches on big blue mats on the floor. Next, we ran up and down the bleachers, which made Meghan Littlejohn's mascara run together with her liquid foundation. After a few minutes, her faced looked something like a cross between Eddie Izzard and Freddy Krueger.

Then, we split up into smaller groups.

Christy Swangin (pronounced like "her titties were swangin' in the breeze!") was my group's cheer coach, president of the eighth grade Junior League and dating the Trojans' star quarterback, Gunther Dupree.

Christy and Gunther made a cute couple, I must admit. I think the success of their preteen relationship lay in its balance. Each one had his or her special talents that the other could appreciate. For example, while she had a way of knocking herself out with her own cleavage during high kicks, he was better known for having the longest nose hair in three counties.

Christy weighed in at about ninety-two pounds and stood about four-foot-eleven on a good day . . . just like everybody else on the Turrentine Trojans squad. At five-foot-two, 135 pounds, I was a veritable monster next to these girls. Walking over to my new group, I could hear them praying for the floor to hold.

Christy took us over to a big blue mat to await further instructions. There we learned about funny-sounding moves like "herkies" (pronounced as in "I done dropped her keys!"), which were no doubt intended for short, stocky girls with big leg muscles. But at my height, with my spindly arms and legs, I stood out like a Christmas tree in a room full of Chanukah bushes. They might as well have tied ornaments to the end of my nose.

Christy was a strict coach. She told us, "Be sharp! Pretend you're hitting a brick wall behind you!" This turned out to be too much inspiration for me. I punched a girl in the ear during a "Swedish fall / Fish" move. When she started bleeding, Christy and everybody else looked at me like I was Godzilla coming to burn down their village.

By the time we started learning our Big Routine, I was ready to quit cheerleading, too.

Christy called the six of us over for a Team Swangin chat. She'd never lost a bet, she said. And this time she'd promised to turn our flabby sixth-grade bodies into "rock-hard spirit sticks! Whaddya say?!"

I didn't exactly know what to say, so I just nodded and smiled. Like in math class.

Good thing, too. 'Cause I was pretty sure Christy would've kicked my butt with any sign of resistance. Quitting wouldn't be so easy this time.

The next day, official tryouts began. Everybody met in the gym, as usual, only this time the whole place was empty. The blue mats were gone. The whole place was quiet as a grave, until suddenly, Christy appeared and ordered everyone up into the bleachers. Below us sat a table. And behind that, three grown-up judges.

About an hour later, they finally called my name.

I stepped in front of the judges to start my Big Routine. Someone in the bleachers pushed "Play" on the boom box. With a loud *bam!* the opening beats of "Too Legit to Quit" started bouncing off the ceiling, then traveled down the walls to the floor. . . .

Where I stood frozen in place.

I looked to my left and right. Two Southern versions of Marsha Brady smiled wide-eyed for the judges. . . .

Who were completely oblivious. They missed the white teeth, the flawless French braids perfectly parted down the middle. Even the matching bobby socks with the cute little ball of pink flopping up and down behind each ankle.

And why?

Because they were all looking at *me*. The fat girl in the center. The sweaty, terrified, unmoving blob of un-cool wedged between two future Miss Americas.

In fact, the whole room saw nothing but me.

Everyone stared at my unmoving feet. My stiff legs. My shaky hands. Wondering, hoping, praying that I'd do . . . something. *Anything.*

I stared back. I couldn't help it. Somehow, my soul had lifted out of my body and was floating above, watching me screw up my only chance at popularity. Then, with another *bam!* the music ended. The judges didn't even bother to check their stopwatches. Nothing else mattered because all eyes were fixed on my total. Fear. My soul whooshed back into my body . . . and it was just . . . over. Without my ever taking a single step . . .

Then, slowly, I took one. Then another. Then my feet started moving faster and faster than I could control.

Suddenly, I was walking, then jogging, then running right toward the exit doors. And with a third huge *bam!* I was outside. Free from all the judges and eyes and perfect ponytails and girls with teeth that would never, ever need braces. . . .

I was jumping into Momma's car, waiting patiently outside.

"How'd it go?" she asked.

"Do they have cheerleaders in Alaska?"

"I don't think so, sugar."

"Good. I'm moving there."

And imagining the next three years of middle school, I meant it.

By the time I left Turrentine, I knew Burlington like the back of my hand.

I knew that old folks ate lunch at the local K&W Cafeteria near the mall. Sometimes, they'd go to the Iron Skillet Steakhouse for a Trucker Dee-light special or drink "Titty-Twisters"—an apple martini with triple sec and a splash of melon liqueur—at the Buckhorn Saloon off Highway 70 going toward Greensboro. Momma used to spend a lot of time looking at tree ornaments at the Christmas Shoppe because Daddy liked the season so much. He'd sing Christmas songs in July. His favorite was Willie Nelson's homemade version of "I'm Dreaming of a White Christmas," where if you play the lyrics backward you can hear coyotes howling in Willie's backyard. If Momma wasn't at the Christmas Shoppe, I could usually find her shopping for frumpy shoes and plus-size stretch pants at the Bass Outlet off Chapel Hill Road.

"Anna Lee," she'd always tell me, "we've got hourglass figures just like every other well-built woman. Only ours have fifteen minutes on the top and forty-five minutes on the bottom."

On weekends, these same folks entertained themselves driving down I-40 to the High Point furniture markets or shopping for hosiery at Jefferies Socks, secondhand shoes at the Wide Shoe Warehouse, old lamps at Granddaddy's Antiques, and everything else at JR Wrangler's General Store. Until I moved up North, JR Wrangler's was the biggest store I'd ever seen. Even bigger than the old downtown Woolworth's or the VA Truck Stop off I-40 West. You name it, JR's sold it. Which was lucky, considering their official motto was "Turn left at the Waffle House. If we ain't got it, you don't need it!"

Except for reading trashy novels I got at JR's, though, there wasn't much else to do except ride bikes, build trailer parks, watch rasslin' on the TV, rent VHS tapes of old movies, sip milk shakes at the local DQ or shoot the breeze at Jim's Service Station on a Sunday afternoon. Since JR's was closed Sundays, this was my second favorite option.

Jim's was a local hangout for hunters, farmers, retired Vietnam vets and Uncle Stu if only Aunt Sandy would let him. It sat right on

Front Street in downtown Burlington. You could drive from one end of Front Street to the other in about ten minutes. Five if you didn't hit the stoplight.

The owner, Jim "Fatback" Sr., was a good ol' boy who didn't mind teaching me all sorts of useful skills, like how to throw a football and open my own can of beanie weenies. Daddy also liked the place because Jim "Fatback" Sr. would let him wear his ball cap inside, didn't clean his spit cups too often and served up the best French fries in town.

Jim "Fatback" Sr. graduated along with my Daddy from Western Carolina University back in the '70s with a degree in animal husbandry. But it wasn't until he moved back home that "Fatback" discovered his true passions: deep-frying potatoes with sliced lard—also known as "fatback." His close second was installing tire tread.

It seemed all Southern men of that generation had the same idols: John Wayne, Clint Eastwood, the Godfather, Hank Williams, Hank Williams Jr., Dale Earnhardt, Al Pacino, Randy Travis, Archie Manning, Tattoo from *Fantasy Island*, Elvis, Jerry Lee Lewis, Russell Stover, Kirk Douglas, Neil Armstrong, the original Batman and the fella who invented tire tread.

A lot of Mommas around town—including mine—used to complain about the atmosphere at Jim's. It sure wasn't the kind of place you'd picture a teenage girl hanging out, especially on a first date.

Jim's son, Jim Jr., was sixteen and weighed about a hundred pounds soaking wet. He showed up at my door that night wearing his lucky "Big Johnson" hat and a tie-dyed Grateful Dead T shirt. It wasn't exactly the suit-and-tie combo most girls envision, but I was just grateful he hadn't brought Chip Townsend along.

Jim Jr. and Chip Townsend were best friends and went everywhere together, or so it seemed. Chip was a self-made ladies' man and all around sketchball. If there was a girl around town he didn't like—or one who'd turned him down, more like—he'd find a dead fox, cut off its tail and tie the thing to the back of her car. That way, folks would start asking, "Who's the fox-tail?" (which, by the way, is another word for "floozy") whenever she drove by. Chip insisted he wanted to stop playing the field and settle down someday, when all he really needed was a good shave and a swift kick in the rear.

Jim Jr., on the other hand, was a perfect gentleman. So Daddy finally agreed to let him inside for a "talk." From the hallway, it sounded like things started off rocky. Daddy got in a few warnings like, "Now don't you ever let me catch you doing . . ." or "When I was your age, fellas didn't go around . . ." and Jim Jr. responded with a few dozen "yessirs" and "nahsirs" before things finally calmed down. After that, it got boring. Some stuff about the weather. Football this. Responsibility that. Which hot dog joints to avoid and other life lessons.

At long last, Jim Jr. and I finally drove off in his beat-up white Ford where he played that "world is a vampire" song by Smashing Pumpkins all the way to his Daddy's restaurant. We ordered the usual—French fries with extra ketchup—then headed off to catch a movie.

Back then, before things like DVDs and Netflix, folks got their movies from the Carmike Cinema on Huffman Mill Road. It was a big round building with velvet seats and curtains over the screen. If you looked real hard, you could see the projector boy changing the film reels by hand.

We watched 120 minutes of Jennifer Love Hewitt in a tight blue tank top driving a whole bunch of high school boys crazy. Halfway through, Jim Jr. bought us a box of Sour Patch Kids candy and when that was empty, he held my hand till it got warm and sweaty.

Afterward, we drove over to JR's and banged on the door till somebody let us in. Jim Jr. bought sliced fatback—the kind you ate right out of the package in sizes "single man's dinner" through "granny's big helper." In the parking lot, he showed me how to do the "chicken leg dance." This was a move only a string bean like Jim Jr. could pull off. He'd roll up his pants leg, hitch one foot and lean back on the other. Then, he'd shake his bony butt around while snapping his fingers to the beat. He'd top it all off with a *whoop* and a holler to the sky. Then he'd turn to me and smile and wait for my applause, which I'd give generously. If maybe not honestly. Jim Jr. was real nice and all, but about as sexy as a school bus fire.

Chicken dance aside, he made a damn fine beau. We'd go off to see a different movie every week. Though nothing too intimate ever happened, whenever he'd rub my hands between those knobby drummer fingers, he made the world seem a warmer place.

When I left Burlington, he was the most heartbroken of all.

"I'll miss you the most, scarecrow," he said with a teasing smile. It was the last day of summer and I was headed off to boarding school in less than a week. "That's what you're supposed to say right about now, Anna Lee."

But I couldn't. There were too many things—too much of a future outside Burlington—to be excited about. So I just smiled and nodded and gave him the biggest hug I've ever given.

Six months later, I was a sophomore at Wellingham Academy and Jim Jr. was getting married right there at First Christian. It was a Christmastime wedding, so the bride's Momma baked a red and green wedding cake shaped like Rudolph the Reindeer to match. The whole sanctuary was decorated in poinsettias and tinsel. I stood up and sang "Amazing Grace," and afterward, everybody sat down for another fellowship hall luncheon: Granny Blanche, Daddy, Momma,

Aunt Sandy and Uncle Stu on one side of the table, Mr. and Mrs. Jim "Fatback" Sr. beside me on the other.

I was taking a big, red bite out of Rudolph's nose when Jim Jr. introduced me to his wife. The newest Mrs. "Fatback" looked just as knobby-kneed and sweet as her husband and, as a result, likely to make him very happy.

Watching them walk through the crowd was a beautiful sight. When they got into their car and rode off into a happily-ever-after ending, it brought a tear to my eye. I suddenly realized that this was where all their—and my—fairy-tale dreams began.

That sanctuary was our home. Where we were all baptized, raised and supposed to be married and buried. The first place I learned to believe in myself—thanks to a whole slew of people who believed in me, too—and where I was supposed to follow in Jim Jr.'s footsteps.

After all, that's the same path my parents, grandparents and everybody else I knew took. The way respectable folks were supposed to live, and what all of Burlington's high society expected of me. All those fine folks had big plans for their wannabe Scarlett.

Only she, as it turns out, had her own.

Chapter Two

Fake IDs and Faker Tans . . . How Scarlett Survives Her First Year of Boarding School:

• Tenth Grade •

I was fifteen years old when I first saw the Penis Building.

Anyone even remotely familiar with Winston-Salem, North Carolina, knows what I'm talking about: the huge, multistory office building occupied by Wachovia Bank. It's tall, phallic-shaped and, every Christmas, lit up by a hot pink strobe. Nobody knows if the "Dick in the Sky" is an architectural disaster or some kind of subversive, anti–Christian Conservative Republican joke.

Needless to say, most everybody under thirty—and thus, still "trustworthy"—hopes it's the latter. . . . Well, everybody who wasn't a future Debutante, anyway. Oh, no. These little ladies were much too busy making straight A's, running Student Council, furrowing brows over the "poor Mexicans, who can't help their 'simple' nature," and finding just the right scoop-neck blouse for Cindy Washington's latest tea party to ever give the origins of that horribly *inappropriate* "building" a second thought.

Anywho, as most "Salemites" know, the "Big Dick" separates Winston-Salem into two distinct halves:

"Winston" is a mishmash of old money Southern businesses. R. J. Reynolds. Hanes Her Way. LabCorp. This half of Winston is where the public school kids go. Where Southern jocks wearing John Deere ball caps, polo shirts and baggy khakis gather in parking lots to drink Bud Light and make out with future housewives and kindergarten teachers. "Salem" is a different story. An alternate universe. A private, cobblestoned community founded in the eighteenth century by Moravian Puritans, with Wellingham Academy as its epicenter. Founded in 1751, Wellingham is the oldest girls' boarding school in the Southeast. Until the mid-1980s, no Wellingham student was allowed to travel in public without her big-ass, wide-brimmed Southern Lady's hat. Until the early 1990s, no Wellingham student was allowed to wear *pants*, let alone jeans. . . .

But at fifteen, dressed up in my favorite Calvin Kleins, staring up at Winston-Salem's favorite phallus in the sky . . . how was I supposed to know I was a future Rebel Deb? Neither Momma nor Granny Blanche went to Wellingham, so none of us knew what to expect from boarding school. Still, I suspected anything had to be better than another three years in public school, where the girls cared more about getting boyfriends than an education, the teachers openly preached that "girls aren't good at math," and the guidance counselors considered graduating high school with fewer than three illegitimate children successful.

Safe haven though it seemed, my first day at Wellingham was

already turning out a disaster. I was nervous, late for orientation and couldn't find the stupid student store to buy my books. I was huffing up the cobblestoned path, following the "Welcome, Students!" signs. My undies were riding up. I'd "forgotten" (read: Boycotted!) today's deodorant and was super sweaty. My flip-flops were rubbing a blister into my big toe. And now, for cryin' out loud—as my Momma would say—baby Jesus was sad and had started crying all over my head!

Translation for the "Yankees": It was raining.

Momma and Daddy had already dropped off my circa two hundred pounds of teeny-bopper clothes, cassette tapes, boom box and—most important—shoes. I don't know a Southern girl alive who isn't obsessed, in one way or another, with fancy-pants footwear. And since it's pretty much springtime all year round in North Carolina, most of my shoe collection were open-toed Reef surf sandals covering all shades of the pastel rainbow. I never went anywhere without a pair of flip-flops, that's for damn sure. And I was bound and determined to squash every last pair into the tiny shoe box of a closet Wellingham provided.

My sophomore-year dorm room was a doubleheader—two desks, two chairs, and a bunk bed in the corner. As my new roommate hadn't yet arrived, I grabbed the bottom bunk and started unpacking. I'd gotten around to the last of my Reefs and was about to prove my Great Aunt Dot wrong—you can, in fact, fit a hundred pounds of collard greens into a fifty-pound sack—when, lo and behold, a knock came at my door.

I opened it, somewhat bewildered, and there stood Brooke Walters. Perfect hair. Perfect nails. Her pale pink sweater set shedding angora fuzz all over my Lee jean overalls. Momma and Poppa Walters standing vigilantly behind as she pushed into the room, stopping dead at the sight of my having claimed the bottom bunk.

It was on.

She looked at the bunk. Looked at me. Looked at the bunk. Placed her laptop on Granny Blanche's favorite afghan, now adorning *my* bed.

John Wayne himself couldn't have thrown down a better challenge.

"I'm Bitsy," she said. Didn't offer her hand, just a smart-alecky smile. "Could we visit a bit about the bunk situation?"

Happy to, darlin'. As I see it: You snooze, you lose. Am I right?

With her nervous-wreck parents pacing the hallway outside our door, Bitsy and I sat down to discuss the "bunk situation." Apparently, young Miss Walters had some kind of brain problem. She'd had surgery on her pituitary gland (or some other kind of fancy-sounding brain stem thingy) and her Momma was afraid, if we didn't trade places, ol' Bitsy would roll off the top bunk in her sleep. Because she'd had brain surgery.

Um . . . yeah.

I tried to hide my smile. I looked over at her laptop, still sitting on *my* Granny Blanche's knitting, on the bunk I'd rightly claimed.

First of all, my new roomie was clearly a rich chick. Nobody had laptops back then. Or used the Internet for anything but "Oregon Trail" showdowns. Not unless they were super-duper nerdy. Back then, we went to school and played outside. We didn't call dibs using other people's Granny's afghans.

"Why don't we compromise?" I offered. A quizzical, arching brow appeared on Bitsy's face as I went on. "Why don't we take the bunk apart? That way, we'll both get a bottom-floor suite?" I said, trying to lessen the tension with a little humor. I even offered a conciliatory,

"Ain't I silly? Now, why don't we go watch *Real World?*" chuckle to sweeten the deal.

No return chuckle came my way. I could tell this whole "girls' boarding school" thing was gonna be a tough horse to break. In the end, she relented to my compromise and we split the bunks. That left us with about five inches of floor space, but hell! At least I didn't get stuck sucking humid air off the ceiling and old broken-brain wouldn't sleep-fall, leaving me with a life-sized squash for a roommate . . . right?

The next day I woke at seven a.m. and headed down to the school auditorium for my very first Wellingham Academy Devotions. Miss Freeze, our Headmistress, and Dr. Burkett, her weak-willed-male, "nutty professor" counterpart, stood on a stage in front of about two hundred would-be Debs to share school announcements, a short sermon and lead the group in daily prayer. I took one look at Miss Freeze with her huge, early-'60s beehive and pinched face, and felt like Matilda, the heroine in my all-time favorite Roald Dahl book. She looked cross and suspicious, and her lip curled like her dog was in the back doing something mighty smelly.

I would soon find that Miss Freeze was as punishing as her name— and her beehive—suggested. That woman could freeze ice with one look, and every time a Wellingham girl got a note in her mailbox to "Please see me" in that chicken-scratch straight-out-of-pharmacy-school writing, she hightailed it to Miss Freeze's office . . . certain the wrath of our Lord couldn't be any scarier.

On this morning, however, we'd been called in special. This was the first day of school—Devotions was more than just group prayer. Today we would learn the basic rules of Wellingham's Code of Conduct:

♡ No smoking.

♡ No drinking.

♡ No boys allowed beyond the two front "sitting parlors"—
stationed on either side of Miss Freeze's office.

♡ No leaving the building without "signing out" where
you were going. And no leaving *period* without an
adult (or "upperclasswoman") chaperone.

♡ No tardiness.

♡ No skirts above the knee.

♡ Class began at eight a.m., finished at noon. A "cookie
break" would be offered at ten a.m. between second
and third periods.

♡ At 12:05 *sharp* all girls were expected to line up outside the cafeteria doors. When lunch was ready to be
served, teachers and faculty were allowed into the dining room first. Then the rest of us could enter. All girls
were expected to sit as assigned at any one of a dozen
circular, tableclothed tables. Each table was headed
by a teacher, who would count attendance as each girl
stood behind her chair, waiting to eat. Miss Freeze
would then lead the Moravian blessing:

> *Come, Lord Jesus! Our Guest to be . . .*
> *And bless these gifts bestowed by Thee!*

which everybody would say out loud in unison. Then,
we were free to pull up our chairs and eat. Each girl
had to stay at least fifteen minutes before she could be
excused.

♡ Study hall began at one p.m. and ended at three.
♡ Cotillion classes, sports practice and/or piano lessons
   till five, when we were expected back in the same cafeteria for dinner. Same routine. Same protocol. Same
   catfish and butter bean salad on Fridays . . . you get
   the picture.

Miss Freeze read through the rest of the rules, including mandatory Sunday school and service every weekend, and finally dismissed
us to first-period Latin. As we filed out of the auditorium, I couldn't
help but stare at the still-pinched look on Miss Freeze's face. Like
she'd had a dose of castor oil for breakfast and was fixing to break
loose a case of the runs.

She watched us all leaving—our T-shirts, Chuck Taylors and L.L.
Bean backpacks facing her old-fashioned indignance—with this
almost painful look of incomprehension.

To give the poor woman some credit, I don't suppose that any
generation has really understood the next, and every generation has
steadfastly insisted that the younger adapt to its particular values and
views. My parents' generation, true to form, sought to bring up its
young in its mold, but also had a firm resolve to do something more
for us. We were children of no real wars, no real struggles. Our hippie parents grew up, paid a few taxes and became the FDR generation they'd once despised. They were, as a result, even more critical,
conservative and fearful than folks in my Granny Blanche's Great
Depression days, when kids who got oranges for Christmas were the
richest in town. This "Way We Were" generation grew up drying
and reusing paper towels. Breaking open thermometers to play with

the mercury balls inside. Their children, if they escaped Vietnam, AIDS, hard drugs and alcoholism, abandoned their strawberry fields and made sure their kids did the same.

Still, looking back, I've decided my parents' generation of Southerners may have endured more hardship and offered more sacrifices than any other previous generation. Sure, they weren't exactly rocked 'n' rolled by the '60s—but most folks in Burlington weren't. Their generation of Southerners was a little too sheltered for the civil rights movement or Woodstock—which, besides integration, didn't seem to affect them too directly. Like a lot of small-town folks, my parents simply went to school and pretended not to notice the new black kids in the next seat. Then they'd go home, have dinner and watch all these radical changes happening through their TV sets. It was just life as usual, and thus, the '60s always seemed distant, like watching a fictional television program. According to Momma, things like "free love" only happened to "big city" people in places like Los Angeles and New York—parts of the country she'd only caught glimpses of through black-and-white coverage on the Channel 6 news. Times were still mighty hard. Sheltered or no, it couldn't have been easy for my parents to grow up listening to tales of the "War of Northern Aggression," and all their own parents complaining about the "damn Yankees moving down here, lookin' to make our nice state into the next Jersey Turnpike." Hell, after all that brainwashing, I was just grateful they weren't yuppies.

Looking back on my relationship with my own parents and others—like Miss Freeze—from their generation, I think they also felt a sense of duty to their children to make certain that, at whatever cost, their children would be spared some of the adversity they'd seen. Momma's childhood friend, Benny Purdue, had seen the inside of a Vietnam POW camp and lived to tell the tale. He'd made it back alive to Carolina and promised to never leave again. And so what if his whole body was covered in scars from machine-gun fire? If his right ear was half cut off? So long as he could get back home to send his daughter, Cindy, to Latin class that first day of school.

Because he wanted her to grow up a Lady. To have it better than he did.

Long story short: We were by God gonna be Debutantes, because anything's better than ending up like poor Benny "Mincemeat" Purdue. Or some millhand at the local textile plant. Or being shipped off to watch all your friends die in "some Godforsaken jungle," as my Daddy would say. Like Benny and every other Wellingham parent, "We want you to have it better than we did," was his motto. The motto of all Southern folks over forty in the '90s.

Heavy stuff aside, Cindy and I made our way to "Hodges"—the Hodges Academic Building, making up half of Wellingham and where all classes were conducted—for Latin I with Miss Krinkle. . . .

The only "Eye-talian" in town.

A tall, stout woman, Miss Krinkle had one of those middle-age paunches in front that stuck out of her blue-jean skirts like a shelf. And she wore those colorful, braided belts our elementary school teachers donned in the '80s, which was kinda groovy. She had perfectly coiffed Donna Reed hair and was fluent in a language nobody could technically speak because it was dead and the original dialect was lost. All that, and her cheery disposition, made Miss Krinkle a cool—if painfully dorky—teacher. Our parents thought so, too . . . well, except for the whole Catholic thing.

Whenever the old women gathered around Momma's stove to talk about Miss Krinkle, it sounded like this:

"You ever know'd an Eye-talian?"

"Where in tarnation's that?"

"Yo-rope."

"Oh, my Harold's been there. In the War. Said them people was hairy, slick 'n' awfully friendly with they hands."

"Reckon that's so?"

"Course it's so. You think my Harry'd lie 'bout a thing like that? Got three wives and about a dozen mistresses on the side, them Eye-talians."

"Got lots of 'em down in Atlanta now."

"Hmph. Like Jesse Helms always say, 'When I look at Atlanta, I see what five hundred thousand Confederate soldiers died to prevent.'"

"Ain't it the truth. A whole city done run over. And them folks stick together like buttermilk sticks to your chin."

"Oooh, but it's good! And a good diet, too, Myrtle. You know I lost eight whole pounds eatin' nothing but buttermilk and cornbread?"

These were the same people who danced and held each other close to "Just My Imagination (Running Away with Me)." Later, they shagged to beach music and we had to listen to their stories of romps at Myrtle Beach and how the neighborhood floozy used white petroleum jelly every time she "shacked up" with some newly minted graduate from the Citadel.

"Eye-talian" or not, Miss Krinkle was the butter on our breakfast bread. With three more years of Latin ahead of us, Cindy and I were happy to have her at the front of the class.

Up front, in what I would learn was her usual spot, sat Diane Sutherland. Beside Bitsy. At the back of the class, chewing the cracked, black polish off her (nine-inch) nails, was Rachel Dobbs. Cindy sat to my left. And to my right, Caitlin Sure doodled something on the insides of her milky white, baby-fat covered arms.

In almost every class it was the same. Diane and Bitsy up front. Rachel in the back. Cindy, me and Caitlin dead center. Every day from right to noon. Latin with Miss Krinkle, English with Miss Ashley, Algebra II with Miss Meade, Biology with Miss Ward, History with Mr. Odmore—the only male teacher at Wellingham, and thus, resident heartthrob—and gym with Miss Bailey, who doubled as the tennis coach and had a habit of totally wigging out whenever she drove the school bus. Then, there were two hours of "upperclasswoman"—proctored study hall. Where Rachel, Cindy, Caitlin and I passed notes back and forth calling each other "My Little Kurgan" and "My Bonnie Lass" after what we'd heard on this week's episode of *Highlander: There Can Be Only One!*

For all its faults, Wellingham's academics were first rate. I've never studied so hard in my life, and neither Brown nor NYU nor any other school challenged me the way Wellingham did.

My sophomore year would be tough, but I had no idea what a learning curve there is between private and public education in the South. Surprise-surprise! After nine years of rural public school education, I knew almost nothing. I was starting at ground zero, and figured out pretty quick that it was either sink or swim in this hole.

After my first day of Latin, where a series of near-unpronounceable verbs made my head spin clean off its shoulders, I trudged along to English Lit, where Miss Ashley promptly kicked my ass with the first of many pop quizzes.

Can *you* define "triangulate"? How about "circumspect"? "Provincial"? "Encumbrance"?

. . . Didn't think so.

I also found out I didn't know squat about "declensions." Or "diagramming" sentences. Or "verb tense." Or anything, really, about any major (or minor) work of English literature. When we read *Silas*

Marner by George Eliot, then *A Tale of Two Cities*, by Dickens, I felt a whole new world opening before me. I learned about Greek city-states from Mr. Odmore, who coached soccer and had a freckly "ginger" wife who was constantly pregnant and didn't say much, and line equations from Miss Meade, a tan, leather-skinned lady with a huge smile and a bowl haircut. I struggled at first. I watched Diane and Bitsy rise to the top of the sophomore class while Caitlin popped Correctol laxatives to get thin and Rachel carved a labyrinth design into her thigh with a ballpoint pen. But I was in it to win it. And every night, when old broken-brain complained that the U2 spilling out of my headphones was disturbing her beauty rest, I prayed that baby Jesus would take my side and let me beat her—just once—at *something*.

And one day . . . I did.

One day, during a sophomore class meeting, I was nominated for Honor Cabinet. And so was Bitsy.

Honor Cabinet was a group of students, two from each of the sophomore, junior and senior classes, who were chosen to "uphold the values, traditions and moral code" of Wellingham Academy. Basically, they were the snooty, rich-bitch version of Hall Monitors. While the faculty treated such girls like royalty, the rest of us looked over our shoulders to see if Big Sister was watching.

So, one day, when Irma Jean Merritt—one of the wealthiest and most fervent members of our Young Republicans Club—nominated me for the job, I was flat stunned. Maybe she didn't like Bitsy. Maybe she thought the new kid wouldn't be such a stickler for rules. Who knew? Who *cared*? Important thing was, one minute I was a little nobody struggling to learn point-slope functions and make friends who didn't pop pills or carve themselves into topiary gardens every day . . . and next thing I knew, I'd been voted a representative of my entire class. Granted there were only forty of us . . . but still. Bitsy hadn't. She'd lost. She was now, for all purposes, a steamin' hot pile of *loser*.

And woo boy, was she mad!

Suddenly, Bitsy—who knew I was a religiously late sleeper—got religious, too. But in a totally annoying way. Suddenly, little Miss Phineas Gage was waking up at six a.m. to press her sweater-vests and read her Bedside Study Bible. With every light on in the room. Suddenly, Diane was inviting me to lunch to discuss "official Cabinet business" and Bitsy was telling me how "the dear, sweet Lord didn't appreciate my using His name in vain." How "I could always make conversation with Jesus."

Oh, my. Was that so?

In that case, I suggested Bitsy converse with dear, sweet Jesus 'bout fixing her broken brain. Or invest in a nice, dim, single-person reading light that wouldn't flood over to my side of room at the crack of friggin' dawn.

She didn't much take to my suggestion.

After that, things started to change around Wellingham. The new kid was getting special treatment, and she didn't like it. Outside our little snow globe of a world, gas hit one dollar a gallon and folks *freaked*. Rachel lent me her Alanis Morissette single of "You Oughta Know," inspiring us less toward Jesus and more toward hating boys forever and ever. But much like my stint of upholding "values, traditions and morals," our little bubble of change was soon to burst. When it came out later that Alanis was writing about Dave Coulier (Uncle Joey from *Full House*), we all lost some respect for the leather-pants-clad rocker girl. Uncle Joey was yucky to the max and we felt a little betrayed. Who in her right mind would get that worked up over a paunchy, middle-aged bald guy? Plus, Burlington's old Carmike theater with its red cloth seats and velvet curtains that closed around the screen started charging $3.50 per ticket. That plus the cost of gas meant the school started cutting back on weekend trips to the movies. And Miss Bailey's away games to Saint Mary's, Wellingham's über-slutty, second-class rival.

Like I said, the bubble was bursting. This Rebel Deb-to-Be couldn't play Hall Monitor much longer. Not with a straight face, anyway.

A few weeks into my Cabinet appointment (don't that sound fancy?) it was time for all the tenth graders to get new ID badges made.

This meant Rachel, Cindy, Caitlin and I had to trot down to the student store—an old stone building that still sold Moravian sugar cookies in long tin cans—to have our pictures taken and printed on tiny laminated cards alongside our dates of birth. We'd heard that some Puritan settler chick had drowned her baby in an old pump well in the store's basement. When Miss Isley, the eightysomething-year-old church lady from Yazoo City, Mississippi, who ran the front cash register and whose job it was to make sure us whippersnappers didn't disorganize the pencil sharpeners, met us at the door, we knew today was gonna suck pretty hard. Everybody knew Miss Isley's grandson, Tarnell, because he used to come by all the girls' school dances, wearing old-fashioned wingtips, too much hair gel, and offering oh-so-quotable words of wisdom:

"Beer is God's way of saying He loves us and approves of sleeping in every other Sunday."

"After my last DUI, the judge asked me, 'Son, would you consider rehab?' 'Not unless they've started serving whiskey,' I replied."

"The only form of birth control I use is the Mason-Dixon Line."

But my all-time favorite was something a bit simpler. . . .

"There ain't nothing," he'd say, "like a sweet Southern girl."

I think I liked this Tarnell Isley–ism best because it rang true.

Especially considering how many of us he tried to lure out to the woods after each dance for "a pull off his longneck Budweiser."

Tarnell used to come by Wellingham after lunch. We'd go on long walks around campus and he'd tell me all about his home and family ties to Colonel Sanders, Stonewall Jackson and Orville Redenbacher.

Tarnell considered himself a "gentleman." A "nice guy."

Throughout the twentieth century, sex, chivalry and the myth of the "nice guy" tended to rotate every ten years. In the '60s, nice guys wore crew cuts and drove Chryslers, and that got them girls. We accepted that.

In the '70s, they bought aviator sunglasses and grew shaggy, "Screw you, Nixon!" facial hair, and that got them girls. We learned to accept (and quietly laugh at) that.

In the '80s, they smiled a lot. They shaped their "fades" and wore acid-washed jeans and pretended to like Whitesnake. They worked in record stores and didn't mind female condoms. Nobody was really that happy; we were all just a little too freaked out over GRID, Tommy Lee's back hair and Bret Michael's lineup of trashy-looking girlfriends. We didn't know how to accept that. Nice girls everywhere were more than a little frustrated.

When the '90s came around, guys suddenly became moody and threw away all their shampoo. They avoided showers, replaced colorful clothes with black, long-sleeved T-shirts and Kurt Cobain envy, and . . . oddly . . . we loved that. That got *us* a few dates once in a while—the "nice girls" milling around in the back of the gym during every school dance. For once, it wasn't just the fox-tails who wore their cleavage pulled up to their necks.

In the '90s, guys stopped caring so much about their appearance and started caring about—shockingly—*what they had to offer.* They were finally becoming sensitive, datable creatures, and "nice girls" caught a break. Chivalry came back. Mr. Nice Guy evolved into men who'd found old copies of *The Art of War* and dared to crack a page, who were finally available because they were "sensitive" and "enlightened" and wore fuzzy sweaters to the beach. Lots of sweaters and sensitivity and "special moments" in the '90s.

Tarnell was a big fan of that all mushy '90s stuff, especially the "special moments."

One time, he showed up after lunch with that look in his eye. He took my hand and led me toward the usual spot—a long staircase leading down from the main campus to a football stadium college kids used during the school year. Only this time, we didn't keep walking and talking. He was unusually quiet, in fact, as we sat down on the first step. He smiled, played with my hair, told me how "bee-*you*-tee-ful" I was. . . .

And then it happened.

He reached for my face. I thought maybe I had something stuck to my cheek or wedged between my teeth. So, I opened my mouth and started digging for leftovers. His hands landed on my shoulders, then moved to my neck, turning me into a sweaty ball of fear. Not only were my teeth fulla crud, but I'd had the ribs for lunch and was feeling mighty gassy.

His fingers brushed my skin, making me blush. *Dang, is she shy? That's hot,* he thought. Or whatever goes through a twenty-seven-year-old's brain just before he goes in for the kill.

Then his braces clamped around my mouth like a bear trap and a slimy, slithery water snake entered my mouth and promptly had its way with my tonsils. He fished and floundered around in there for what felt like an eternity. Finally, he pulled away. He had this fat-cat smile like we'd just shared this special, romantic moment that would be written in the stars. He held me close and we rocked back and forth. Then he started blabbering about all sorts of stuff, like his favorite bird dog, Floyd, and how I should take care to scrape the burnt pieces off his Momma's cornbread when I came over for Sunday dinner. Oh, and not to mention the mole over her lip because she was getting that one removed.

Meanwhile, I never wanted to kiss another "nice guy" again.

All this ran through my mind while Caitlin, Rachel, Cindy and I played "rock, paper, scissors" in the bookstore. We finally decided Caitlin had to ask Miss Isley to show us downstairs.

Poor Caitlin.

She was a new kid, too, but her roommate situation was even worse than mine. Caitlin lived with Jenny Lee Crumple. Jenny was the spitting image of her Daddy, Bo Crumple, whose neck was thicker than his head and who talked with a Texas drawl you could ride out till sunset. The Crumples were big people, and Jenny Lee's Momma always reminded me of "Chyna Doll" from the WWF. Jenny Lee was essentially her Daddy in a blond wig. One hand could cover your whole face, and her thigh and shoulder muscles rivaled any boyfriend I'd ever had—or ever would have, for that matter.

Caitlin, on the other hand, was chubby, big-lipped and timid. When Caitlin walked in with her Momma and found Jenny Lee's man-panties ("manties") sitting right there in the middle of the floor atop a half-eaten mushroom pizza, she knew the next year of her life would be tough.

But now, cowering before Miss Isley's crotchety old wrath, Jenny Lee didn't seem all that bad. In the end, Caitlin whimpered enough to get us down into the basement "to get printer paper," which Miss Isley couldn't—and wouldn't—deign to get for us, anyway.

So, she unlocked the basement door and we tiptoed downstairs.

"You gals get back here quick, ya hear? We got them dang badges ta make!" Miss Isley shouted from the stairs.

Somebody upstairs was playing Caitlin's favorite song. An old 45 record (yep, they still had those, too!) of Elvis crooning "Don't Cry Daddy" that kept scratching on the "Daddy." The needle must've been kinda wobbly, so all the words kept running together into a sloppy King soup. I 'spect that's pretty close to how Elvis sounded during his last tour, anyway.

But we were too excited by what we'd found to pay attention. While there was no pump (nor mummified settler baby) hidden downstairs. . . .

About a dozen boxes of ID badges and laminating equipment lay waiting instead.

Rachel turns to me and we share a look. Who wants to be fifteen with Tarnell Isley when we could be twenty-one with college boys?

It was around midnight when I finally reached Wake Forest University and talked my way past the campus police. Tonight was the Phi Kappa Psi fraternity's annual gathering to initiate their pledges . . . and, needless to say, I was counting on a little "initiation" of my own.

Southern fraternities get real passionate about this kind of thing, and some of them even have special things they do in the fellas' honor. On this night, the Phi Psis even had a polite buffet dinner preceding the party. Somebody even put out fancy pewter cups and laid a blue carpet with the Phi Psi crest on the floor.

Watching all this, I was more than a little disappointed. I'd seen *Revenge of the Nerds* about a hundred times (while Granny Blanche was at her bridge club) and was hoping that times were still fast at more than Ridgemont High.

Back in the Southern '60s and' '70s, Wake was supposedly a fun-lovin', greased-lightnin' school where frat boys spent their days "gettin' it on" to Marvin Gaye music, playing beer pong and hazing their pledges by sticking Icy Hot down their underdrawers. Or, at least, that's what my Daddy told me. Besides *Revenge of the Nerds*, the only visual references I had for "frat boys" came from his stories of the Kappa Alpha house back in 1974. Back then, Alan "Stinger" Fields and his friends were star football players, who were given big athletic scholarships so they could win championship titles, major in Animal Husbandry and make "C's" in classes like "Insemination 101." Theirs was an uninhibited time full of fun, laughter and flirtation. A good way to delaying growing up and joining the "real world" for another four years. Five, if you got red-shirted and sat the bench, my Daddy said.

By the '80s, however, things had changed. The "real world" had won out. By then, the most partying this campus ever saw was when Ronald Reagan got elected, or when a bunch of seniors protested till they were finally allowed to dance in public.

The Phi Psis on this night looked less like party animals and more like a bunch of repressed kids just grateful for a dance floor. They were humble and solemn and quiet—like Big Brother was watching from the Dean's office. Instead of the cocky, sexy frat boys *Revenge of the Nerds*, *Sixteen Candles* and *National Lampoon*, I got a whole bunch of Richie Rich impersonators dressed up in their daddies' clothes. The atmosphere was tentative and polite—like we were waiting for the president to show up. Or worse, George Wallace's ghost. I felt like I was at a wake, folks were so reserved and quiet. Nobody dared speak above a whisper, and if any sudden laughter broke out, it was quickly silenced by the crowd's stern, disapproving looks and unspoken *tsk-tsks*.

After laying out the fraternity carpet, the brothers changed into their uniforms: matching seersucker suits they were supposed to wear every day—even to parties. Then they all got together and stood around in a big clique on one side of the room with their dates: Stepford Wives in monogrammed cardigans with crispy bangs, drawn-on eyebrows and fake-bake tans.

After a few minutes, everybody abandoned the pewter cups for chilled glasses of punch or white wine spritzers. Then they paired off into couples and chatted softly about taxes and "the gawddamn i-legals" invading our state. It was like watching a bunch of speed daters—or worse, our own fortysomething parents at a country club brunch.

On the other side of the room, dorky, underage girls like Caitlin, Rachel and me huddled in corners avoiding eye contact with our elders and clutching the cups we'd worked so hard to access but were now too afraid to drink. We were terrified and not about to touch the punch bowl, which seemed verboten and probably not even spiked.

Only with this crowd, and much to our eager-to-rebel chagrin, there wasn't much to fear. All in all, this was the kind of party I could've safely invited my Momma to.

Welcome to a fun night out in the middle of the rural South. As I'd always known, but wouldn't acknowledge, there was literally *nothing* to do at fifteen in Winston-Salem in the late '90s. Even in a frat house with a fake ID and three sets of virginity to endanger.

Back then, outside of Wake and Wellingham, most of the city streets were covered with prostitutes and criminals. Kids our own age got mugged just walking downtown, so we weren't about to go that direction. The nearest high school with boys, North Carolina School of the Arts, was full of would-be artists who wore spiked dog collars and thought our school even weirder than theirs. So, in the end, it was either Wake or go home.

After the pledges were formally introduced, the whole chapter stood as one to sing "American Pie," leaning on one another's shoulders and swaying back and forth in one huge circle. Later in the evening, a few couples started slow-dancing cheek to cheek. Much to my disappointment, however, everybody kept their eyes up and their hands to themselves. So much for my "initiation." At any moment, I expected good ol' George Wallace might indeed jump out of the closet to give an impromptu lecture about the evils of "forn-eye-cation."

Not exactly the wild, zany times a Rebel Deb was hoping for. It was like Jesse Helms could jump out of the closet at any moment, and with all these tight-asses in the room, probably would. Where were the six-packs? The panty raids? The fun-loving guys whose roaming hands we were hoping to slap away? Rachel, always the subtle cynic, took one look at the Phi Psi president's tiny, round fingers and size 8 loafers and grimaced. "Little hands and little feet all add up to little meat," she said.

True. Putting some of these boys in suits was kinda like bothering to perfume-up a pig. While they represented some of the best families in Winston, the lacy edge of the inbreeding slip was beginning to stick out beneath a few skirts here, fellas. Rufus T. Polychron, whose Daddy invented some kind of adjustable elastic to keep your panties from falling down 'round your ankles, sported the biggest set of ears in three counties. Henry "Mac" Hanes was heir to a hosiery empire but, due to his huge schnoz of a nose sucking up every oxygen molecule in the room, couldn't find a dinner date with enough lung power to survive the appetizer course.

Needless to say, Phi Psi—dull as it was—housed some of the heaviest hitters in the South. This was no Wellingham dance, where all of us gathered in the gym to grind up against the boys from Christ School, who'd ridden their activity bus all the way from Boone to fetch us Diet Sprites before a quick make-out session behind the field hockey clubhouse. We were little girls playing dress-up in our Momma's shoes. What if all these rich college boys discovered three charlatans in their midst?!

I finally took a sip from somebody's "Titty-Twister" and tried to calm down. . . .

Too late.

Seems Kimmy Lee Linklater's older sister had ended up at Wake, too. Only she was a senior studying art history (or whatever M.R.S. degree was currently most fashionable), and we were underlings in too much makeup, leaving telltale lipstick stains on our beers.

The elder Miss Linklater took one look at me and blanched. That wasn't no sorority girl. That was her kid sister's tomboy playmate, sans overalls and catfish stains on her hands.

I leaned over to Rachel. "We gotta make a run for it," I whispered.

But, again, too late.

Miss Linklater was marching straight in our direction, with about a half-dozen very irate Chi Omegas behind her.

Next thing I knew, we were dumped off at the curb outside Wellingham, sneaking around in the bushes. It was already way after "lights out" when Caitlin knocked on Cindy's first-floor window and she finally agreed to let us in. Rachel crawled in first, scraping her knees something awful in the process. Then Caitlin, with me pushing her big tush from below. It seemed we'd get away with this one scot-free, but by the time I was ready to jump across Cindy's sill, our jig was already up. Miss Freeze came bellowing down the hall, flung open Cindy's door and all four of us were in a whole mess of trouble.

I looked back through the open window as Miss Freeze laid into first Cindy, then Caitlin, then Rachel. After some pretty thorough questioning, they were taken away to await the dawn and, with it, a new onslaught of questions and punishment. Their ringleader, Miss Former Honor Cabinet member, would be last on the chopping block. A warning to the others.

Above, through the trees, the "Dick in the Sky" looked down on our plight.

Only this time I didn't smile. Didn't laugh. Didn't stare. It was suddenly the most unfunny building I'd ever seen. A modern symbol of "separate but equal," keeping us Wellingham girls on one side and a whole world of happy kids doing happy things on the other.

For my punishment, I was "campused" (forbidden from leaving the building) for three weeks and got my butt kicked straight off Honor Cabinet. During my "period of confinement," as Miss Freeze politely referred to it, the girls and I ruled the school. We held daily *Sixteen Candles* and *Pretty in Pink* marathons after school. We watched old reruns of *My So-Called Life* and fell in love with Jordan Catalano all over again. We stole Ella Mae Abernathy's prize Daisy Dukes and held fashion shows, flaunting our pubescent fannies in front of any and every reflective surface. As the school beauty queen,

Ella Mae took especial pride in carefully cutting and molding her cutoff blue-jean shorts. So we had to make sure and return them before she made curfew—for upperclasswomen this was ten p.m. *sharp*—or else all hell might break loose. You just don't go filching the beauty queen's Daisies. And not that Ella Mae wasn't a perfect lady and all, but had hers in particular turned up missing . . . well, our asses would've been handed to us by a five-foot-ten Debutante with raging PMS. We listened to "Ordinary World" by Duran Duran and took Polaroids of ourselves wearing tuxedo pants and boleros and crazy hats our parents would've made us donate to poor folks loitering 'round the Goodwill. We snuck out after study hall and spent hours rifling through prom dresses at Tina's Treasures, the local consignment shop, which also featured pinto beans and peanuts in its weekly two-for-one sale.

Once I wasn't on Honor Cabinet anymore, Diane stopped asking me to lunch. Which was fine with me. I was getting heartburn from all the cucumber sandwiches. She always insisted we go to Tea for Two, where socialites gathered after bridge club and before drinks at the country club. Instead, as Wellingham's newly minted Rebel Deb, I ate in the cafeteria every day like everybody else. Well, everybody except Caitlin. She stuck to bran cereal, grapefruit juice and navy beans with rice.

The minute I got sprung from the joint, we went cruising in Rachel's brand-new VW Beetle—mint green with a convertible top. We did a lot of that kind of thing. Days are long and hot in the humid South, and in the late '90s there wasn't much else to do. We blasted "Heart and Soul" by T'pau and got our ears pierced at Claire's. We watched public school boys playing Hacky Sack outside Morning Dew Coffee Shop. Besides the parking lot of Lowe's or the local city hall, Morning Dew was the cool-kid hangout and our main source of escape from Wellingham. We'd sign out to the library and then spend the next several hours drinking espresso and flirting with older boys who smoked pot, shaved their heads into faux-hawks and affected English accents. That way they could pretend to be from London instead of Rural Hall. They taught us the difference between "naked"—when you don't have no clothes on—and "nekkid"—when (in the words of Lewis Grizzard, Jr., a fellow Southerner and a great American) you don't have no clothes on and you're up to something. We learned crude jokes we'd giggle about later. Like, "Why do Southern Belles avoid orgies? Too many 'thank-you' notes," and such bathroom-stall humor. Some of them had thick accents and, when enraged, called each other "sumbitch." Some of them were addicted to coke. Some of them played bass guitar and braided hemp necklaces to sell to surf shops. Some of them tried to lure us into the bathroom to make out. Some of them were even gay . . . which, at fifteen with Ronald Reaganism not too far behind, we'd never really encountered. Hell, till I went to college, I thought a blow job was something you got at the hairdresser's.

We boycotted clubs. We avoided sports. We went cruising around Winston every afternoon . . . except Wednesdays. Wednesdays we had Cotillion at the Piedmont Club.

Tuesday nights, ten or twelve of us "riches"—Wellingham girls from the oldest, most established Southern families—wouldn't wash our hair. We'd take our Momma's advice and cover our scalps with baby powder to "keep the curl" from our hot rollers. The next morning, you could tell who the "riches" were when they wore their rollers to Latin. Sure, there'd be whispers and jealous snickers from non-Cotillion girls behind our backs, but we didn't care, 'cause we got to skip study hall. We'd cram our food at lunch and spend the next three hours pile-driving ourselves into whalebone corsets laced with cotton. Then came the dresses. Mine was always a scoop-neck lilac frock with frilly, poufed sleeves and a crinoline bustle. Top that off with about a pound of cover-up, eye shadow, Lip Smacker bubble-gum-flavored gloss and Aqua Net hairspray, and we were ready to rock.

Scarlett woulda been proud.

Just so you folks know, these Cotillion classes were supposed to prep us wannabes for more than one Deb Ball.

According to Ella Mae Abernathy, who spilled her secrets in exchange for the location of her "missing" Backstreet Boys CD, there are at least *two* "coming out" occasions. And by the time a girl's got her learner's permit in western North Carolina, she's already prepping for her first, preliminary Debut: the Shelby Ball.

There's a whole schedule laid out for these ladies to show their stuff properly at the Ball:

By March of their senior year in high school, the Debs get their invitations, and approximately ten girls from each city (including Winston) are chosen. About a hundred girls (total, from all North Carolina cities) come out at Shelby. Debs come from as far as Greensboro, Hickory, Cleveland County and Asheville for the big event.

By late April, the Debs are shopping at Poffie Girls in Charlotte to pick out their Deb Ball gown from miles of poufy, white silk material. The pushy Poffie ladies are basically the drug dealers of Debbing. How they fit a Deb for her dress is basically the same thing my Uncle Stu Hogphill, mechanic and bird-dog raiser, does to size up a pig for market. Well, minus the hog-tyin' rope.

They take each girl's measurements, standing her on the fitting block and pushing the pouffiest dresses available. Each Deb is required to "try out" her dress by posing on a high-backed stool, her crinoline immediately popping up to resemble a big marshmallow. On average, these gowns cost anywhere from thirteen hundred to eight thousand dollars.

What is this, a wedding or something? Can you imagine spending that kinda money on a little girl's party dress? My Daddy's first Cadillac DeVille—red with red interior, so it resembled a moving hickey more than anything—only cost about five hundred dollars. And the in-state tuition to UNC was only about seven grand at the time.

Then again, where I come from, getting a girl "out" and married off seemed far more important than a college degree.

After choosing her gown, each girl receives a Debutante Handbook containing detailed instructions on choosing her "Marshal," or her date to the Ball. These instructions are designed to make sure the Marshals are clean-cut, sans earrings, long hair and/or tattoos. Essentially, nobody interesting was allowed to escort you "down the aisle." Uncle Stu once got invited to one of these things. He was a young son-of-a-gun, fresh out of the Marines, and when his Deb-to-Be girlfriend took a look at all those "God, Country, Corps" tats, she almost fainted. Made him buy a whole bunch of Cover Girl concealer, and by the time she was through, Uncle Stu looked like he got hit by a paint truck.

Both Marshal (usually the Deb's steady boyfriend) and Grand Marshal (the Deb's Daddy) have to wear fancy-tailed, white-tie tuxedos with gloves to the Shelby Ball. Grand Marshals have a much bigger role than Marshals—Marshals thankfully don't have to wear gloves. Once a Deb receives her Handbook, she mails back her check (about two grand, made payable to the Terpsichorean Society of North Carolina). Then she fills out a form with the names of her father and his title in *French*. For example, Mr. Beauregard the worm farmer would become M. *Beauregard, fermier de ver.* (Fancy, huh?) Also printed on each invitation are the words "All Debs are required to meet at the home of Mr. Beauregard for a pre-Deb orientation."

Make no mistake: The Beauregards are the *crème* of the crop in Debutante culture.

The family home sprawls over fifty acres of land standing by a lake. The house itself is about ten thousand square feet. Very *Gone With the Wind,* Tara manor. Classically expensive china. Tudor-style portraits throughout the house. Columns. Green, sloping lawns. Fountains with angels spouting water and the like. Once the Debs arrive for pre-Deb orientation, they feast on chocolate-covered strawberries, sparkling cider and mimosas (for the Mommas, of course). All the Debs already know each other because they've been at pre-Deb parties all summer long. Mr. Beauregard—who always reminded me of Big Daddy from *Cat on a Hot Tin Roof*—usually gives the Debs a speech about how proud they should be of representing their communities, and that they shouldn't drink at the Deb Ball.

Coming from a fella who serves mimosas at orientation, this speech of his is the biggest hoot of the evening.

Meanwhile, from late May to late August/early September, the Debs host theme parties: Discos, Country-Western Line Dancing (where Debs take supper in barns with horses still standing around in their stalls, eyeballing them as they eat) and pool parties. The parties in western North Carolina—as opposed to Raleigh—are kinder, down-to-earth and nicer. To most folks, that means you're allowed to eat all the barbecue you want and undo the top two buttons on your pants, but I'm pretty sure Mrs. Beauregard wouldn't approve. So what if her husband already popped through his a while back? You let loose those floodwaters, and you might end up with a whole crowd of unbuttoned Daddies with their pants falling 'round their ankles, trying to line-dance with future Debutantes. And that just don't look right.

Before each party, all the Debs and Debs' Mommas get together and meet at fancy restaurants to plan each event. Here, all the Mommas try to out-dress and out-class each other. Some Mommas want really fancy food (like caviar and stuff made out of yucky duck bladders), while most of the teenage Debs want things like Diet Coke and chicken fingers.

In general, the Mommas are much more invested in the Deb parties and Ball than the Debs, and competition amongst them is rampant—a lot of boob jobs going on, as well as comparing their husbands' jobs at the LabCorp plant or Moses Cone Hospital. As expected, these arguments usually lead to fights about fancy versus modern, often resulting in pseudo catfights at the table. And then you'd better watch out. Most of these gals are about as big as a double-wide trailer. You get that many pounds of ladylike behavior, bouffant hairdos and acrylic nails passionate about a cause . . . and you're on a ride you just can't stop and get off.

Please don't take all this to mean only the older women get catty at these things. Heck, no.

There are certainly Deb duels as well. Usually involving the Humble versus the Haughty. For example, while their Mommas fight, some of the more down-to-earth Debs are arguing, "What's all the fuss? We're just here to dance and eat brownies!" while other, snobbier-type Debs refrain from replying. They smile sweetly, silently wondering, "Where on *earth* did these low-end rednecks come from?" Which, of course, was directed at fat wannabe Debs like me.

It's all a wash. Ultimately, the younger girls have little say in such matters, anyway. Their only comfort is getting to choose the band, DJ and menu, while the decorations are handled by their Mommas.

In September, Debs collectively hire a hairdresser and makeup artist to stay with them for three days before the Ball. The local favorite is Neely Ray Privat, a fortysomething beautician from Chapel Hill whose perfect eyeliner and flamboyant "flock of seagulls" hairdo makes him the safest bet for hanging around teenage girls on a Friday night.

After Neely Ray's put his final touches on a hundred or so French twists, the Debs practice what's called the "Wedding Rehearsal" with their Grand Marshals.

This happens in a local civic center or community college, and whereas the whole summer is about the Mommas, the Shelby Ball itself is about the Daddies. A faux stage, catwalk and arbor with flowers are decorated for this Friday evening rehearsal. Each Deb walks from backstage, steps through the arbor, smiles then proceeds down the catwalk. The Grand Marshal waits at the foot of the steps, offers each arriving Deb his arm and then escorts her to the couple's selected "mark" in front of the audience. The Marshals are also there Friday night to practice the "cutting in" dance, wherein each Marshal stands behind the Grand Marshal, and when the father takes his daughter's hand and walks her to the bottom of the stage, the Marshal steps in to take her hand. More specifically, each Grand Marshal holds out his hand (gloved), the Deb takes it and curtsies. They then proceed together, walking down the stage steps to form a semicircle at the base of the stairs. While the Grand Marshals are escorting the Debs to their positions, the Marshals walk behind the Debs and stand behind them and the Daddies. Once all the Debs are in their spots, the Debs move to waltz with their Grand Marshals for about one minute. Then the Marshals "cut in," while the Grand Marshals go out into the audience and fetch the Debs' Mommas. The rest of the evening is a formal dance party.

Ella Mae Abernathy put it best: "The Shelby Ball always has great barbecue . . . and that's about it. There aren't any stores or anything to go shopping beforehand. There's a swimming pool at the hotel. That's the only advantage. My younger sisters were too young to be invited, so they lay by the pool and drove up and down the two-lane highway the whole day while I was gettin' my hair done. Oh, and I don't remember there being any black people. Ever."

On Saturday (the day of the Ball), families rent hotel rooms at the Deb Hotel—a local Holiday Inn or whatever—near the local civic center (or wherever the Ball is taking place). Some Debs aren't used to staying in anything other than Ritz-Carltons. This usually kicks off the inevitable fit-pitching about the noticeable absence of spas at the Deb Hotel.

The hairdresser and makeup artist start "formal" hair at nine a.m. and basic makeup at eleven, with multiple retouches throughout the day. Then the Debs have lunch with their Daddies at the Cleveland Country Club, where they "meet and mingle" with other Deb-Daddy duos. Steak and potatoes are usually served at this meal to satisfy the men, and the grazing lasts till about three p.m. Full-bellied and fancy-free, the Debs venture back to the hotel to collectively take a nap, Scarlett O'Hara style. Around four, the Debs' grandmothers and aunts come in and flower trucks start delivering gifts and bridal bouquets.

At about four-thirty, the Debs start putting on their dresses. Some have up to thirty-two buttons along the back. This is where Neely Ray's fingering skills really come in handy. Meanwhile, the Debs'

Daddies usually have somebody watching the door. "You just let me know if anybody comes by here lookin' to peep. And by anybody I mean any swingin' dick" is the usual set of instructions.

With all thirty-two buttons buttoned, Neely Ray endures another round of makeup retouching. Then the long kid-leather gloves (above the elbow) come out.

These babies need talcum powder to roll them into place, with an extra sprinkle or so underneath to prevent too much sweating. During all this, the Marshals are stuck together in a little "holding" room, where the Debs' Mommas have finally found something to pass the time—giving a whole room full of anxious teenagers a lesson in tying bow ties. Once everyone is dressed and ready, the Ball begins and follows the procedure from Friday's rehearsal. Typically, shrimp, pasta, sweet tea and fruit are served, but *no alcohol is allowed* . . . well, until after the Ball, that is, when the more down-to-earth Debs head off to Hersey's Barbecue or a local bar joint to finish the night.

Don't get me wrong: Shelby's fun for practice. Like a good pair of training wheels.

But the *real* event is the Raleigh Ball a year or so later.

In early May, toward the end of a Deb's freshman year of college, she'll receive an invitation to the Raleigh Debutante Ball. She's usually at UNC getting her degree in English Lit or Education, so the mailman doesn't have to go far. She'll also receive another Handbook, including the same forms with a schedule of events laid out for her to follow. Approximately 130 girls are chosen for the Raleigh Ball, mostly from Wake Forest, Chapel Hill, Winston-Salem and Rocky Mount.

Debs have up to a month to pick out their Marshals and submit their payment forms with the boy's name included. This part's pretty important. If a Deb doesn't have a Marshal last minute, she'll have to withdraw from Debbing or grab somebody from the audience during the Ball.

Once again, in May and June, the Debs travel to Poffie Girls for another fitting—only this time, the Debs are older and much more direct about what they want and *don't* want in a Deb gown. Some girls still cling to the traditional poufy skirts . . . while a few skintight rebels opt for modern, slinky silk. I didn't get either one, unfortunately, because I'd already been rejected as a potential Deb by this point. But having witnessed a boatload of these fittings, I will say: the bigger the pouf, the better.

From June to late August, the Debs once again get together to plan the same kinds of theme parties, only this time the DJs (and the catfighting Mommas) are out. Also gone are the days of wiggling around to the Electric Slide. The Debs are supposed to be grown women now, and expected to hire the same time-honored, local North Carolina oldies band—Chairman of the Board. Mostly, these pre-Deb parties involve shagging, barbecuing, luaus, and pool events at the local country club. What's slightly different is that the Raleigh Debs continue to receive more invitations for Christmas parties, weddings, birthdays, baby showers and such *after* the actual Ball has taken place. Also, kinda like the fitting room at Shelby, each pre-Deb party now has its own Daddy "bouncer" at the door—mostly because of problems with college-age Debs sneaking in their college-age friends.

Beside the occasional crashers, there are *big* alcohol problems at this point. Debs and their boyfriends sneak it in and get plastered, and then the night is filled with girls throwing up in various bathrooms. While more traditional Debs don't enjoy it being less proper than when their grandmothers did it, the food, decorations and music are generally much better at this level. By "better" I mean no more electronic remixes of "Way Down Yonder on the Chattahoochee" or "There's a Tear in My Beer over You."

No, siree.

Becoming a Debutante now meant live musical talent through which to put our years of dancing lessons to good use. Like, for example, trying to box step whenever Misti Krystal Truelove (Chairman of the Board's lead singer) belted out her rendition of "I Fall to Pieces."

Even with the lovely accompaniment, I'd say the boys have it worse than the girls. At least, in some respects. Besides being forced to dance in new, hard-soled tuxedo shoes, Marshals now are cut from their former starring roles during the actual Ball down to a mere cameo here and there. In Raleigh, the poor kid is nothing more than a "teaser" horse, making appearances only as needed for specific duties. The Daddies, on the other hand, are a different story. While a Deb's Marshal stands to dance with her only after her presentation (there is no "cutting in"), the Grand Marshal takes over as the second-most important figure of the evening.

From September to early December, the Debs attend their sophomore year of college, but by late December, the Ball schedule is back in full swing.

In December, the Debs reunite to reenact the same rehearsal schedule as Shelby. Friday is still practice night, with Debs in formal hair and makeup and wearing cute "lily" (taffeta) dresses. The actual Ball occurs the next Saturday. As in Shelby, when each Deb takes her Grand Marshal's arm and the couple walks to its "mark," all the Daddies and daughters form a full circle around the room. On Saturday, hair and makeup are done in the afternoon (around three) instead of the morning, and then the Debs head to the country club auditorium, while their Mommas, siblings and boyfriends stay in the audience waiting for pictures to be taken. At about four-thirty the Deb picks up her bouquet of roses and sits for formal photography with her immediate family and her Marshal—who then leaves once again to sit in the audience.

The next few minutes are funnier than watching my Aunt Dot "break in" a new pair of panty hose.

First of all, the Debs and their Grand Marshals have to head down into the club's basement to await presentation. Mind you, they're formally dressed, coiffed, perfumed and starry-eyed from all the camera flashes. Then the Daddy does his balancing act. He takes one hand, helping her down the basement stairs with her huge hoopskirt and bouquet . . . carrying her "Deb Stool" in his other. "Deb Stools" are traditional, high stools painted and decorated by family members (like with fake flowers and pictures laminated on them) for the Deb to sit on in her big crinoline skirt as she waits to come onstage. Kinda like a sorority sister's painted paddle, Deb stools are *huge* within Debutante culture. Especially in North Carolina. When they reach the bottom, the couple gets a break. The Deb usually perches high up on her stool while poor Daddy loiters around at his next job: waiting for the family name to be called. Again, this was another ritual I was banned from as a "rebel"—which was probably a good thing, considering my bootyliciousness might've broken the stool, destroyed all my handiwork, and heartily embarrassed Daddy Fields.

So, basically, a Deb's Daddy spends much of his time helping her walk down flights of stairs in high heels with his left arm, carrying a huge stool with his right arm, finally coming to rest in an entire room filled with "Brides" and their dozens of hand mirrors, all jittery 'cause they're waiting to "come out."

Just before formal presentation, the Debs are called in groups of fifteen to line up in alphabetical order. The comedy routine starts again as each Deb and her father walk back *up* the mountain of stairs they've just conquered, back toward the stage.

This time, instead of a simple arbor, the stage is set up like a Southern mansion. At either end, two pillars, two windows, two rooms (usually, one with red wallpaper, one with green) form an actual house, which the Debs must all pass through before they take their Daddies' hands, curtsy and then move down to form a full circle. Every Deb picks up another, larger bouquet of white roses (stationed at a nearby table) to carry when her name is called.

Once all the Debs and Grand Marshals have passed through the "mansion" and taken their places downstage, they're surrounded on all sides. The audience moves in to form a square around the Debutante circle, and multiple cameras are readied on all sides to photograph the Debs. The Head Debutante comes out last, positioning herself in the middle atop a big platform where she can pick up a huge ball of ribbon attached to a maypole. The Head Deb's job is to pass this ribbon around till all the Debs hold a piece of it and are (symbolically) interconnected within their social class. The Debs then raise the ribbon (along with their bouquets) and walk around in a circle like a carousel, with the Head Deb in the center. After one full rotation, they drop their ribbon to the floor and enter the audience. The Debs keep their bouquets, however, as they receive big hugs and kisses and other mushy displays from family and friends and as they pose for individual pictures. The Head Debutante is chosen by the Deb Ball Committee based on any number of factors, including family ties, reputation and—most of all—wealth.

After the Ball, the entire audience and all the Debs attend a *huge* party at the Raleigh Country Club. Invitations to this event are probably the most sought-after in the Southeast, and the place is usually *packed* shoulder to shoulder. As expected, the Chairman of the Board plays shag music for the crowd. The party lasts till about two a.m., when shuttle buses start running to and from the party to the Deb Hotel to prevent all the drunk, rich folks from embarrassing themselves by trying to flag down limos along the highway.

W̶ay before all this happens . . . before any Debutante becomes a lady and full-fledged member of adult society . . . she's a little girl waiting in line for her first box-step lesson.

And like most new kids, when I arrived at the club for "upper-level" Cotillion classes—for high-schoolers—my sophomore year, I didn't exactly know what to expect. Caitlin, Cindy and Rachel were old hands at this. They'd been here since age eleven. I, on the other hand, was fifteen and had only ever engaged in "lower-level" cotillion—for middle-schoolers and younger. Thus, in their world, I was *way* behind the eight ball. Altogether, Rachel and Cindy already had close to two dozen pairs of pearl-lined gloves between them, and Caitlin's Momma had long ago insisted she wear a latex girdle zipped up to her neck. Still, they assured me I was better late than never and wouldn't suffer immediate bodily harm as a result of the fox-trot, so I took a deep breath and dove in.

We gripped hands and pushed through the French doors, treading nervously down the red-carpeted hallway. We were a harmonious threesome of teenage awkwardness. Caitlin was pudgy and self-conscious, Cindy tugged constantly at the elastic rubbing track marks into her thighs, and Rachel was dour and still covered in the remnants of black eye shadow her Momma's washcloth just couldn't scrub away. And donning soccer shorts just beneath my crinoline, I was clearly leading a one-woman revolt against the tyranny of "girly stuff." At the end of the hall stood our Escorts-to-Be: Christ School boys wearing khakis and blue sports coats, forced to accompany us by their equally hoity-toity families.

At that point, the entire group lined up—Debs on one side, Escorts on the other—and filed into the ballroom. Chandeliers. Flowers. Huge bay windows with lace curtains and gilded chairs circling the floor. Each Escort was paired with a Deb-in-Training as an older lady stood in the center cueing the music and clapping along to its rhythm to keep us in step. Each couple joined hands, with the boy's right hand at the girl's waist and his left cupped around her wrist, trying our best to avoid eye contact. We started with a box step. Side, back, side, forward. A clap with every step. The rest of our night followed the same routine. A room full of wannabe Debs in fluffy dresses, itchy tights, crinoline and huge hair bows swaying like Rothschild dolls to their Grannies' Big Band records. When class was over, each Escort took his Deb's hand and led her to a chair. It was then his job to fetch pink, heart-shaped cookies and Kool-Aid from the long tables waiting in the wings.

I looked up at the nervous boy—my "Escort"—standing over me. He wasn't allowed to leave until I'd finished eating, so I bit into my cookie . . . wishing Brent stood in his place. We could blow this joint, ride our bikes into the sunset and eat chili dogs when we got there.

To his credit, my Escort looked just as miserable. Suddenly realizing he'd forgotten to let go my hand, he jerked away, leaving a sweaty wet spot on my glove. Later, I caught a sniff of his Gap cologne and accidentally sneezed into his face.

I'm pretty sure Scarlett wasn't proud anymore.

Chapter Three

Scarlett Faces the Inquisition . . . and Becomes a Rebel Deb:

• Eleventh Grade •

irthin' babies is where it's at!" my good friend Alma Claire used to say.

As Wellingham's self-proclaimed Queen of the Queers, this was her favorite joke. Curvy, flirty, and openly bi-curious, Alma had a sense of humor that stemmed from all the hell she'd caught growing up in Lexington, "L-Boogie," North Carolina.

The only child of a "Glorified! Sanctified! Vilified!" Moravian minister, Alma was the stereotypical preacher's daughter running wild in girls' school. This included "ladyscaping the flowerpot" every morning before class.

"Ladyscaping" was a certain private activity involving an electric razor, a "flowerpot" and a very anxious wannabe Scarlett, who'd been forced to watch her new roommate's "demonstrication" because they shared a bathroom.

"It'll do you some good," Alma said. "Ain't nobody a lady till she learns to trim her fanny!"

Girls like Bitsy and Diane didn't exactly approve of this. When word got around about Alma's grooming habits, they'd call her "gay," which meant stupid, or "queer," which meant "why don't you straighten up and use the stall like everybody else?"

As unique as she was, Alma didn't suffer these insults alone. There were lots of other "queer" gals at Wellingham. There was Lisa Scuppernong, whose entire closet was filled with '70s-era bell-bottoms, fringe vests and tank tops. Lisa drank her whiskey straight out of a screw-top flask and loved Robert Plant more than most folks loved ham biscuits for breakfast. And, let me tell you, nothing hits the spot like a ham biscuit for breakfast.

Then there was Darla Granger, with her tiny, pterodactyl-like frame and thick Georgian accent. Darla was sweet but barked her words like a Chihuahua, especially when talking about her fear of "them dern Hisp-*ann*-aks!"

And who could forget Ida Mae Grumble, the anorexic who survived on oatmeal and graham crackers? Or Mary Sue Wrinkle, the pixielike ballerina whose obsession with fairies bordered on the psychedelic? Or finally Martha and Maple Johnston, twin croquet champions whose body hair put Sasquatch to shame?

Nobody could forget any of them. Especially Alma Claire, their self-proclaimed Queen.

In the beginning, she'd keep me up at night telling stories about her childhood. At the time, Lexington ("L-Boogie") was the pulled-pork capital of the world. Every corner of town was decorated with a fake plastic pig, and no wedding was complete without a pig pickin' reception. Local custom dictated that every groom pull the first piece of pig meat straight out of the pit and feed it to his new bride as a symbol of their love. Then they'd wash the whole thing down with sweet tea and blackberry cobbler with clotted cream. By the end of the night, somebody would fetch a fiddle or an old Hank Williams record and the whole party would slow-dance, cheek to cheek and hip to hip.

At L-Boogie Senior High, girls didn't go to Cotillion or wear ballgowns. They didn't even know what a "Debutante" was.

Oh, no.

Folks at L-Boogie High ("L-Boogers," Alma called them) knew other ways to have fun. They drank beer and smoked rabbit grass out of the backs of flatbed trucks. They spent their weekends listening to Toby Keith and riding four-wheelers through the woods, not learning about useless, uppity stuff like social etiquette or birth control.

Their elders weren't any different. According to Alma, the only fella in town who used condoms was old Dr. Garfunkle, a certified pediatrician-slash-mechanic, and only because he'd caught the clap during the war.

To an outsider like me, L-Boogie High sounded just like Wellingham. So what if it was a world away from our formal traditions and discipline? Its students weren't too different in their treatment of "queers."

When it came to girls like me and Alma, the L-Boogers thought we were freaks. Their notion of a "Debutante" was somebody's boring old granny who sat around sipping tea and listening to chamber music.

And to them, preparing for a Ball sounded like a flat-out waste of time.

Nope. L-Boogers went "swamping" instead.

Swamping was a time-honored tradition among L-Boogers. Imagine two good ol' boys, Chip and Scooter Gerringer, jumping into a dirty watering hole behind their house (which some folks called a "lake"). In L-Boogie, these "lakes" are often filled up with catfish. And Chip and Scooter are well versed at this kind of fishing. They know catfish—besides being scaly, full of bones and requiring entirely too much mayonnaise to eat—like cool, deep spots. So, Chip and Scooter tread water over to the nearest fallen tree, reach in up to their elbows and pull out two live ones per fist.

A bonfire, a jar of mayonnaise and a loaf of Merida white bread later, and Chip and Scooter are helping themselves to a couple fresh catfish sandwiches.

Later, all the L-Boogers would get together and sit around the fire. Scooter would hop onto his Daddy's prized four-wheeler and Winnie Mae Whippersnapper, L-Boogie's newest Squash Queen, would take up the rear. Then they'd speed off into the woods with Winnie Mae squeezing Scooter's belly till he turned blue in the face.

Maybe Chip, eager to outdo his brother, would bring his 1971 International Suburban out for a spin. This baby would be the talk of the town: thirty-five-inch Super Swamper tires, one-ton axles and a 502 military-style engine—black, with flames licking the sides. Truly the Holy Grail of monster trucks, able and willing to leap fifteen Toyota Corollas in a single bound!

Back at L-Boogie High the next day, Chip and Scooter were usually involved in another fun activity most of us at Wellingham had never even heard of: hazing.

According to Alma, hazing in L-Boogie involved something called the Duck Squad. Basically, Chip and Scooter and every other upperclassman at L-Boogie High would grab a freshman, head back to the water hole and paddle the poor kid with a wooden stick till his behind shone pink as lobster meat. If he whined or complained, the usual response was something like, "Boy, you keep that up and I'm-a bust yo head down to tha white meat!"

Sometimes, the elder L-Boogers would pick an especially scrawny underclassman and tape him into a cardboard box before tossing him to the fish. And if he lived, he passed the test.

"Only Yankees and queers," they warned Alma, "ever fail."

That being said, Alma didn't too much like her hometown or talking about it. She'd much rather make up more stories to tickle both our funny bones. She'd come from money and—just like me—felt stifled and held back by giant public school classes with thirty-plus students to every teacher, redneck classmates who'd rather go deer hunting than learn to read, and a chauvinistic atmosphere that made it clear girls were to be seen and not heard. Clearly, Alma hadn't fit in with the public school crowd any better than me, so her Daddy sent her to Wellingham for a real shot at an education.

One of her favorites was making up pretend boyfriends. Her latest was a "townie" named Jack "Jerk-a-Lerk" Black.

Alma'd whisper and I'd giggle all the way through breakfast, morning prayers and down the hall to Biology II. We'd choose two seats by the usual suspects—Cindy, Rachel and Caitlin, who didn't like Alma and, as a result, didn't like me anymore. I was tainted by association.

Bitsy and Diane sat a few feet away, up front and center, pencils poised. Their pink frosted lips puckered and ready for any potential ass-kissing opportunity.

All through class Alma and I would pass heart-shaped notes. We couldn't whisper anymore for fear that Ms. Spencer—Wellingham's biology-teacher-slash-snake-haired-Medusa—would give us the stink-eye and immediately turn us to stone.

Alma's messages were always written in purple ink from her troll doll pen. Whenever she leaned over to write, I couldn't help myself: I'd stare at her humongous boobs. I was totally fascinated with everything Alma had and I never would. It reminded me of how it felt looking up at my half-nekkid Granny Ruth before I realized I had zero chance of inheriting breasts.

Besides being "queer," Alma was a symbol of all things Southern and womanly—blond hair, brown roots and enough Cover Girl concealer to hide a Dalmatian's spots. She bought the stuff with a jumbo applicator that looked like a caulking gun. This made smearing it on every morning resemble grouting tile.

Every other weekend, she'd get her fingers plastered with big acrylic nails. They were always bright pink or blue with unicorns painted on them. Sometimes she'd even tease her hair to look just like Loretta Lynn. Problem was, whenever it got humid outside—and, hello, this was the South, so humidity was everywhere!—her hair spray evaporated, making her look less like Loretta and more like Vince Gill. She was in Cotillion classes, too, and because of her family ties was headed down the Debutante route, but she'd much rather spend her time chasing boys and catching trouble.

I loved all this about Alma. To me, she wasn't a "queer" or a "redneck" or any of those "bad girl" labels . . . she was just my friend.

And also something of a fibber.

One day in English Lit, as I was translating Chaucer, Alma leaned over and told me that her real Daddy was Rod Stewart. By the time we got to the Wife of Bath's tale, I was supposed to believe that Alma's Aunt Dot owned a gift basket business in Los Angeles that delivered cookies to Cindy Crawford's doorstep every morning. Apparently

Cindy wasn't the tall, gorgeous supermodel she played on billboards across America.

Oh, no.

According to Alma, Cindy Crawford stood about five-foot-four on a good day. And she sneered all cockeyed like a pirate whenever Aunt Dot forgot the macaroons.

As junior year went on, Alma's stories became harder and harder to believe. She told whoppers like I'd never heard. One of the biggest went something like this:

"I was once at a party at the Playboy mansion. Folks were engagin' in three-ways and orgies and all sorts of stuff. All of a sudden, I spotted this ex-boyfriend I hadn't seen in years sitting across the living room. All I could think to say was, 'I thought I told you to wait in the car.'"

Years later, I found that passage in Tallulah Bankhead's biography. But, woo boy, was Alma inventive.

As my Uncle Stu would say, Alma was a professional junk-talker.

She made school feel like summer camp . . . only with Debutante training. And when I tried to joke back and accidentally called it a "flow job," she laughed. That made me laugh right back. We were like black-eyed peas and corn. Which, for all you Yankees, is just about the yummiest combination ever.

After a while, I started noticing clothes disappearing from my room. Wellingham's rules wouldn't allow us to keep locks on our closets, so since Alma and I were roommates, she had easy access to my stuff. She'd wait till I went to sleep and then ransack my latest JCPenney catalog delivery. Inevitably, I'd show up for Bio the next morning and find Alma in yet another sweater with "AF" embroidered across the collar.

I tried to ignore it. I tried to pretend I didn't notice when first my clothes, then my favorite CDs, were suddenly missing. I chalked it up to Alma's Daddy being so lenient. He thought his baby girl deserved whatever she wanted, whenever she wanted. From, apparently, whomever she wanted.

Still, as much as I loved and accepted Alma, it sucked coming back to our room at night to find her reading the new "Scarlett" sequel Momma sent me from JR's.

I guess, in the end, I was just so grateful for a kindred spirit that I pushed it all aside. Alma was the spunky, sarcastic cheese to my macaroni. When she sang real loud during Glee Club practice and her boobs and bangs bounded up and down, I laughed. I forgot about being "finished" for a few precious moments each day. And even when her stories got so wild and absurd that nobody in her right mind could believe them . . . I did. Because I knew she'd do the same for me.

I was happy just to have a Queen on my side, queer or otherwise.

So, to cement our friendship and show Alma I wasn't holding a grudge . . . that she actually filled out my sweaters quite nicely and I didn't mind sharing my books . . .

I invited her to the beach for spring break. And she said yes.

The first day was like a scene out of *Thelma and Louise*. We propped our feet up on the dash of Alma's Chevy Malibu and sang "Highway to Hell" all the way to South Carolina.

This wannabe Scarlett and her best-friend-slash-Queen-of-the-Queers were spending an entire week—*unchaperoned*—at my Granny Blanche's condo in North Myrtle Beach.

We imagined hordes of much wilder, snarkier, rebellious public school kids all around us. Middle-class hoodlums with tattoos and cars and siblings, who maybe didn't care if we knew how to bake perfect lemon squares and do the fox-trot . . .

Who maybe weren't even *Southern*. Can you even imagine?

Along the way, we stopped for lunch at Bojangles' Famous Chicken 'n Biscuits. The fella behind the counter informed us that he'd just moved here from Texas and showed us his name tag that read "Keep Austin Batty."

Between taking our orders and pointing out the new slurpie machine, he was nice enough to warn us about the three things all Texans apparently hate: taxes, the federal government and, most of all, "e-legals." Then, he suggested we get ice cream cones from Dewey's Sugar Shack and make plans to share a funnel cake first chance we got.

Once we'd settled into Granny Blanche's condo, Alma suggested we explore the main drag—Ocean Drive. There, she got her belly button pierced and tried to convince me to do the same. We shopped for beach clothes at Wings Beachwear. Alma got a polka-dot bikini and chewable candy cigarettes, while I finally settled on a modest one-piece with a frilly skirt long enough to wear to school.

We spent the next few days on the sand. Alma basked in the midday heat while I hid beneath a huge hat and SPF 75. Boys wandered by, staring at her huge God-given floating devices. They'd watch us from a distance as we ate frozen lemonade and listened to Duncan Sheik CDs. Sometimes one of the more shy ones would stop to ask me for the time, staring at Alma over my shoulder. If he was especially brave, he'd ask for a cigarette.

I never had one and that never mattered because he was already down to business: Did Alma have a boyfriend? How old was she? Eighteen, he hoped.

That question always made my stomach do backflips with jeal-
ousy. Alma was much closer to "legal" than me, a fact that some guys
ignored . . . until it was almost too late.

One night, Alma and I decided to chance it and go cruising for
older boys on "the Strip." Our plan was simple: We'd have dinner at the NASCAR Café—South Carolina's finest!—and then
go man-hunting around the Pavilion amusement park. This whole
area was a dangerous place we'd only ever seen in old beach movies with Frankie and Annette. This was where college coeds rented
cheap motel rooms for Senior Beach Week and slept six or seven to a
room after a long night of barhopping. South Ocean Drive ran right
through the middle—a two-lane highway with soda joints and hot
dog vendors on one side, and shops that sold T-shirts spray-painted
with Confederate flags or pictures of nekkid women on the other.

You could even drink beer outside on "the Strip," as long as you
wrapped it up in a paper bag and didn't puke on anybody. The rules
here were those of the Wild West—fast and loose, with little if any
regulation.

Back at Wellingham, you weren't allowed to bring a glass of lemonade out of the dining room cafeteria. The rules were clear, strict
and—fair or not—swiftly enforced. So when it came to Myrtle Beach,
a place where all bets were off and all the rules abandoned, I imagined freedom—a paradise of free teenage will! Where I could sow my
oats and walk on the wild side; smoke and drink and make out with
rough chins attached to big shoulder muscles . . .

Only after so many years of sheltered childhood and Debutante
training, I couldn't really enjoy any of it. I was a puppy who'd been
cage-trained and didn't know how to walk around off her leash. I
didn't know what beer smelled like, let alone how to swill it from
paper bags like a wino.

When Alma and I arrived, the party was in full swing. This wasn't no Farmers Market dance among the haystacks with Eulice Barlow. The sidewalks were crawling with soldiers on leave and surfer dudes with tattoos and oily muscles. They showed up with truckloads of bikini-clad girlpersons wearing not much more than a couple Band-Aids laced together with dental floss. They whooped and hollered as they jumped out. Some jumped too hard and let loose a peep show of free-falling girly parts.

We'd prepared ourselves for public school kids to be different . . . but these were way wilder than we'd imagined. None of Alma's pretend characters could even compare.

We finally ducked inside the NASCAR Café where Alma grabbed my hand and made a beeline for the ladies' room. She spent the next half-hour in front of the hand dryer curling her bangs around a round metal brush. It acted just like an iron when you heated it up and left tiny burn marks all over Alma's forehead.

Our U.S. History teacher, Ms. Hootenanny, had the same marks on her chin. Only she'd had a face lift.

One day, Alma asked her about them during our lesson on the atrocities of the "War of Northern Aggression." Ms. Hootenanny's face turned bright red and we were all afraid she might blow a fuse. I expected Alma to get slapped with twenty hours of detention and about a thousand demerits. But no—Ms. Hootenanny just smiled. Of all things, she was tickled to death. She took Alma's questioning as a compliment.

"Ooooh, little dahlings! So ya'll fiiiinally noticed!"

. . . Uh. Yes, ma'am. We did.

"Well, be sure you don't tell anybody about the onion skin."

Do what?

"*Onion skin*, dahlings. It works wonders. It's much better than regular cover-up! Just add a little moisturizer to make it stick and— voilà!—it even covers those nasty curling irons!"

Next thing you know, Alma's switched out her caulking gun applicator for a vat of Vaseline and sack of sweet Vidalias.

By the time her NASCAR beautification ritual was complete, I'd passed out on a nearby love seat. We finally exited the bathroom and entered the main dining area. Alma pointed out that the walls were decorated with life-sized cutouts of the Pettys, Garth Brooks and an advertisement for Russell hunting boots. I barely noticed. I was starving and a little nauseous from Alma's onion smell.

Our waiter, whose name tag read "Mr. Hush," seats us toward the back. He's got a big nose and two bigger fists carrying a basket of hot wings. He sets it down on our table and I dig in like a half-starved orphan.

Alma ignores the food and starts whining about our seats being so near the kitchen. I'm happy so long as nobody spots me with a face full of buffalo-flavored chicken. I've already got so much sauce on my chin that Mr. Hush grimaces like he's just witnessed a car wreck.

He dumps a couple Wet-Naps by my side, then leans over and spots Alma's bulging particulars. He slinks over, offers her a menu, which Alma opens and skims like a pro.

She's smiling, flirting, acting very much in charge . . . only there's a problem: some funny words in small print on her menu. She squints and gives it her best shot. . . .

"We'd like some . . . *whore-da-vores*. Please."

He blinks. Not once . . . *three times*. His mouth moving but no words coming out.

"I'm sorry, ma'am . . . what was that?"

She flashes a smile, turns on the drawl.

"I'd like some *whore da-vores*, sugar. Right away," she says. And this time, she's a little impatient. Like she's just asked for a simple bread basket, and how dare he question her stunning NASCAR Café menu-ordering prowess.

He smiles back. The lady wanted "whore da-vores" and "whore da-vores" she was gonna get!

Moments later, our "whore da-vores"—deep-fried shrimp with a side of hush puppies—arrive. Free of charge. And, he asks Alma, did we maybe wanna come back to his beach house later for the "after-party"?

"Suuuuure, fella," she responds. But now I'm blinking. Not once . . . *three times*.

Doesn't an "after party" entail . . . like . . . a *party*? And how can we be doing something *after* something else when that something's not happening right now?

Alma takes my hand. Gives me another look. Then she bends down and pulls the troll-doll pen out of her purse.

She grabs a napkin, bends down and writes the phone number to my Granny's condo. That's when I can't help myself again. And between her ginormous boobs I spot my Momma's pearl necklace.

Seeing those pearls is almost comforting now. Makes me feel like we're back at Wellingham and just having a quiet dinner in the cafeteria, creeping kudzu and Miss Freeze's favorite azaleas dipping their dusty leaves into our glasses of sweet tea. We're safe and protected, not alone with some sketchy waiter inviting us to happenings that aren't happening and staring at Alma in a way that makes my skin crawl.

She finishes writing, folds the napkin into a heart and presses it into Mr. Hush's hand.

His smile suddenly reminds me of a lizard we'd dissected in Ms. Spencer's class. Or maybe one of those crocodiles from *National Geographic*.

Was this really the kind of man Scarlett would kiss and call a scalawag and marry someday? Not likely. He took the note and promised to call as I swallowed my fears. . . .

Gulp.

Who wants to be Scarlett in Myrtle Beach when we could be ourselves at home?

If you've ever seen that old movie *Shag*, you know that in the 1960s, Myrtle Beach was divided up into three areas: South Myrtle Beach, North Myrtle Beach and Cherry Grove.

By the mid-'90s, NMB was still a ritzy spot covered with privately owned condos, where old folks still held local shag contests. The winning couple would get their names carved into the sidewalk. Runners-up scored dinner at Duffy Street Seafood Shack off Ocean Drive at Highway 17.

A few miles north in Cherry Grove, you finally escape the '60s. Here, regular kids shacked up in their parents' summerhouses. These places looked weather-beaten and awful on the outside . . . but inside, they were shrines to Southern youth.

Confederate flag bedspreads, crystal pitchers of iced sweet tea and empty cartons of Marlboros and Virginia Slim cigarettes everywhere. If you stared through the backdoor windows, you could see the welcome sign to Fat Harold's Beach Club: "Come boogie where yo' Momma did!"

These Cherry Grove folks were "high steppers," as my Uncle Stu would say. That meant they wore tuxedos to play tennis and cocked their legs up real high and fancy to dance.

South Myrtle Beach, on the other hand, was what he'd call "No Woman's Land." This was a place where Southern girls took chances. Sometimes they lived to tell wild, sinful tales full of near-escapes, police chases and scandalous Debauchery. And sometimes, they got knocked up and shipped home. I'd heard of that happening once. Her name was Bessie Andrews, and I only knew her by reputation. She'd supposedly gone down to tour Fort Sumter with her youth group and wound up in South Myrtle and very much in the family way. Then her Momma sent her to a home for unwed mothers in Siler City and we never heard from her again. After that, the old folks always warned us girls about going down to "No Woman's Land." We were told that "good girls" came back as girls and "bad girls" came back as women.

In the case of me and Alma, two hicks from Squat Bucket, North Carolina, your best bet was on the former. As wild as we pretended to be . . . in the end, we were just two innocent schoolgirls from Wellingham with only half-cooked oats to sow.

The first time the phone rang, it was some old lady named Jeanie Williams.

See, Granny Blanche had more than one condo on the beach. Whichever one we weren't using at the time, she'd rent out to one of her friends at a discount. It was a friendly thing to do and gave her bridge club biddies an excuse to eat seafood and play cards with a view of the ocean.

When I picked up the phone, I expected to hear Mr. Hush's deep, syrupy voice on the other end. Instead, an aging Chihuahua started barking her orders.

"Huh? Hell-ow?!"

"Mrs. Williams, is that you?"

"Uh, yeh. I uh need someone to help me. Uh. Hell-ow?!"

"Yes, ma'am, I'm listening. Can I help you with something?"

"Uh, yeh. Thay's this co-wad outside mye how-as and it's po-lin' on a bo-wad."

That's when Alma started pulling on the cord to get me to hang up. "He's gonna call!" she mouthed. And I nodded, "Yeah, I know. But what do I do?!" I finally had to rassle the receiver away so she wouldn't hang up on Jeanie.

"Uh, yeh. Hell-ow?!"

"Yes, ma'am. You were sayin'?"

"Uh yeh, so it's po-lin' on a bo-wad on the side of my how-as and I need someone to come ow-at and fix this fo' me."

"Um . . . okay. I'll tell Granny to have somebody come by and . . ."

"Now-a I have a doctor's ahpontment on Monday, so wha-hen do you thank you'll be ow-at to fix that?"

Just then, Alma gave the cord a good jerk and it came out of the wall socket. So much for respecting your elders.

When Mr. Hush finally called, we hurried over. Inside, his apartment was an Eden for eager teenagers: lava lamps, peeling paint, gray carpet, a half-filled pool filled with lawn furniture. . . .

And, of course, the "townies."

These were folks who'd grown up in the South, didn't pay their income taxes and didn't give a damn what happened anywhere north of Blacksburg, Virginia.

Mr. Hush was definitely a "townie." He'd graduated from College of Charleston with a dual degree in turf grass installation and animal husbandry.

Mr. Hush had a hippie roommate, Pop-Tart, who played "What's Going On?" by Marvin Gaye on a loop the whole night. He had a whole crate full of other CDs, but said he liked this one best because the lyrics talked about stuff like "smoking up" and "making it."

So there Alma and I sat on their dingy couch, our bellies full of hot wings and our ears full of '70s Motown. Since Mr. Hush had already laid his claim to Alma, Pop-Tart quickly focused his attentions on me. I like to believe a chubby chaser, much like a sucker, is born every second.

First, he offered me a bottle of Mike's Hard Lemonade that took me three hours to finish. Even so, he insisted this was the liquor "chicks dug most." Then Mr. Hush showed us the huge tiger tattoo across his back. He said it was the symbol of his college fraternity, which made me turn to Alma and mouth, "He thinks we're in college, too, doesn't he?!"

She just smiled coolly and kicked my shin. Then she upped the ante, pulling up her own shirt to expose the butterfly "tramp stamp" on her lower back.

I'd never seen Alma's tattoo before, and suddenly understood why that particular detail was added to her pretend slut stories back at school. Her sudden move made everybody's eyes go wide. The boys with expectant desire, and me with total shock as I tried to keep my cool and my legs firmly closed—a difficult task in Alma's borrowed black miniskirt.

It seemed like I'd finally arrived. Like this was the kind of "after party" I'd yearned for back at the Phi Psi house. Only with Alma it was all finally possible.

For that short while, we pretended to be regular girls doing regular things with regular guys. And, then, out of nowhere . . . the question.

"So, what school do you gals go to?" Pop-Tart asks.

Gulp.

My face turns bright red. I can tell because my pulse is racing and my palms feel all sweaty. I look at Alma. *"OmigodhelpmeJesus!"*

She ignores me this time and locks eyes with Pop-Tart.

"Um, just somewhere nearby," she says.

"Like where? Maybe we know some of the same people . . ." Mr. Hush chimes in.

"Oh, I don't think so," she responds, then gets up to go. "It's been real fun, ya'll. But we'd better get going. . . ."

"But it's only ten p.m."

"Yep. We gotta make curfew. All-girls' college. You know how it is . . ." with a slight quiver now.

For a few seconds, I was so afraid that I floated out of my body like in the sixth grade. Then the air shifted in the room and, suddenly, I was watching both sets of male eyes level on Alma.

"You have a ten p.m. curfew? In *college?*"

Alma and I spent the rest of the night driving along the beach. We stopped only to share a cherry-flavored slushie to wash away the hard lemonade and ogle the bare-chested boys who seemed to fill up every inch of sand.

All things considered, the night was a total bust. Our plan hadn't worked at all. Instead of enjoying nookie with older boys at a real party, I'd gotten kicked out once again.

It seemed like I'd never grow up. Like I'd stay underage and awkward—too old to play with Barbie, too young to date Ken— forever.

It made me think about Ella Mae Abernathy's Debutante Ball. All those Cotillion classes and dress fittings were behind her, and all she could do was await bigger adventures. It must've been so exciting knowing the rest of her life was about to begin. I remembered her spotless dress and kid-leather gloves and how alive she looked that day. . . .

When out of the corner of my eye, she was right there. I blinked at first. I thought it was my daydream. Then I stared out the window at a lone figure tumbling along the sidewalk, and realized it was really her.

She didn't look excited at all. She looked so pitiful and blind drunk I could barely recognize her face.

"Alma, look . . ."

"What is it? I can't see . . ."

"Pull over."

"What?"

"*Pull over*," I said.

And, without thinking, I rolled down my window.

"*Ella Mae!*" I shouted out. "*Ella Mae, come here!*"

And thank goodness she did.

She climbed into the car, breathless and crying. Runny mascara staining her perfectly makeupped face.

I'd gotten so used to imagining Ella Mae in her dress and crown that it shocked me to see her sandy hair, wet clothes, torn pants and underwear. All the telltale signs of rape we'd memorized in Sex Ed classes. Ella Mae leaned back and said just a few words before dozing off in the seat.

". . . Anna Lee? My crotch hurts."

When we got back to school, I got another note in my mailbox: "Please see me," in Miss Freeze's familiar script.

She led me to Ms. Krinkle's classroom and asked me to wait there. Next door, Diane, Bitsy, Miss Freeze and other members of the

Wellingham Academy Honor Cabinet—aka the Inquisition—were gathering for my so-called trial.

This whole thing started when word got around about Ella Mae's assault. Even though we'd rescued her, that also meant we'd been out on the Strip, too. And that meant Alma and I became "bad girls"—tainted by association.

This new label applied especially to me. I'd already been thrown off Honor Cabinet for making fake IDs sophomore year, and now Miss Freeze was on the lookout. Fool me once, fool me twice was her motto. Besides, she already expected this kind of behavior from Alma.

As I'd soon find out, getting called in front of the Inquisition went a little like this:

1. You did (or didn't) do something really, really naughty.
2. Somebody smelled the smoke or found the bud or found a cheat sheet or saw you with windowsill scuff marks on your thighs at one a.m., when you were supposed to be in bed . . . or whatever. The evidence was witnessed.
3. Somebody ratted to Miss Freeze.
4. She sent you a "blue note" in your box: Please see me.
5. You saw her. She interrogated you with her poker face on to see whether you needed to go to Honor Cabinet or whether a slap on the wrist would suffice instead.
6. You, invariably, went to Honor Cabinet.
7. They sat you in a room—usually Miss Krinkle's Latin class. Sometimes with your accomplices; most times, by yourself. That way, you couldn't come up with a story or corroborate one another.
8. You sat there for what seemed like *hours.*

9. Some Narc (probably from your Latin class) came to fetch you from your "holding cell."

10. She took you into a nearby classroom and sat you down in a single chair with a tape recorder sitting beneath, primed for "testimony." Around the chair, a semicircle of teachers, faculty and Honor Cabinet members like Diane Sutherland smiled at you with shit-eating, Cheshire cat grins to try and make you feel "comfortable." Before they cut off your head, that is, like Uncle Stu used to do to live chickens before turning them into Sunday dinner.

11. They asked you questions.

12. You *had* to answer. On tape.

13. The same Narc took you back to your room, after which you were expected to return quietly to class, Cotillion, sports practice (or whatever) until the Council decided your fate. This part could take anywhere from minutes to hours but always felt like forever.

14. If you got kicked out of school, they'd announce it the next day during morning prayers.

Welcome to merry old England. What was next, debtors' prison?

So there I sat awaiting judgment by a jury of my teachers and peers. And not sure Scarlett even cared this time.

After my Honor Cabinet Inquisition, I was "campused" for sneaking off without permission.

That meant I couldn't leave Wellingham for three whole weeks—

for any reason whatsoever. Well, unless I fell down and broke my neck or contracted whooping cough. Then Miss Freeze might consider letting me walk to Health Services for a cough drop. My parents were livid about all this, but what could they do? Stick me back in Burlington public schools? Wellingham was the best school—hands down—in the whole state, and ultimately, I decided to suck it up and stick it out rather than blow my chances at the best education I'd ever had.

In the meantime, Alma and I had three whole weeks to turn our Southern Belle angst into full-fledged Rules of the Rebel Debutantes:

> Rule #1: Love the South. (Well, anything above Jacksonville, Florida, that is.)
>
> Rule #2: You Can't Make Chicken Salad Out of Chicken Shit. (Translation: Cowards Never Amount to Much.)
>
> Rule #3: Someday, the South Will Rise Again. And Dale Earnhardt, Jr., will be President.
>
> Rule #4: Size Matters to a Real Lady.
>
> Rule #5: If Your Man's in the Klink, Go Get You Another'n!
>
> Rule #6: Edumacate Yo'self.
>
> Rule #7: Cotillion Sucks!
>
> Rule #8: Never Pass Up a Good Opportunity to Shut Up.
>
> Rule #9: If Nobody's Buying the Milk, It's Probably Spoilt. (Translation: Don't Date Older Men!)
>
> Rule #10: You'll Never Catch a Husband if You Don't Wash Your Fanny!
>
> . . . and about a thousand more, most of which were too naughty to write down.

We'd gotten so used to rules and procedures that it felt only natural to make our own. Besides, what else were Alma and I going to do? Nobody had cell phones or used the Internet much back then. All we had was a big, clunky dorm phone attached to the wall in the middle of the hallway. This allowed everybody to eavesdrop on everybody else's conversations.

Miss Betty, an old biddy Wellingham paid to ruin our lives, made sure nobody stayed on the phone for more than an hour. Then she'd walk down the hall screaming "Lights out!" and stand outside our doors till we fell asleep. And if you were up past ten p.m., Lord help you. You'd better get ready for an ass-whooping.

Most nights, Alma and I would wait till Miss Betty finished bed checks and sneak down into the basement to watch *Dazed and Confused* till the sun came up.

When this got old, we'd make up dance routines to songs like "Brass Monkey," "Saturday Night," and the "Macarena." Sometimes, we'd practice our Tootsie Rolls or do the Shoop Shoop, sliding across the floor in our socks and underdrawers. Children of the '90s did stuff like that. We fantasized about college and boys and being old enough to risk getting pregnant. We "saw The Sign!" with Ace of Base, and went to coffee shops to meet new people. Back then, nobody came to Starbucks to sit alone and stare at her laptop. We had relationships with our friends, not our Facebook.

Anywho.

For those three weeks, Alma and I went nowhere and did nothing but go to class, suffer through Cotillion and make stuff up to entertain our busy imaginations. Still, even with all this nothingness, the "Big Brother" of Wellingham became suspicious.

The last day of my punishment, Miss Betty accused Alma of smoking crack.

She was skipping up and down the main hall to make us laugh. As she approached the top of the hall, Miss Betty throws open her door, drags Alma inside and demands to know if she's has been "smoking the crack?"

"Nah. I'm just playin'. You know, being retarded . . ."

She stopped right there. Miss Betty's scowl said it all.

Apparently, she'd grown up with Gilbert Grape for a brother. And now Alma was on her shit list.

Alma got stuck cleaning Miss Betty's room for the rest of that night and every weekend for the next six weeks. After that, she threw in the towel. No more Miss Nice Deb.

She started ignoring all the rules and making out in the hallways with Molly Dinglehopper. Some girls at Wellingham were LUGs ("lesbians until graduation"), but Molly was a "hundred-footer": a butch for life you could spot from across a football field.

First, Molly gave Alma mono. Then, Molly started making out with a girl from Reynolds High School and all hell broke loose. Heartbroken, Alma went from slutty and sweet to uptight and surly in about a month. She played the same Cranberries CD over and over till the player broke. Then she refused to leave her room or eat anything but salted sliced tomatoes.

I finally forced her into a strict John Hughes movie-marathon recovery program. It took a few days' worth of several late fees on my rented copy of *Pretty in Pink*, but she eventually reverted back to the old Alma I knew and loved. Thank goodness, too. A couple more days of Alma's moping and I would've resorted to impersonating Gilda Radner.

Since she insisted on taking revenge on Miss Freeze and Miss Betty, I proposed we go on "demerit hunts." In boarding school, this is the same as trying to get yourself arrested.

We'd wait till after lights-out and her shoe shadows disappeared; then we'd follow Miss Betty around the halls, lurking in the corners, trying to get caught and punished. Anything was better than studying for another Trig test or gathering in the TV lounge to watch *Dawson's Creek*. Sometimes, Alma and I would dress up in costumes and follow her down the hall. Once she caught on, though, the wheels were in motion. . . .

And that's when we started getting blamed for *everything*.

Much like the penal system, once we were in, we were tainted for life. Of course, girls like Diane could be snobby and cliquish and make our lives a living hell, but they were just "assertive," while we were "bad."

That's how Wellingham worked. Girls that never spoke up, never complained, always did all their homework. Girls who ran track or played field hockey. Girls who got up in the morning for every prayer devotion, every bun ceremony. Who went to church. Who shunned boys. Who played the part of the doting, respectful, submissive yet studious virgins. Girls like Diane, who joined the Honor Cabinet just to rat each other out, were the twinkle of Miss Freeze's eye. . . .

Those girls were "good."

They got medals. Awards. They sat beside Miss Freeze at lunch and never missed catfish-and-coleslaw dinner in the Wellingham cafeteria. Like snitching was some kind of public service. And that meant they could do no wrong . . . ever.

Alma and I, on the other hand? We were not those girls.

We got bored; we'd hide in the yearbook room at two a.m. and hack into the school's computers. And, sure, we pulled our fair share of pranks. But it got to the point where every time Miss Freeze smelled smoke in the basement . . . every time a window was found unlocked, a door cracked, a study hall missed or a test failed . . . we were to blame: The chubby girl who talked back. The "white trash" slut who slept around. To Miss Freeze, we were nothing but rude, ungrateful, uncouth girls who hung out with "low class" people in "low class" places. Who burped in public, skipped lunch and questioned adult authority over our hearts and minds . . . to her, we were just plain old "bad."

Over the past two years, we'd gotten used to this. Maybe we'd even believed it. Only somehow, right before school let out, something changed.

During our yearly awards ceremony, Alma and I watched as girls like Diane—the embodiments of our snobby upbringings—walked across the stage to pick up their medals for making our lives a living hell. And, somehow, during her acceptance speech, a lightbulb came on. Somehow, Alma and I decided to get *unused* to all the labels we'd been given. To throw away all the mean gossip and accusations we were supposed to ignore or put up with. Somehow, during that one ceremony, our whole self-images changed.

We were no longer that easy to label and discard. We weren't just "white trash," or "gay," or "different," or "loose." We'd joined forces. No longer simply "bad girls" or "good girls," Virgins or Whores, wannabe Scarletts or Queens of the Queers . . . but everything put together into two complete women:

The Rebel Debutantes of Wellingham Academy.

Chapter Four

How a Rebel Deb Semi-Steals a Car and Still Lands on Her Feet:

• Twelfth Grade •

By senior year, Alma and I were full-fledged Rebel Debs. And that meant we no longer paid attention to any rules or bothered showing up for Cotillion.

We rolled out of bed at seven-fifty for our eight a.m. classes. We skipped the required meals and ate bowls of cereal in our room instead. On weekends, while the other girls grabbed their monogrammed Koozies and piled into activity buses headed to Episcopalian football games . . .

Let's just say Alma and I were out looking for a better time.

We were sick of the usual entertainment: school dances with preppy, Wall Street mullet-wearing types trying to bump 'n' grind us into corners. The same boys wearing the same Duck Head polo shirts, asking girls like Diane out to dinner at the Wake Forest Country Club.

I'd finally passed my driver's test that summer, and Granny Ruth bought me the best present *ever*—a cherry-red Chevy convertible I nicknamed "Connie."

Once the bell rang for lunch, Alma and I would hop into Connie and be gone with the wind. She kept us from spending even one extra second at school outside of classes—curfew be damned. Most days, we didn't come back till ten p.m. Sometimes, we didn't come back at all.

In that time, Alma and I would go back to her house and make a mess of the kitchen. We'd bake lemon squares that fell apart in the middle or chocolate sour cream cake that we left out all night so it spoiled.

Alma loved to cook. When she wasn't chasing girls and causing trouble, she'd spend her time whipping up homemade chicken salad (which, like I said, you can't make out of chicken shit). Sometimes, she'd even make her semi-famous jalapeño-pimiento-cheese sandwiches.

Among all our recipes and Rules, Alma and I also wrote a handbook for Northern transplants . . . a sort of *Southern Living* for Yankees, if you will. It included definitions for common Southern phrases like "She do be gettin' tonky," which means she drinks too much, and "Bless your heart," which really means "Screw you."

Portions of our anthology wound up on the Internet and went something like this:

A whistling woman and a crowing hen never come to a
very good end. *(Be who you are.)*

Ain't that the berries! *(That's great!)*

Cuter than a fat country baby eatin' peaches off a hard-
wood floor. *(Very pretty)*

As easy as sliding off a greasy log backward. *(Very easy)*

Barking up the wrong tree. *(You're wrong.)*

I'm to' up from the flo' up! *(I'm upset.)*

Ya got hair on yer peaches er what? *(Are you brave?)*

Be sweet! *(Behave yourself.)*

Don't be ugly! *(Don't be unkind.)*

Be like the old lady who fell out of the wagon. *(You aren't
involved, so stay out of it.)*

Busy as a stump-tailed cow in fly time. *(Very busy)*

We also included some Southern slang that people in earlier generations—folks like my Uncle Stu, for example—made up and later used to describe almost every boyfriend I ever brought home:

Biggity, worry-wart, sorry, tight-ass, hot mess, spring chicken, laid-up, airish, clodhopper, carpetbagger, scalawag and coon-ass.

Then we included a few Southern words that when drawled out sounded dirty, but weren't:

Fussbudget, crab cake, Poupon (as in Grey), ratchet, grizzled, shiskabob, rustle and cusp.

By the time my "campused" punishment ended, our lexicon of Southern language was complete and Alma and I were long gone. We were now emotionally, physically and socially liberated . . . and very, very tired of boarding school.

Problem was, we'd already scoured Winston-Salem and Wake Forest and were getting tired of those, too.

We'd run all over local hangouts like the Morning Dew, the Missing Link and every other coffee-shop-slash-teen-scene. The only place left to explore was a big condemned building called "the Wherehouse," where we'd heard "hippies" lived.

"Hippies," in those days, were basically the watered-down versions of the 1960s icons: Janis Joplin, Cat Stevens, Lenny Bruce, Captain Beefheart, Steve Winwood, that Wavy Gravy fella and Ted Nugent. They were also responsible for Alma and me learning about something called "weed." And not the kind you'd find strangling azaleas in your Momma's flower bed.

Alma seemed to love the stuff, though she complained about it afterward. She said it made her nose itch and her taste buds feel like she'd swallowed a bottle of Liquid Paper. When she offered me a hit, I decided to pass. I could eat cooked turnips and get the same results.

The bottom floor of the Wherehouse was a huge basement occupied by Cashius McTooth, a forty-eight-year-old Vietnam vet who smoked stinky clove cigarettes that left his teeth greenish-brown.

Cashius told funny stories about his military days, and Alma and I enjoyed listening. Until he offered to give us a tour of his bedroom—to supposedly show Alma and me "the ropes"—and we got smart and cut him loose.

The second story was a crude-looking dance hall where garage bands banged on pots and pans and called it "industrial music." The audience was usually made up of folks with names like "Juju Bee," "Moonstar," "Blu" and "Hemp," who worked construction all day and head-bobbed to the sounds of banging pots all night. When they weren't making music or watching *Fear and Loathing in Las Vegas*, these folks would braid their hair into cornrows and threaten anarchy if weed wasn't legalized before the next presidential election.

On the top floor was an artist's studio. That's where fellas with black eyeliner, nose rings and baggy pants made sculptures out of car parts. "Moonstar" once showed me a Jesus figurine he'd made out of scrap metal and old tires. If he'd had any kind of aesthetic ability, I'm sure my Uncle Stu would've taken a liking to it. After all, the word "MICHELIN" was printed right smack across Jesus' forehead, and I'm sure Uncle Stu would've appreciated our Savior sticking with domestic.

Despite all its resident hippies, the Wherehouse was a fun place where anything could happen. And by "anything," I mean you could fall down and break your neck at any moment.

This was mostly due to the building being condemned. The floor was so old that it quivered with the slightest weight. The main staircase that allowed movement from one floor to the next was so covered in jagged metal you were likely to need a tetanus shot on your way. But, in a way, that's what made the whole place so dangerously cool.

At seventeen, Alma and I didn't care if we caught the plague. We were gonna have fun, even if it killed us.

We spent the rest of junior year at every pot-banging concert the Wherehouse hosted. One night, Alma and I showed up dressed up like characters from *The Craft*. I was supposed to be Neve Campbell with my skin all flaky and dried up. Alma was that weird chick with the bug eyes and huge mouth, who I later saw straddling some rocker dude in *Almost Famous*. She slow-danced with some gal dressed in a David Bowie costume—another clove cigarette smoker who bought VHS tapes of artsy, pretentious movies I was pretty sure you could get off PBS for free. At the end of the night, we went parking in Reynolda Gardens with a couple pot-bangers from the band and felt pretty foxy for two sheltered Rebel Debs.

When we weren't at the Wherehouse, we'd sneak out of Darla Granger's window and walk around Cherry Street. Darla always warned us against doing that—Cherry Street was dangerous back then and only streetwalkers, hoodlums and "e-legals" went there after dark.

Darla was a fellow "queer" with a phobia of prostitutes and "e-legals," which didn't, as it turned out, mean underage girls like Alma and me. She thought hanging out at the Wherehouse would get us attacked by "them dern Hisp-*ann*-aks!"

Not even Miss Betty would suspect Darla had a social life. That meant whenever Alma and I sneaked through well past curfew, the coast was sure to be clear.

It was just like sophomore year, only way more fun and no Miss Freeze to lay into us afterward. You'd think we'd have learned our lessons a couple years ago, but as Rebel Debs we felt invincible.

Back in the safety of our beds, Alma and I made up snarky nicknames for girls we didn't like: slut-bucket, whore-bot, skankalicious, skankatron and "has-bian," which meant a girl who was once a lesbian but then turned straight, or "taint," which Alma said was a really mean nickname because it referred to a part of your fanny that required a good washing after gym class.

Our names and sayings and lists were endless. By the end of the year, Alma and I had compiled thousands and put them all into a huge notebook we called the "Confessions of the Rebel Debutantes"— our very own anti-Handbook for surviving boarding school and life in the South. It also included definitions of common Wellingham phrases like "the school acts *in loco parentis*: in place of parent."

Translated, this had two possible definitions: (1) you're never getting out alive; or (2) your real parents will have no idea what's going on in here.

That being said, none of the other parents were as clueless as Alma's Daddy, Reverend Claire.

A tall, statuesque man with bushy eyebrows and a beak for a nose, the Reverend was himself an only child just like Alma. His Great-Granddaddy, Reginald Claire, was the first hosiery baron to patent seamless stockings back in the 1940s. Back then, ladies like my Granny Blanche wore stockings with a long seam running up the back and held up their underdrawers with garters made out of plastic tubing. Real elastic was too expensive and being rationed by the government for WW II.

When Reggie Claire came along, times changed. Ladies said good-bye to long seams and plastic tubes getting caught in their hoo-ha hair, and a happier era of fitted underdrawers emerged.

Reverend Claire never seemed too proud of his family fortune stemming from unmentionables. I suppose that's why he never mentioned it. Instead, the Reverend fancied himself a pig farmer. He even kept a great big ol' tract of land up in Virginia, which I was lucky enough to visit more than once or twice.

Alma sometimes brought her local public school friends up to the farm with us. Most of these folks were straight country. They smoked like chimneys, drank like fish, married local and sometimes wore jewelry in places only underdrawers should go.

We had a grand ol' time. We'd ride around on four-wheelers, eat seven-layer cake and romp in the outdoor Jacuzzi till late at night. Sometimes, once everybody was asleep, Alma's Cousin Randall would get a little eager with the liquor.

Those nights, I'd awake to the sound of him screaming out "*Dadddy!!!*" into the night. One of us would invariably wake up to find poor Randall hugging the toilet or passed out in a fetal position. Seeing him like that always made me queasy. And I wasn't even drinking.

Then again, neither was Clementine Footwhistle.

Clementine Footwhistle was another of Alma's cousins, twice removed. Reverend Claire insisted Alma invite her along, too, because she was family and also something of a Professional Debutante.

I never did quite understand how somebody's cousin could be "twice removed." Did that mean somebody tried to oust her from the family . . . twice? Or that she got something cut off? The latter I could understand because Ella Mae Abernathy once had a hairy mole removed from her nose 'cause it made her look like a witch. And I can't imagine a real Debutante walking around in her ballgown with a hairy witch nose.

Anywho.

Clementine was maybe eighteen but acted like she was forty, just because she'd already come out in Atlanta. Besides being a bit too big for her britches, she wasn't quite as classy as most Professional Debs. For one thing, her underdrawers were too tight. One time, she wore a pair of eighteen-hour panty hose that turned into a twenty-four-hour camel toe. She also wore big, floppy hats that screamed, *"Look at me! Ain't I gorgeous?!"*

I soon found out that, besides floppy hats, Clementine loved anything and everything about Debutante culture. For example, she played field hockey, never missed a garden party and wore pastel sundresses over top her camel toe every day.

Unlike me, Clementine was successfully following her Scarlett O'Hara fantasy. She showed me pictures from her sister's *Gone With the Wind* wedding. Each one was full of teased hairdos, wide-brimmed hats and hoopskirts that barely fit into frame. The groom's family had even rented out Graceland for the event. Problem was, it started raining. And that turned the red clay into sticky Southern glue quicker than you could spell "secession."

In their hoopskirts, the bridesmaids had a helluva time escaping the weather. Getting into the limo without flashing their knickers was near impossible, and more than one groomsman got an eyeful of Miss Scarlett's undercarriage.

Then she showed me the picture of Mr. and Mrs. Footwhistle beaming with pride.

Clementine's Momma was herself a Debutante back in the 1970s. Once she got a little age on her, she started teaching her daughters' Cotillion classes. It became her ambition to make sure Clementine came out at nearly every Debutante Ball in the country. Thousands of dollars and dozens of ballgowns later, little Clementine was way beyond most other Professional Debs. She'd curtsied and waltzed around New York, Washington and even the International Debutante Ball in Europe—all for the sake of preserving her heritage.

For Professional Debs and their Mommas, Debbing is a culture. And there's something to be admired about that, I think. Much like a Bat Mitzvah or Quinceañera, a Southern Belle's Deb Ball is her cultural rite of passage symbolizing her break from childhood. With about a pound of Aqua Net to cushion her fall, of course.

Clementine was the kind of girl who, at seventeen, still believed in the rules. She never rebelled against the system. Whereas I'd morphed from wannabe Scarlett to Rebel Deb, Clementine had kept her childhood dreams of poufy crinoline skirts and acceptance to the cool kids' lunch tables alive.

Like many outsiders and parents, Clementine was so engulfed by Debutante culture that she had no real idea what happened to those of us inside Wellingham. She was too focused on finding the prettiest—and *poufiest*—Deb ballgown. Hell, you even mentioned the word "pouf" around Clementine and she'd blush like a whore in church. It was *that* exciting.

Trust me when I say that the proof was in the pouf.

To Debs, the amount of pouf in a girl's gown determines her level of class. Much like how my Uncle Stu sized up a man by his hunting boots: A professional Deb knew her own by her level of pouf.

Wellingham was a world *full* of pouf.

It was also brimming with SUVs, ponytails, trust funds and pampered lapdogs in custom-fitted dresses with yellow bows in their hair . . . and that doesn't even count the Debs' pets.

Yet somehow, it always seemed that following all of Wellingham's rules and regulations—living such a restricted, borderline Victorian lifestyle—gave girls like Clementine great pleasure. . . .

If you think about it, this might explain why she wore her panty hose so tight.

Most folks who aren't Southern by birth or didn't know any rich folks growing up don't understand what this culture is like. They don't understand girls' schools or Debutante Balls. They don't get how special Clementine felt stepping up on her fitting block, turning her profile to each side and imagining which hairdo would go with which gown. Her kind of preparation is a way of life. And her Ball was a professional Deb's once-in-a-lifetime moment to be captured and treasured alongside her wedding.

As crazy as all that sounds, I knew it had to be better than bouncing out of your bikini like all those regular girls at Myrtle Beach, right?

Those girls didn't go to Deb Balls or fancy country club parties—they jetted off to Cancun and drank margaritas laced with date-rape drugs. Or at least that's what Clementine said. She also said those girls got rolled up into carpets and sold off as sex slaves—same as the ones who ate too much chicken-fried steak or dared wear red panties to Sunday school.

Clementine knew all sorts of stuff like that. Facts and figures and measurements and whatnot—everything a Rebel would want to know about Deb culture in the New South. If you looked past her crazy hats and camel toe, Clementine was a fountain ready and willing to shower us with knowledge.

For example, the proper way for a lady to curl her eyelashes.

Alma did pretty well at this, but I poked myself in the eye during Clementine's first lesson. After that, Clementine stuck to the basics.

We learned how a Debutante flosses her teeth. Then, how to properly clean kid-leather gloves. If we begged and pleaded enough, she'd teach us how to tastefully wiggle our hips while doing the Roger Rabbit.

Clementine belonged to something called "the Assembly."

According to Clementine, Ora Lee Footwhistle hid her love of moonshine well enough to be invited to come out by "the Assembly." This was one of the oldest and most exclusive of all Debutante clubs and didn't operate like its peers.

Oh, no.

The Assembly wasn't Fat Harold's. Not everybody with an old-timey name and some cash in her pocket got invited to come "boogie where yo' Momma did!"

In the Assembly, just because your Aunt Ora Lee was a Deb didn't mean you got to be. This club was *way* too exclusive to allow that. Of the eighteen or so girls who came out each year, a full *eight* of them were chosen by the Assembly *alone*. So that meant, years later, when Ora Lee wound up an old maid, Clementine was the only child left to take her place.

Clementine's "Assembly" stories were all about parties and luncheons and teas her older sisters and friends threw the summer before their balls.

Teas were held at the Poinsettia Club, cooking lessons at the Fox-fire Café, jewelry-making at the Beaded Frog Boutique, and everything else in the living room of somebody's mansion.

Each party was full of other professional Debs—"good girls" who wore matching silk pajamas and spent their summers at Camp Seafarer. Girls like Clementine and Diane Sutherland went to Camp Seafarer. Girls like me and Alma did *not*.

And why?

Because Camp Seafarer was for straight, skinny girls who listened to Jimmy Buffett and made head cheerleader.

"Good girls" who got together for themed bonding sessions to make pasta and play Bunk. Sometimes, they'd go out for movie nights, ladies poker or BBQ-'n'-bluegrass shindigs. They'd drink punch and virgin piña coladas and gnaw on pork shoulders roasted in big pits dug into the ground.

Naturally, there was a dress code:

Only white or pastels allowed. One-inch heels, *nothing* strapless, and the word "Casual" printed on your invitation did *not* mean "denim."

During "waltzing parties," girls were expected to wear white, closed-toe shoes and stand around sipping tea out of porcelain cups. Clementine didn't have any problem with this. By tenth grade, she'd already scoured the racks at David's Bridal so her wardrobe was ready to go.

The dress code for picking the actual Deb ballgown was just as iron-clad:

One-piece, floor-length, princess-cut or sweetheart neckline and, again, *no* strapless allowed.

Once a Deb picked out her gown, she had to call and register it with the Terpsichorean Society. That way, no two girls ended up in the same frock on their big day.

The most pressure is put on the unspoken Top Deb, who represents the *crème* of the *crème* of the Southern Belle crop. Only she's not really chosen on her own merits, but her parents'. So, if you think about it, she's not really all that creamy as her Momma and Daddy.

Once she's chosen, a Top Deb's wardrobe becomes super important.

That's why old money up front made all the difference if you were looking to be Top Deb. Without it, you'd never afford all the new clothes!

"The chosen girl could never *ever* be poor or disreputable," Clementine said. As a Top Deb back in Atlanta, she was a staunch supporter of such rules and regulations. She'd even taken up a community petition to ensure no one would ever change the dress codes.

"If we don't preserve what *was*," she went on, "we'll lose what *is*."

Somehow, I had my doubts. I was pretty much sickened with Clementine's attitude at this point and didn't ask for any more lessons. Then one morning as she was cleaning her eyelash curler, a miracle happened.

"Ya'll have no idea," she said suddenly. "By junior year, everybody's given up. We've already come out, anyway."

And with that, my doubts started to vanish. Was it possible that Clementine's Top Deb façade was just that? Were there, indeed, more rebels out there besides me and Alma? Could one of these self-proclaimed "good girls" secretly be . . . dare I say it . . .

Bad?

That's when we met Janelle Somersby, Clementine's archrival and a self-proclaimed "accidental Deb."

Janelle was staying at a nearby farmhouse with her own family. We met her riding four-wheelers one day and quickly realized she had quite a reputation, too, though the exact opposite of Clementine's.

Janelle represented the other side of Debutante Culture. She'd come out in Raleigh last year. Her two older sisters, Donna and Drusilla, came out in Charleston and Dallas.

The Somersbys were the exact opposite of the Footwhistles.

They started out as ranch hands until somebody down the line started manufacturing turf grass for golf courses. Once a few hundred thousand of those puppies sprung up all over the Texas heartland, the Somersbys were set. After a few years, they invested in tobacco and relocated to Winston-Salem.

Debbing meant a lot to the Somersbys—especially Janelle's Daddy.

"Baby girl," he whispered as she ascended the stage, "if 'n ya trip and fall, go ahead and roll down the aisle. We'll swing by and pick you up at the bottom."

And like any self-fulfilling prophecy, that's exactly what happened. Janelle took one step and fell flat on her dumper, and a whole room full of Winston-Salem's finest citizens sat there thinking, "Told you so."

"They only invited me 'cause I lived on the right side of town. I was the 'accidental' Deb. They expected me to fail."

Janelle knew a lot about Debutante culture, too. And when she started talking, everybody listened. Even Clementine.

She told us all about necking at tea parties, getting it on with Chuck Muffinstomper after a Sip 'n' Sun pool party, and chugging liquor in the bathroom before her Ball.

According to Janelle, all the girls would sneak airplane bottles inside their crinoline. You had to tuck them real far up to keep the glass from clinking—even into some naughty places. Then they'd scurry into the ladies' room and chug till the bathroom attendant came in. They flushed the rest, but not before ingesting enough Jägermeister to strangle a cow.

Janelle was already a full-figured woman and the drinking didn't help. It was no wonder she'd fallen down onstage in front of everybody.

She did her best to stay cheerful and ladylike for the rest of her big day. Her date, however, was a different story. Chuck was nothing but a cowpoke from backwoods Texas. He was too wild to act right around rich folks, and Janelle was too young at the time to tell him no. So when she got pregnant after the Ball, nobody was too surprised. That last shot of Jäger landed her smack-dab in the "family way."

Janelle's lessons were entirely different from Clementine's. She wasn't a Top Deb with curly eyelashes or an M.R.S. degree from UNC Chapel Hill. On the bright side, she avoided camel toes by boycotting underdrawers altogether.

"The only reason some girls at the Ball were even nice to me was 'cause my parents were rich," she said. "It must be hard being so prissy. Me? I trim my fanny right there on my bathroom sink."

That alone made Alma beam with pride.

Girls like Janelle were the wilder, faster versions of Wellingham Debs. They drank and smoked and walked around without any underdrawers on, for goodness sake. Some of them even peed standing up. But at least they were enjoying life.

Sure, Janelle made some choices most folks wouldn't agree with, but she also smiled more than any Deb I'd ever met. She didn't take herself too seriously . . . even if, in the end, she wound up the only pregnant Deb in town.

The most important lesson she and Clementine taught us up at the farm was to set ourselves apart.

Janelle wasn't actually a Debutante—not anymore. She was just a Rebel. And good girls like Clementine were just regular Debs, plain and simple. But me and Alma? We were a little of both. That's what made us so special.

Still, both girls were considered family. Reverend Claire insisted Alma bring them both along "to add more class to this sinful endeavor."

Reverend Claire didn't like Alma's non-Debutante friends, especially Billy Ray Horn. Billy Ray was a sweet country boy whose deep-dark secret was his love of baking. You gave Billy Ray some flour, sugar, a can of Abilene's Homemade Peaches and twenty-five minutes in your Momma's kitchen . . . and you'd end up with an edible peach cobbler masterpiece.

Why Reverend Claire didn't care for Billy Ray I couldn't figure.

I pondered this while watching him down a bottle of Wild Turkey with a peach schnapps chaser. The stuff looked like motor oil with a splash of orange.

This kept up till around two a.m. By then Reverend Claire and Clementine were fast asleep, and Alma, Billy Ray and Randall were usually so drunk they wouldn't wake up till around noon the next day.

That meant I had the whole house pretty much to myself.

Most mornings I'd wake up at dawn and sit around drinking breakfast tea and watching the sun rise. Nothing much compares to watching the sun rise against the Blue Ridge Mountains. The sky is black for a while, then blue, then green, then orange, and then yellow before its big yellow face finally peeks over the rocks to wink at you and say, "Mornin'!"

About an hour later, I'd be zoned out in front of the TV watching *Saved by the Bell* and Tom & Jerry cartoons.

Once, I woke up at five a.m. to find Reverend Claire sitting in my usual spot by the windows. Outside, a wraparound porch and about two hundred acres of farmland were the only things separating us from that sunrise. He turned and looked at me, surprised anyone was awake. Then he smiled.

"Want to do me a favor?" he asked.

The scarf was wrapped so tight around my face that I couldn't see them. But I could smell their poop from a mile away.

I was strapped to his four-wheeler facing backward, so I guess the scarf didn't make much difference. By the time Reverend Claire stopped I'd inched the fabric down far enough to let my eyes and nose poke out. . . .

Then I immediately tried to stuff them back inside.

We'd parked right in front of two huge steaming mounds of fresh manure. They were oddly colored: one black and one white, and by the smell I knew they were ripening quickly in the morning sun.

I cupped my hands over my mouth and looked around. What kind of animal could lay such enormous turds at our feet?

All I saw in either direction were cows, pigs, mountains, rock caves . . . and then they came into view:

Two llamas named "Chocolate" and "Vanilla." I'll give you two guesses why.

When we'd finished shoveling sawdust and dirt all over their poop, it smelled like the stuff our janitor at Wellingham used to sprinkle all over throw-up whenever somebody got sick from the cafeteria food and spilled her guts in the hallway.

Next, it was time to feed the pigs.

Strapped back on the four-wheeler, with about fifty pounds of grain cradling my mega-huge German ancestry, I wondered if maybe I should start drinking. That way, I could just run around doing wild-ass stuff with Alma and the rest of them all night long and not have to shovel llama poop at six a.m.

That grain was just about the heaviest stuff I've ever lifted in my life. It was only fifty pounds, but for some reason, I just couldn't get in the mood. The pigs sure were grateful, though, and Reverend Claire looked mighty proud as he helped me lift the mouth of the sack. When we'd finished, and I started toward the back of the four-wheeler, he stopped me.

"Appreciate your help," he said. "Billy Ray always turned me down, lazy boy."

And then he handed me the keys, took my place sitting backward in the rear and let me drive all the way home. Best of all, I didn't crash or stall out the motor, even once. I think he especially appreciated that part.

I thought of Reverend Claire at Alma's own gown fitting, about a month later.

We'd driven Connie the convertible all the way down to Fuquay-Varina. "FQ" was home to some of the fanciest dress shops in Carolina. Inside, three ladies waited on us for hours while I sat there like a bump on a log, waiting on Alma, who was waiting on just the right gown and for just the right shade of cream tulle to come along.

It was Alma's big moment, though, and I wanted everything to be perfect, too. So I sat. And waited. And sat some more. And waited some more. Finally, one of the shop ladies asked me to choose between a couple gowns. She called one "alabaster" and the other "blanch," but I couldn't tell the difference and called them both "white."

I was getting thirsty from all this color coordinating, so I headed next door to the Save-A-Coin truck stop for a bottle of Coca-Cola. I would've picked us up a couple ice-cream cones, too, but after all that poop-shoveling, chocolate and vanilla ice cream weren't as appealing as they used to be. Besides, I'm sure Alma didn't want any dripping on her hand-stitched, elbow-length kid-leather gloves.

A few days later, the gown arrived. The corset and bustle made Alma feel fat, so we decided to skip dinner—green bean salad, ambrosia and country-style steak this time—and snuck out to Biscuitville instead. How sausage biscuits and sweet tea were supposed to make Alma feel skinnier, I'll never know.

When we got there, the drive-thru was closed so we had to go eat at the counter. When we emerged about a half-hour later, I pushed the handy-dandy "Unlock" button on my remote control key chain and *click* the car doors unlatched.

I got in, sat down and was about to stick my key into the ignition when all of a sudden, I heard a rustle in the back.

Alma looks at me . . . was there someone . . . some*thing* . . . in here with us?

Then it happened. From the backseat, a furry head and two dilated eyes appeared in the darkness.

Arfffff!!!! Strrrrrrffff!!!!

"Holy fuckballs!" Alma screamed. "It's a *dawg!*"

I turned to look.

Behind me, a tiny, shivering ball of pink and white fur with a little collar that read "Snuffles" buckled around its neck yapped at full volume. With a name like that, how dangerous could he be?

Strrrrrrffff!!!!

Snuffles snapped into the air, and then started growling and gnashing his teeth. Clearly, Snuffles wanted us *out* of his Master's car—*fast.* To prove his point, he tried to lunge out the window, held back only by a thin leash. When that didn't work, he tried peeing all over the dashboard, all in the span of about three seconds.

We grabbed our stuff, jumped out and ran toward another Chevy Cavalier—the *right* one—a few yards away. For once, I was glad to get back to school that night.

Alma and I ate the rest of our meals in the school cafeteria. When we walked in for dinner, the whole room went quiet. Everybody looked shocked to see us show up; they just sat there and stared for a good thirty seconds. Just long enough for Miss Freeze to clear her throat and Alma and me to grab some PB&J sandwiches and skedaddle.

A couple days later, everybody got another shock when I became the second Wellingham student to ever be accepted at Brown University. Brown was way outside of the South, and thus, highly suspicious. I'm not sure to this day whether Miss Freeze thought Brown was a school or a color.

Once I got into college and everything was set for Deb Ball, Alma and I were free. We could finally have all the fun we'd been dreaming about. The kind we were determined to have, even if it killed us.

Since graduation was coming up, we made plans to revisit Myrtle Beach. We weren't going to let Mr. Hush and Ella Mae ruin our trip this time.

Maybe this time we'd eat saltwater taffy and fudge from Barefoot Landing. Maybe we'd even lose our virginities, Alma suggested. Or maybe we'd wait till Senior Beach week to do that. The only thing that was certain was we were *definitely* getting tattoos.

We spent the next few days lounging by the pool and sipping virgin piña coladas. We rode rides at the Pavilion and ate dinner *anywhere* but at the NASCAR Café. The next day, we sipped lemonade smoothies and drew our names and faces in the sand.

When it got dark, Alma and I lay out on the beach and watched the moon. It told her we'd be beautiful and skinny and even famous someday. That we could be anything we wanted, even though we were "queers."

Neither of us had ever heard that before.

When Alma told people she was going away to Wellingham, they thought she was some sort of bad kid or something. Like she'd stolen stuff and needed to be sent off to reform school. And that meant she didn't have a clique to hang out with or protect her.

Since public school cliques were kind of like prison gangs, that meant trouble. You had your jocks, your weirdo theater people, your blacks, your Mexicans—all separated into their own groups, sitting in different parts of the cafeteria, avoiding eye contact with other cliques. They even segregated themselves in movie theaters. Everybody—black, white, red—separated themselves by color or class. Nobody wanted to mix in or shake things up.

Alma and I were all about shaking things up.

We'd never be pretty or skinny or cool enough for everybody else's rules. We wanted our own. And we were so eager to regain control over our own lives, our own bodies, our own *anything* that we'd sacrifice everything to get it.

With that kind of control over our destinies, she said, we could do anything. Even pull out into oncoming traffic on Ocean Drive.

I remember I'd asked Alma if she could pick up some doughnuts from Krispy Kreme for the drive. It was cloudier than usual that morning, and we were supposed to leave in an hour so we could make it back to Wellingham in time for dinner.

She grabbed my keys and left in a hurry while I showered. The water was hard and salty that day. It stuck to my face and made my eyes tear up, so I turned it off to let the water filter do its job. That's when I heard the phone ringing.

"Hello, Mrs. Williams? I'm very sorry, but I can't talk right now . . ." I said. But there wasn't anybody on the other line. "Mrs. Williams?"

Then a man's voice answered. It was shaky, like he wasn't sure what to say. Like he was trying to find the words.

"Ma'am, this is Officer Sherry from the Myrtle Beach Sheriff's Department. I've got an accident victim here who's asking for you. Could you come down to the corner of . . . ?"

But I couldn't hear anymore.

The whole world was slowing down and I was floating above myself again: *I'm not here. I'm somewhere else, and you'll never find me.*

Alma had taken Connie, so I got in a cab and told him to just drive. By the time we got to the highway, he didn't need any more directions. Car parts were all over the road and I watched a box of regular glazed fall out onto the road when they put her on the stretcher.

I ran over to the firemen and EMTs. Officer Sherry led me over to a sheet with a tiny face sticking out. He tried to keep her head covered while we talked.

After a few minutes, she finally smiled and nodded off and one of the doctors said something to us both . . . but I couldn't hear again. The blood was rushing too loud in my ears. What I wouldn't give for one of Alma's jokes. She was the only one who could cheer me up right then.

"Ain't nobody a lady till she learns to wreck a Chevy!" she'd say. If she could speak.

If she weren't already dead.

ack at Granny Blanche's condo, I stepped back under the salty water and felt my eyes tear up.

My ears were ringing. My head throbbed. I leaned against the shower wall and slowly sank to my knees, then my side, the water beating down on me from above. I could barely think.

I'm not here. I'm somewhere else. Somewhere you'll never find me again.

For a second I was dreaming. In my dream, we were still happy. We were dancing in the basement and sliding across the floor. In my dream, the fat kid inside me felt pretty just to be alive. It was the same feeling I got the first time my Daddy ever played his Santana vinyls where I could hear them. I was so excited, like Alma and I could do anything. Like we could go back to staying up past bedtime and breaking all the rules like we used to.

Those kinds of girls, some folks say, are Rebel Debutantes. They're "bad" because they ask too many questions and kiss too many boys and make up their own rules and live their own lives.

Sometimes they go to Myrtle Beach where they take chances and lose things, like their lives. One of them died right there on the side of the road. An officer pressing a towel to her head and me holding her hand and whispering, "Alma, it's gonna be all right."

We were the originals, though there was only one of us left. The girls who started out as Debs, became Rebels, then grew into our own and became both.

Sometimes, Scarlett inspired us to be brave, to have fun even if it killed us—to think about the consequences tomorrow. Sometimes, she was a good role model and the voice we needed to hear.

And sometimes, I wished she'd just shut up.

At Alma's funeral, I couldn't stop laughing.

It was a windy afternoon—common for Southern springs. I stood beside this boy named Jax, who couldn't stop laughing, either. Jax had cut all his classes that day, had driven all the way from L-Boogie to see Alma and say good-bye. His hair kept falling into his face with each laugh, and he couldn't stop. It was the only way either of us knew how to keep from crying.

The rest of the year, I was almost a lost cause.

I was finished with "finishing" school. I'd learned all the "lady-like behavior"—horseback riding, ballroom dancing, corset mainte-nance, wear and lacing, tennis, bridge and all forms of ladies' billiards and "parlor pleasantries" I could handle. Without Alma, Welling-ham wasn't fun anymore—it was just another camp or dance class or after-school activity I wanted to quit.

By the age of seventeen, I was tired of dancing and singing and riding classes. I was sick of seeking acceptance by wearing Keds ten-nis shoes and cashmere cardigans and keeping my mouth shut at all times. To me, these just seemed like good ways to get an ulcer. I could no longer repress all of my real thoughts and emotions just so other folks could feel more comfortable.

At that point, I considered the girls who actually enjoyed Welling-ham a little passé. To me, the only difference between boarding school Debutantes and public school rednecks boiled down to a single rivalry:

Scarlett O'Hara versus Norma Jean Baker.

Make no mistake, in the South there is a *great* difference between Scarlett and Norma Jean. The latter being a complete and total red-neck, and the former being an appropriate role model for any future young lady.

First of all, Scarlett enjoyed fuzzy J. Crew sweaters, vacations at Hilton Head and perfectly rolled-up bobby socks. Her Momma would insist on her engaging in dance competitions to practice strutting her Cotillion-learned stuff in front of crowds of people . . . as she would (with any luck and a lot of elitist support) have to do at her own Debutante Ball.

Norma Jean, on the other hand, entered beauty pageants and got her nails done at Truvy's Salon, where she enjoyed ham biscuits, hair spray and gossip. These two gals were entirely different classes, who rarely interacted with one another except to demonstrate their mutual distaste.

With Alma gone, I had time on my hands. I started taking a closer look at the girls I used to be friends with—and no longer liked what I saw. Years of passive-aggressiveness had now blossomed into full-blown repression. Girls like Caitlin, who'd tried way too hard to fit in our sophomore year, now had control issues and resulting eating disorders that left them addicted to laxatives or covered in gray peach fuzz. Others like Rachel and Cindy had started out sweet, but were now full of rage and morphing into drug dealers. As bad as it was, however, I knew Wellingham had saved us all from a fate far worse in public school. Despite all the carnage Diane, the Honor Cabinet and Miss Freeze left behind, Wellingham gave us self-confidence, focus, ambition and—most of all—the intellectual tools to make our dreams realities. All the things that would've been lost if we'd stayed in public high school, competing with boys for each teacher's attention, and praised more for our bodies than for our minds.

And though Rachel, Cindy and Caitlin had scorned and abandoned me back in tenth grade for befriending Alma, I could see her inside of them now. By senior year, they were budding Rebel

Debs, and wanted what Alma and I had always craved: freedom to *live*—not just keep house and birth babies forever.

By now, I would've rather shaved my head like a topiary garden than keep trying to fit in. Not that I wanted to do that either, but the snobby cliques, frilly dresses, flowery perfume and six years' worth of Cotillion cookies and red velvet cake had taken a huge toll on my psyche. I was sick of the games and hypocrisy I found all around me. I'd successfully turned from Debutante to Rebel and wasn't going back.

I'd even abandoned my childhood Scarlett O'Hara fantasy. Or so I thought.

Since I'd been "traumatized" by my best friend's death, I had free license to do whatever. So instead of fantasizing over my storybook wedding to Rhett, I'd much rather skip class and cruise for boys in late-'90s coffee shops or go to the mall and surf around for the latest Indigo Girls CD. At night, I'd wait till everyone went to bed to hide in the basement, watching reruns of *Highlander*, working out to MTV's *Grind*, and listening to Alma's old Boyz II Men mix-tapes till the sun came up.

By the end of senior year, I figured everybody in town knew I was through with Wellingham. I assumed they'd all taken the hint. I was rebellious, impulsive and generally snarky. Not exactly Debutante material.

The kinds of girls who *were* Debutante material still included Diane and Bitsy. Unlike Rachel and Caitlin, Diane hadn't changed through her years at Wellingham—she was a confirmed victim of chauvinistic patriarchy and a well-seasoned manipulator long before she ever came to boarding school—and still as conservative, doting and pretty as ever.

In short, she never embarrassed her Momma and never caused any trouble at school.

I, on the other hand, had now been *thisclose* to being kicked out of Wellingham a total of four times. In girls'-boarding-school terms, this is equivalent to having been impeached from the presidential office . . . twice.

But, in the end, who cared? I'd survived, hadn't I? And would be starting at Brown soon, aka moving to "Yankee Land" (otherwise referred to by my extended family as "any area above the Mason-Dixon Line"), and transported into another world entirely. So what if I'd been a Southern social failure? So what if I'd made it through seven years of Cotillion classes? I was beyond my childhood, right? Beyond all the Southern good ol' boys who proclaimed their superiority over women, and the women who accepted this treatment because their own mothers—their entire society, in fact—had brainwashed them into believing it. I was beyond the girls in history class who'd question, "Why do we need feminism?" and make me want to scream and cry and run away from school. . . .

Right?

In May of 1999, when I crossed the stage and picked up my diploma, I sure thought so.

I was done with Wellingham. I was going to Brown, where things would surely be different. I was grown-up and mature and way past all my wannabe Scarlett days. . . .

Right?

Like Alma once said, you can take the Belle out of the Ball, but not the Ball out of the Belle. Whether I liked it or not, I would always carry parts of my Rebel Deb past with me—and thank goodness! Because as it turned out, I had a few more lady-making lessons to learn.

Chapter Five

(I Wish I Were)
Charlotte Simmons:

• A Rebel Deb Goes to Brown •

rowing up, folks called me a "queer."

A troublemaker. A nerdy, big-butted tomboy listening to opera while everybody else rocked out to *NSync. A wannabe Scarlett turned full-fledged Rebel Debutante. And after I graduated from Wellingham, these folks thought they'd seen it all. . . .

They hadn't seen nothing yet. Neither had I.

In August of 1999, I went to Brown. Compared to the wild-ass young'uns holding nekkid parties on Waterman Street, streaking around Wriston Quad, storming University Hall and making out at every LGBTA "Sex, Power, God" (or whatever that was supposed to mean) party . . . I was, let's face it, small potatoes.

"AnnaBelle!" one of the girls in my freshman dorm shouted down. "Come talk for us!"

Heather Goldstein was a bigmouthed, big-haired girl from Long

Island, with a face like a Moon Pie. If you aren't familiar, a Moon Pie is a perfectly round cake sold at gas stations, Woolworth's and JR General Stores across the South. They're about the size of an uncooked sweet potato minus the trimmings.

Big-Haired Heather was a shining example of Yankee prejudice. She demonstrated this by assuming every gal from the South had a name ending in "Belle." And when she wasn't taping Polaroids of herself all over her front door, she would make fun of my accent.

"What's a 'grit,' exactly?"

Well, um, it's kinda like ground-up corn only you take the . . .

"Whatever. Too complicated. So, do you guys still own slaves and stuff?"

Um . . . no.

"Did you grow up on a plantation?"

No.

"Do you, like, hate black people and junk?"

What?

"Could you say something Southern?"

Bless. Your. Heart.

"Okay, kewl. Now say, 'I don't know nothin' 'bout birthin' no babies!'"

. . . Um, I gotta get to class. See ya'll later.

"Ya'll?! *Omigod*, that so wicked cute!"

That was the gist of every single conversation between Heather and me. Every. Single. Day.

After an entire semester of answering Heather's asinine questions, eating horrible cafeteria food in "the Ratty" and bumping and grinding at all-night frat parties, I needed a change. And new friends. And neither the SSG—Southern Support Group, a handful of folks who weren't too keen on cold weather, rude people, cobblestone streets or paying four dollars for a cup of coffee—nor my roommate, Jamic, were gonna cut it.

What I wouldn't give for another fellowship luncheon down at the First Christian UCC. Or a Saturday morning gospel concert with Called Out Ministries, The Hall Boys, Christian Wolfe or the Resurrection Quartet playing *Under the West Texas Sky* and *Down on the Bayou*.

For the first time since leaving for Wellingham, I was homesick. One night, I was even bored and lonely enough to follow Big-Haired Heather to Frat Row. She entered a brick-lined building with a big flag over the door. On the flag were Greek letters I couldn't read printed in red. Inside, another big-haired girl with a gold pin on her shoulder offered me a rose before leading me into a lounge filled with other big-haired, snobby-looking JAPs.

I didn't know they were JAPs at the time, of course. I didn't find out what a JAP—Jewish American Princess—was until a girl named Farah Kurtz with a Jewish Momma and a Mormon Daddy took pity on my ignorance and sat me down for a talk behind the sciences lab.

Apparently, Providence had a huge Jewish population. It also had strip clubs with all-day "Legs and Eggs" Sunday brunch, and a whole lot of mob bosses who hung out in pizza parlors that never seemed to sell any pizza. They were otherwise empty except for the greasers, their laptops and a few shredders toward the back. It also had an ex-mayor, Buddy Cianci, whom everybody was half in love with. This was mostly because he'd cleaned all the industrial waste out of the big river that ran through town. Never mind that he'd gone to federal prison. It seemed the sight of clean water flowing through a wasteland made up for many a man's faults.

Even with all this *Sopranos*-like drama, Farah explained, Providence had a lot to offer.

First was its food. Here were smells and tastes I'd never experienced down South. I tried sushi, chickpeas, pesto, Nutella and all kinds of foreign dishes with lots of spices and flavor.

Then there were its people. Down in Little Portugal, you could buy whole fried catfish with the eyes still inside. Not even Chip and Scooter ever thought of eating one of those, bones and all.

At the campus Hillel House, I tried gefilte fish, matzo ball soup and whitefish on bagels. I liked the "bitter herbs" best because they tasted like the horseradish folks ate on roast beef back home. I was relieved when Farah and the rest of her friends treated me better than Heather. They even called me by my name instead of "the Hick," "that girl" or "shiksa."

Everybody else I met looked and sounded so . . . well, *angry*. I started to get paranoid. Even the Starbucks barista seemed to hate my guts. Who knew that her forceful way of screaming out "Skim *latte*! Did somebody order a skim *latte*?!?!" was just the Northern version of being polite?

Then there was its weather. My first year out of Carolina was a hard adjustment. I didn't own a coat thicker than a tablecloth. And in case you didn't realize, the wind in Providence will literally break you in half. Plus, the whole place sits on a big-ass hill. So if you're a skinny white girl with tiny muscles, a poor sense of direction and not much willpower, this gets old *fast*.

Then there was its geography. Providence was the biggest place I'd ever seen. What's worse, the streets didn't have lanes, so folks just sorta drove wherever they damn well pleased. Surviving as a pedestrian was anybody's guess, and I'm pretty sure my Southern fashions were the only reason I avoided being hit by oncoming traffic. I was a blond beacon in a sea of brunettes. A vision of pastels in an ocean of black clothes, black sunglasses, thick makeup and thicker hair gel.

I once set out to find a grocery store and wound up somewhere around South Cranston—which, in case you don't know, is one of many "*Omigod! The ghetto!*" parts of Rhode Island. Or at least that's how two girls in my Bio class reacted. They were both from Beverly Hills, though, so I guess theirs might be a skewed perspective. Still, who knew a gal could go out for a gallon of milk and wind up in harm's way?

And what the sam-hell was Providence doing with a ghetto, anyway?

Weren't *we*—Southerners—supposedly known for segregation? How was it that, come lunchtime in the Ratty, all the black students sat apart from all the white students? That all the KAT House girls laughed at me whenever I tried to pronounce "Ashkenazi" or "rugelach"? That all the Asian kids sat together in Neuro 101, whispering in Korean so the rest of us couldn't understand? Wasn't *this* the place I'd been taught was so much more progressive than anything below the Mason-Dixon?

Why did the North feel so much like the South?

At eighteen, no answers came. So I decided to make the best of things.

There were no core classes at Brown, which I found even more refreshing than sticking my naked toes in the sand and squishing them back and forth till my corns came off. That meant I could take a few English classes, hate them, and quickly opt out. Which I did. The conversation I had with myself went something like this:

"Self, I have no idea what I want to do with my life. So I guess I'll pick the hardest major at school. Something even harder than what Heather's doing."

. . . which, back then, was something called Cognitive Neuroscience.

Big-Haired Heather was also a Neuroscience major. And don't get me wrong—that's pretty impressive, and for good reason. "Cog Neuro," however, was more specific, and thus, required *way* more credits to graduate. For example, I'd have to pass a whole heap of Statistics, Calculus, Applied Math and a couple of chemistry classes I didn't like and didn't do that well in but was too afraid to skip. Cog Neuro was by far the hardest subject to grasp. But I was determined to do just that—*and* make a big splash at AXO. And, by default, beat Heather Big-Hair at both.

Once I returned from South Cranston alive, I made a self-promise: Survive the North, make straight A's, and—most of all—make Heather sorry.

Let me explain:

Farah and the kind folks at the Hillel House didn't represent the total Jewish population at Brown. In fact, this group was big enough that one of only two sororities on campus was entirely devoted to recruiting girls of the Tribe.

They were known as the KAT House—Kappa Alpha Theta sorority. And once she received her rose that first night, Heather pledged to become a bona fide member.

Brown also had an all-Jewish fraternity named AE Pi, but religion never seemed to make much difference to these fellas. They were just as disrespectful to women as all the others. In fact, the only real difference I saw between AE Pi and the non-Jewish frats was the level of violence when hazing their pledges. Let's just say I never heard any rumors around campus of the Jewish boys being forced to "perform" on their elder brothers.

Anywho.

Once I heard about Big-Haired Heather pledging the KAT House, I decided to check it out, too. They took one look at my blue eyes and blond curls and before you could say "hush puppy," my butt was back out on the street. They weren't about to rush a White Anglo-Saxon Protestant from Carolina. I might as well have had "I love Jesse Helms!" tattooed on my forehead.

Instead, I joined AXO—Alpha Chi Omega—which the KAT House lovingly referred to as "A-Chi-Ho." And I entered a world *way* more rebellious than anything I'd ever seen. This wasn't tuck-it-in, slick-it-back Wake Forest. These gals came from all over—big cities like L.A. and New York and Chicago—places I'd only ever seen on the *Today* show, and did way worse than fall down at Deb Balls and sneak in through first-floor windows. They were serious trouble.

There was Katy, our sorority president when I joined, who wore bright red lipstick and her underdrawers on top of her clothes. Her favorite pledge-bonding activities were playing beer pong, snorting cocaine and bragging about how she'd screwed her boyfriend in every room of our sorority house. Then there was Ginny Dee, the curvy California girl with tattoos in places that would've made even Alma blush. She once lived off Greek food for an entire month, she claimed, and had the B.O. to prove it. And then there was Emma, the six-foot-tall track star from Washington. She wasn't nearly as wild as the others. Poor girl had been threatened by kidnappers as a child.

Every weekend, we AXO girls got all dolled up in our sorority uniforms: halter tops, tight jeans, bright pink boas and shimmery silver eyeliner. Then we'd head off en masse to a local bar.

All the bar-slash-pick-up-joints back then had names like Liquid Lounge, GCB, Fish Co and Oliver's. Oliver's was the closest to the AXO house, and thus our favorite. Plus, it hired bouncers who didn't laugh at my fake ID. I'd bought it through Farah once she became my pledge sister. I was shocked but pleased that she didn't join the dark side at the KAT House. To cement our sisterhood, we walked into Kinko's one afternoon for a "passport photo," and walked out with social lives. The only reason I even bought the thing was because, like most Ivy League schools, Brown was kind of boring.

Since we were both Cog Neuro majors, Farah and I had the worst of it. Before AXO, our social activities included doing homework in the sciences lab or sipping cranberry juice that we pretended to mix with vodka at departmental parties with Entomology majors. In case you're not familiar, those fellas study bugs for a living.

As new pledges, we found that our social options exploded. They now included doing homework in the sorority lounge or standing around ogling frat boys and coughing up secondhand smoke at Oliver's. Only one of these involved dressing up in skimpy outfits, so our choice was clear.

Attendance at the bar was pretty much mandatory during pledge week, even though neither of us was twenty-one. But I needed all the fun I could get. So like Gordy Mae Paisley—the Health teacher back at Wellingham—used to say, "Smoke 'em if ya got 'em."

So I did.

The first time I used my fake ID, Mike "Diseased Monkey Boy" Zaconi was guarding the door. I started sweating a bit as he glanced over the measly piece of plastic, and then at me, with hesitation in his eyes. I already knew that DMB was the campus mambo (man-bimbo), who'd pretty much let anything with boobs through that door. That would normally knock me out of the running. But I'd paid attention during Clementine's man-catching lessons and came prepared with an entire arsenal of Top Deb weapons. One hair toss and a couple batted eyelashes later, and DMB waved me through without comment. Feminism be damned.

Inside, my sisters and I would flirt mercilessly with all the pseudo-jock frat boys Brown could offer. And unlike the Phi Psis at Wake, not a single one looked anything like Ronald Reagan.

Oh, no.

This was a Brave New World. The "frozen, heartless" North. A land of slick, greasy roughnecks with big eyebrows and loud voices who came from funny-sounding places like Hackensack and Braintree.

Back at the AXO house, our initiation was in full swing. A whole semester's worth of fun and games and getting locked into basements awaited us. Oh, right—and we made paddles. That was fun, too! There were only five of us newbies in my pledge class: Me, Kit, Emma, Farah and Jackie.

By then, most folks started to realize that I didn't fit in up North any better than I had down South. As a result, my initiation was a bit rougher than the rest. For example, since I was also the only real blonde for miles around, I had to put up with Heather and some of the other KAT House girls calling me "Shiksa Barbie." Also, besides weekly trips to Oliver's, we lowly pledges were required to memorize the history and heritage of AXO. This meant spending a few weeks in Pledge Class.

Second semester freshman year was all about Pledge Class—which was just like Cotillion, minus the frilly dresses and ballroom dancing and table setting. We studied workbooks full of sorority facts and passed exams that tested our knowledge of all things Greek. We learned about our sorority flower (the carnation) and musical instrument (the lyre). We took field trips to plan parties with other sisters from Providence College and University of Rhode Island. They were mostly trampy-looking gals with bad skin and hairy hoo-ha's, but we were still required to like them. Or, at least, pretend to. We had to treat them like sisters even at their worst moments—like when one of them fell down drunk on the dance floor during a semiformal and ripped Emma's hemline clean off.

"Whoa! Like, that was sooo hella stupid, right?!" said drunk girl.

"Whoa! Like, I'm glad they're teaching you to walk erect at your public school, right?!" Emma replied.

That reminded me of Alma and made me smile. Finally, I thought, I've found a group of Rebel Debs, just like me! Having grown up in a part of the world where sororities are a religion, where folks wear T-shirts like "Go Greek or go home," I decided right then that AXO (as opposed to birthin' babies) was where it was at.

Toward the end of freshman year, Pledge Class ended and we moved on to bigger projects—like practicing our sorority songs.

These were cute little ditties the older sisters made us memorize and then sing to all the frats. Each one was about how much we *loooooovvved* the Theta Delta Chis (or whomever we happened to be facing at the time) and how much we wanted to date-slash-hug-slash-make-out with every single one of them. Next, we moved on to building a beer pong table in the basement. When that was finished, we built a huge green bench with the words "Class of 2000" in silver letters on top and donated it to AXO as our pledge class gift. As our final task, we held tryouts for the Greek Olympics. This was a traditional relay race where all the pledges from both sororities sprinted around Frat Row, passing colored batons to one another in front of a massive crowd of shirtless frat boys painted with Greek letters.

Since Providence didn't warm up till sometime in early May, this month was also designated as streaking season. Mostly boys took part in this, until a couple bolder AXO sisters decided running around nekkid (not "naked," as we were definitely up to something) was way more fun than puff-painting paddles.

And, hell, if that didn't suit . . . they could always fake a kidnapping.

One night after tryouts, the five of us gathered in the sorority lounge for yet another pledge-bonding activity. I think it had something to do with cutting and pasting letters onto poster board for an end-of-year dance. We were all getting cozy, taking our shoes off to relax, when suddenly . . .

Bam!! Bam bam bam!!!

About a dozen boys wearing all black with panty hose over their heads burst through the window.

"Get down and shut up!!" they screamed.

One of them threw a burlap sack over my head, hitched me over his shoulders and escaped with the others back into the night.

All I remember is trying to catch my breath while some big hulk held onto my fanny so I wouldn't fall.

"What a gentleman," I said.

And against every kidnapper code of conduct known to man, he talked back.

"No problem," he said with a slight Midwestern accent. This made my ears perk up. I immediately recognized my captor as none other than Larry Bizwitz.

I'd already met Larry at an AXO mixer during my first semester. He was introduced to me as captain of the rugby team, Heather's off-again, on-again "boyf," and a turkey sandwich lover. From the way he held on to my fanny, I suspected he was a Rebel Deb lover, too.

"Don't I know you . . . ?" I said, feeling him up, still blind as a bat.

My groping spooked Larry so much that he handed me over to one of his fellow kidnappers. I suddenly wished I'd put on some makeup before being thrown into a sack.

Through a thin spot in the cloth, I spotted Jackie's legs dangling over another kidnapper's shoulders. Looked like my other pledge sisters were being kidnapped, too.

We finally landed inside some dark, cramped room. Only they forgot to remove our sacks, which made me giggle and Emma freak out.

"*Omigod*, where are we?!" she screamed.

"Sssh! It's just their basement," I said.

I finally ripped through the top of my sack and helped the others to do the same. By this point, Kit was bored, Emma was terrified, Jackie looked oblivious and Farah was giggling. When we finally got the sackcloth off Emma's head, she took a few deep breaths and that seemed to help.

They finally let us out and we trudged upstairs into a huge party. Even covered in dust, sackcloth and sporting a big ol' blush, Larry Bizwitz couldn't keep his eyes off me.

He was wearing his kidnapper's 007 uniform—a black turtleneck with black slacks, perfect for Rebel Deb hunting—and pretended to make conversation with the short fella standing in front of him. The short fella would speak. Larry would nod. The short fella spoke again and Larry nodded again, pretending to keep up. He kept up his staring game for about an hour until, finally, it was time for the pledges to go home. We still had paddles to paint and benches to fix and songs to sing. But my heart was soaring—there he was: Heather's beau! The rugby captain! Staring at *me*. The Rebel Deb reaping revenge on all the big-haired betches of the North.

The next day, Emma and a lot of other folks got riled up about our fake kidnapping. She kept going on about how sexist the whole thing was and how our older sisters had endangered our safety and whatnot. But I didn't care a lick. In fact, I was thrilled! Getting fake-kidnapped was way better than sitting around, painting paddles. Nobody back in Winston would've *dared* try that with a Wellingham girl. Not unless they wanted somebody's Daddy showing up on their front porch, locked and loaded. I'd enjoyed watching Larry watching me all night, and I suspected he had, too.

And as if to confirm my suspicions, guess who paid me a visit?

I was headed to my room right after a shower when there it was: the telltale turkey sandwich. Half eaten, and sitting on my desk . . . right next to Larry.

One of the older sisters had let him in. He saw me, did a double take, then blushed bright red and ran out of the room. Not easily deterred, I took a shortcut past Larry's room that night. When I approached his door, he was half naked and leaning against the doorframe talking to Pete Wallsley, a fellow Southerner from Atlanta.

I'd worn my cutest pink camisole sweater-set that day, with a sweetheart neckline and beaded pearls that screamed out, "Ain't I just the purdiest thing you've ever seen?!"

Larry saw me and did another double take. Pete smiled, extended his hand like any good Georgian gentleman, and started polite conversation. I tried to concentrate on Pete's questions, but my eyes kept darting over to Larry. "The boy was built like a brick shit-house," as Alma would say.

We all have memories we treasure forever: When we lost our best friend; when we first fell in love. That moment in the hallway was one of mine.

Once Pete found some excuse to leave the two of us alone, Larry and I walked over to the local Starbucks on Thayer Street and had our first official date. We spent the next two hours making out.

By sophomore year, I was now nineteen, Larry was twenty-one, and both of us spent way more time making out, making love, and riding a huge tidal wave of infatuation than ever going to class. We were inseparable. We spent so much time alone together that we'd even invented our own makeshift sign language:

A nose wiggle meant "I love you." A sigh meant "I'm happy." A "Humph!" meant I'm pouting because that makes you smile.

While my sorority sisters were out at Oliver's, we'd stay in watching Rocky II and Dead Poets Society till I could recite the dialogue backward. One night during Rocky's victory scene, Larry revealed himself as one of those math geniuses who invents futuristic lasers in his garage.

No, seriously.

Back when he was seventeen, Larry made some kind of eye laser thingamabob that got him featured in Time magazine. Then he flew off to some big-ass conference where he ate whore-da-vores and shook hands with James Earl Jones. A couple years later, Larry came to Brown to "find a Jewish wife." This was apparently why he'd been dating Big-Haired Heather. Problem was, she'd been cheating on him and he found out the night of our fake kidnapping. One cheating JAP and several double takes later, and here we were: the Scientist and his Shiksa. Two mismatched peas in a highly unlikely pod.

First, he taught me about Judaism. That's when I found out what a "shiksa" was. Suddenly, the KAT House sisters' taunts made a lot more sense. In return, I taught him about Gentiles—specifically, Debutantes. A few months into our relationship, he managed to say "Momma, that ain't right!" and "You do go on!" with a straight face. I baked him one of Granny Blanche's famous chocolate cakes with cinnamon icing for his birthday and for Halloween, he was the Popeye to my Olive Oyl.

After a while, I even got him listening to country music. Hank Williams, Ol' Waylon and even some Randy Travis. We came up with a couple of our own. Some of my favorites included "Your Cornbread's Hot 'n' Tasty, but You Ain't Got Nothin' on My Baby," "There's a Tear in My Beer over You," "He's a Ten-Shot Drinker and a Ten-Second Lover," and "We Met One Night in Tijuana . . . Now She's My Baby's Momma." We danced to those made-up songs till our shoes fell off.

Though we were very much in love, our cultural and religious differences were obvious. He got drunk at parties, but I didn't. He sometimes did cocaine, which I'd never seen, and didn't sleep those nights, which I didn't understand. He was cynical, distrustful and generally tormented by his own impossible standards. As a Rebel Debutante, I wasn't.

On the other hand, I was also too afraid to drive a car in a place without any street lanes, so he had to. He was brave when I was afraid, and when we ate together in the Ratty, he'd build huge turkey sandwiches and cram them into his mouth to make me laugh.

When junior year rolled around, we got closer. Our differences didn't seem to matter so much. We kissed in hot tubs and ate matzo brie and fooled around in the backs of limousines on our way to semiformals. Every night, we cuddled and planned for the future. We were happy. And for once, this Rebel felt accepted and understood . . . whether she was a real Debutante or not.

In 2001, Brown was that kind of place.

Where a Jewish boy and a Southern WASP could find each other and fall in love and, until their Mommas found out, live happily ever after. The kind of place where the past didn't matter because you were here to build a future. Dating Larry was my first real step toward growing up. And he made Brown into the kind of eclectic American pot this Rebel Deb needed to melt into. He gave me what I'd been searching for for so long: the Real World of Boys . . . or, as much as he could offer at twenty-one and I could grasp at nineteen. Somewhere in the back of my mind, I hoped Larry and I would last. I tried to relax. I ate his strange, slimy gefilte fish balls and giggled at his late-night puppy noises because for once I could be as silly and rebellious as I wanted. I let my shoes fall apart from dancing. I trusted Larry to be there to pick me up, shoeless and all.

Until, one day, he wasn't.

One day, the Rebel Deb wasn't cute anymore. One day, I wasn't the girl who loved him, laughed with him and hung on his every word. I was now just the "Shiksa Barbie" his friends disliked and his Momma called "that girl."

We all have those memories locked inside us forever: the first time our heart broke. The face of the one who broke it.

One day, he woke up and remembered why he'd come to Brown in the first place: to find a Jewish wife. He didn't want to marry me, didn't want to have children with me and never understood me, anyway. Or so he said. With that, my heart broke into a million little pieces I never knew existed. Not until I sat crying on our floor, alone, with them spread out all around me. So like most first loves, Larry and I came to an end. We had to.

In the words of Lewis Grizzard, Jr.: The fella ripped my heart out and stomped that sucker flat.

But that's another thing all first loves have in common: They fill us up, tear us apart and then force us to put ourselves back together again.

By now, I was twenty-one and had been dating Larry for most of my college career—from my second semester as a freshman to my first semester as a senior. That meant the whole rest of my senior year at Brown was spent getting over the first love of my life.

First, I listened to sad music. I set Bryan Adams's "Heaven" on repeat, which only made me feel worse. Then, I threw myself into school—a much smarter decision—and that actually made me feel better. I ended up with solid A's that semester. Sure, I was still heartbroken, but part of my self-promise was now in the bag.

Only it wasn't enough. I still had too much time to pine over Larry. So, I did what any self-respecting Rebel Deb would:

I got a job.

Just so you know, at twenty-one I'd worked only one summer of my entire life.

At sixteen, while on vacation from Wellingham, I suddenly got a wild hair up my ass and decided to accomplish what no other woman in my family had done before: make my own money. So, I trotted down Main Street, took a right on Maple Avenue, and found myself outside Burlington's finest (and first) coffee shop: Schlabach's Café.

At the time, not too many Southerners frequented coffee shops. Sitting around, drinking hot liquid with your feet stuck in clay and your lungs sucking in humidity, never seemed too appealing.

In fact, there wasn't a single Starbucks or Dunkin' Donuts for nearly a hundred miles—not till you reached Charlotte or Myrtle Beach. Burlington was the land of Krispy Kreme, Waffle House, Biscuitville and Bojangles, all of which made damn sure that Scarlett never went hungry again. At fifteen, I became a waitress at Schlabach's, the only coffee shop in town owned by the only Jewish fella in town.

Mr. Schlabach was a fair but hard-nosed old man with a big mustache that caught every piece of food his mouth ever attempted to eat. As a result, his breath smelled like a mixture of cough syrup with Listerine.

Mr. Schlabach was not only the owner but the chef of his café and served homemade chicken salad for lunch. When I say it was homemade, I mean that I personally chopped and slopped the stuff together and poured it into a big vat stored in the basement. Once our lunch shift ended, he'd recycle what he hadn't sold and re-serve it the next day.

Though my slopping and chopping skills were excellent, Mr. Schlabach suspected he'd made a mistake. I was sweet to folks, sure, but made a miserable waitress. Like my Aunt Sandy back in the '60s, I had the backbone of a wet dishrag. So when it came to hungry, demanding customers, I was a total pushover. I also couldn't write down the orders fast enough and never remembered which one went to which table, anyway.

Mr. Schlabach got so frustrated that he stuck me with permanent chicken salad duty. In return, I'd get so bored chopping and slopping that I'd lock myself in the bathroom till my shift ended. When school started and I moved back to Wellingham, both of us were relieved.

Years later, at twenty-one, my stint at the Paragon Café didn't turn out any better.

It was only a block away from campus and the most popular restaurant on Thayer Street. Waitresses there made lots of money, folks said. Tawanda Jenkins, a girl from my chemistry class, paid her way through school just working weekends. I'd heard about girls stripping their way through the Ivies. Like this girl, Heidi, whose real name I can reveal because she published a book about being an Ivy League stripper called *Ivy League Stripper*. She made a whole lot of dough showing her moneymakers at the "Legs and Eggs" brunches around Providence and graduated cum laude in the process. But how could Tawanda the waitress make as much money as Heidi the moneymaker-shaker?

"Give it a try and you'll find out," she said.

eth Paragon was the thirtysomething co-owner with her fiftysomething husband, Mario. She started the interview by asking whether I'd be old enough to serve alcohol . . . but by the time I answered, "Ya'll have *canned* iced tea?" she was hooked. No résumé required. She was sure her customers would be charmed by the Rebel Deb.

And she was right.

Who could resist my klutzy footwork around the kitchen? Or the adorable way I dropped steaming clam chowder into the laps of children and old folks? Or my clear ignorance of the wine list? Or how I spelled out "tiramisu" in flowery, girlish print with little hearts dotting the "I's"—just like Alma taught me?

Apparently, nobody.

None of that seemed to matter at Paragon. The customers had so much fun laughing at the Southern Belle serving them pasta in pearls and three-inch pumps that they didn't care about the clam chowder all over their Armani suits.

Mrs. Paragon loved me, too, and we only had one tiny problem arise. . . .

Mr. Paragon.

Oh, yes. The fiftysomething was well known for making his waitresses uncomfortable. Even better known was his policy against hiring male servers. The first thing everybody noticed upon entering Paragon—besides the blaring techno music and the hostess's well-pruned unibrow—were the waitresses. All of them were blond, big-breasted. . . .

Or, in my case, "wicked sweet." Better than sour, I suppose.

Point is, the fellas used to wink at me constantly, and the kitchen staff followed suit. One of the busboys used to lick his lips like some kind of perverted monkey. He hollered at me one day on Thayer Street as I was walking to class.

Do all Yankee men do this kind of stuff? I asked myself. Does it ever actually work?

Ultimately, it didn't matter. After I caught Mr. Paragon staring down my shirt for the hundredth time, I snapped. I "accidentally" spilled another bowl of clam chowder right into his lap and walked out.

"Don't mess with the bull, cowboy—you'll get the horns," as Alma would say.

Shortly afterward, Mrs. Paragon threatened to sue me over her husband's burnt manly parts. She even telephoned my mother. But to her surprise, Momma got on the line with a warning.

"What goes around comes around, honey," Momma said. "Just wait till one of your young'uns goes out and gets her first job. Then you'll reap what you sow. And so will that rascal husband of yours."

That shut her up good. Normally, any decent Southern Lady would send a fruit basket or a hanging plant to someone she'd offended. In this case, Momma had Hattie boil a live chicken and lay a curse on the whole restaurant. Mrs. Paragon called only once more after that, and I accepted her apology.

Though by now I'd fulfilled my promise—making straight A's, stealing Heather's "boyf" and surviving all the way to senior year—I wasn't sure my coming all the way up North was even worth it anymore. What if Uncle Stu had been right? What if birthin' babies, staying home and living the simple Southern life really *was* where it was at?

That same day on my way to class, I passed a flyer:

"Theater auditions! Come by today!"

This made me wonder. I'd grown up in the South surrounded by three generations of histrionic Blanche DuBoises, the kinds of women who could fake a smile through a Pap smear. These weren't waitresses—these were master performers. Wasn't I one, too, by birth? Was it perhaps time to test my luck on the stage?

Auditioning for student theater felt like breaking into a mental ward.

I walked inside Lyman Hall and into a hallway full of playacting crazies. There were rows and rows of girls shaking and writhing and wiggin' out on the floor. Some of them held themselves in the fetal position and stared blankly ahead at a whole bunch of nothing. Most of them held little sheets of dialogue that they'd glance at every few seconds between rocks.

Was this "acting"? Sitting on the floor, pretending to have the shakes?

I'd seen the same thing happen in church whenever the preacher held up a snake. Sometimes, old ladies in Surry County got so excited whenever the Carolina Opry came to town that they'd faint afterward.

There had to be more to it than *that*. Right?

I'd expected something on par with Debbing, with all its stages and choreography and intricately beautiful costumes. Instead, I got a whole bunch of half-baked crazy chicks shivering and convulsing in a hallway.

Besides my numerous Honor Cabinet "trials," the last time I'd truly "acted" was in a Wellingham production of *Alice in Wonderland*. Granny Ruth slathered green paint all over my face to match the turtle costume she'd sewn by hand. The next year, I dressed up in pantaloons and sponged blackface all over my chin to play Lieutenant #3 in *The Taming of the Shrew*. I had more lines as a turtle, so I don't think that one counts.

I moved down the hallway full of crazies and spotted what looked like a hall monitor—some girl holding up more sheets of dialogue—and headed her way. . . .

"Hey, there!"

". . . Hi."

"Howdy! Ya mind if I get one of them there papers you're holding?"

She just looked at me and blinked like she'd seen her first three-headed monster.

". . . You mean, 'sides'?"

And she handed me one of the sheets full of "sides."

"Thanks! Say, dahling, what's the play we're doin' called again?"

Another couple blinks followed by a long roll of the eyes, then . . .

"*We* are auditioning *you* for A *Bright Room Called Day*, by Tony Kushner."

"Thanks! And, uh . . . what role am I auditioning for again?"

". . . 'Die Alte.'"

"Do what?"

Another eye roll. Somebody was gonna lose a cornea here in a minute. Then, instead of answering my question, she grabbed the rest of her "sides" and disappeared back into the audition room. I looked down at my sheet. The one-line description of "Die Alte" said it all:

I was basically reading the part of some heartsick German chick white enough to pose as a ghost and with a strange penchant for fattening foods.

Yep. This one was pretty much in the bag.

I stepped into the room, acted out my Granny Blanche's worst case of the runs, and that was that. I became the next star of Brown University's Production Workshop and, for once in my life, knew I fit in somewhere.

As I was growing up, folks thought I was a freak. A tomboy who climbed into fountains at the mall and shouted, "Kiss my tail at the wishing well!" once she got to the top. A nerdy, big-butted Deb scribbling on her Converse sneakers at country club luncheons. A girl who talked too loud in mixed company. A wannabe Scarlett turned full-fledged Rebel Debutante, who catfished in overalls with dirty nails and skinned knees. After all the trouble I'd caused, folks thought they'd seen it all.

Bless their hearts, they hadn't seen nothing yet.

Chapter Six

From "Dollywood" to Hollywood:

• A Rebel Deb Goes to Los Angeles •

*I*n May of 2003, I graduated from Brown. As you can imagine, completing my bachelor's degree from an Ivy League school made me expect big things. And you can also imagine my embarrassment when, about a month later, I still hadn't landed a paying acting gig . . . and was thus stuck auditioning for the role of "Dollyrella" at the Dollywood Ranch and Theme Park.

Don't get me wrong—Dollywood is one of the finest places in the South. First of all, it's built over 125 acres of land smack-dab in the middle of Pigeon Forge, Tennessee, the only place on earth you can buy home-brewed Smoky Mountain beer on Sundays and turnip greens mixed with real ham hock every other Friday. Next, you've got your rides. The Elvis Tilt-A-Whirl, in my opinion, beats the Disneyland Teacups to a pulp. Then, you've got your scenery: the Smoky Mountains. They'll take your breath away quicker than riding Elvis till you upchuck the catfish sandwich you had for lunch.

Then, you've got your bluegrass music, your arts and crafts—glassblowing, blacksmithing and wood carving like settlers did back in the day—and finally, Dolly herself. She's the last role model for would-be Southern Belles, now that Scarlett's been replaced by Miley Cyrus. You can find her on the Dollywood website wearing her usual teased bouffant and perfectly sculpted lips.

Ms. Ennis, my twelfth-grade history teacher back at Wellingham, went to high school with Dolly. She used to defend Dolly tooth and nail, and flatly insisted that Ms. Parton's "dollies" were all natural. Truth be told, the last time Ms. Ennis glimpsed them was back when dancing was a sin and beer was served in a bucket. So her memory might've been a little shaky.

Uncle Stu used to visit Dollywood every fall with his favorite bird dog, May Bud. He'd plan his trip a whole year in advance and leave a few extra days for hunting around Pigeon Forge. First, he'd order boots, then long johns, socks, hats and finally hunting gear especially made for deep snows. The boots were most important, because according to Uncle Stu, there's a hierarchy of fashion for that kinda thing.

"I always order me a pair of Russell huntin' boots," Uncle Stu once told me. "You stand with each foot on a piece of paper and trace your foot with a pencil so the bootmakers get your sole just right. Then you measure your arch, your toes, your ankles—all the way up to your calf—and send 'em all off to the Russell factory. And four to six weeks later, what arrives in your mailbox? Pure huntin'-boot *heaven*."

There are all kinds of Russell boots, Uncle Stu went on. Swamping, fishing, waders and snake boots were the most popular. All of them custom-made and worth at least a hundred bucks, which is a whole lot to spend on shoes you're gonna soak and drag through mud puddles and basically destroy, in my opinion.

But to Uncle Stu, a nice pair of Russells was about the best thing a man could wear.

"I can glance down at another fella's special-made, hand-stitched, rubber-soled toe, and know if he's a Russell man or not," he'd say.

To men like my Uncle Stu, Russell boots were the be-all and end-all of outerwear. The couture of bird-hunting fashion. They were status symbols, like driving a new Mercedes or having a whole bunch of dough stashed away in a private account in Switzerland.

With his Russells laced securely on each foot, Uncle Stu and May Bud would jump into his pickup and drive well over fourteen hours before taking a rest at a local VA truck-stop-slash-motor-inn. One time, he and May Bud stopped about halfway in Tennessee to spend the night. They got up before dawn the next day and were about to check out of the motel when what looked like two "ladies of the night" wandered up to his door. They smiled and leaned inside, spotting Uncle Stu's bottle of whiskey sitting on the nightstand. He'd been digging some quills out of May Bud's jaws from chomping down on a porcupine the day before and sterilizing the wounds with the liquor. Long story short, the bottle was still almost full and Uncle Stu was so shocked to see these two jezebels at his door that he just stared—barely able to move.

"I was right scared one of 'em had a knife or a gun or something. Who knows what kinda John Wayne Bobbitt stuff these floozies do!" he described it later.

I doubt Uncle Stu had ever seen a floozy to know one. He was a prime example of how sheltered Burlington folks could be. They didn't read books because, as the writer of *Steel Magnolias* put it, if one was any good, somebody would make it into a miniseries. And they didn't watch movies, 'cause they were all "trash" full of "nothing but nekkid people." And they didn't go to plays, 'cause there weren't any around except old-timey musicals, religious reenactments and the yearly *Nutcracker* they'd bus schoolchildren down to see in Raleigh. Don't get me wrong, Uncle Stu loved those musicals. He once went all the way to New York to see *Oklahoma!* But beyond that, he didn't go to the theater, "'cause I can nap for free!"

So there he was: big, tough, wild-ass Uncle Stu with a penchant for sappy show tunes and a reputation for hiking fifteen miles through the woods, fending off wild dogs and bears and all manner of creatures . . . now terrified of two hookers standing in his doorway.

When one of them asked if she could share the rest of his whiskey, he got so nervous he up and handed her the bottle. He and May Bud tore out of that place like the Devil himself was chasing.

Poor dog. Uncle Stu hightailed it out of there with quills still hanging from her lips. I'm pretty sure she never tasted porcupine meat again in her life.

Anywho.

My Dollyrella "audition" lasted all day. I was supposed to put on a big blond wig and a hoopskirt, then spend the next six hours bending down to shake a whole bunch of sticky kids' hands as they entered the park . . . without revealing too much cleavage from the Victoria's Secret water-bra that also came with the costume.

I didn't get the part, but, boy, did that hoopskirt bring back memories of Debbing.

By now, however, I was far beyond my Debutante days. I was now twenty-one, a college graduate, and now a struggling actor still living in Providence. In my short career as an actress, I hadn't yet faced much rejection, so when even Dollywood didn't want me, I didn't shed a tear.

Instead, I picked myself up by my bootstraps, grabbed a copy of a local *Entertainment* newspaper and made my way to Worcester, Massa-*tu*-setts for another audition. The role this time? Catherine, the leading lady in *Proof* by David Auburn. She was a geeky math genius who was having trouble fitting into new surroundings after her Daddy died. Much more appropriate! And at least I wouldn't have to don fake cleavage in the form of a Victoria's Secret water-bra.

I got lost a few times along the way. I didn't know how to read a map and didn't know anything about Worcester other than Momma insisting folks there put "papa-*rika*" on everything.

I finally arrived around five forty-five. The audition was supposed to end at six, but I'd just driven over fifty miles and wasn't about to give up and go home that easily.

This was my very first professional audition. So when I stepped inside the theater, I didn't realize that I had to be in the union to audition for a *union* production. All I knew was what I'd learned from other student actors: Wear black and bring a headshot so they can remember you. A "headshot" was a black-and-white photograph of my face. I didn't have one of those, so I brought the best-looking thing I had: a picture of me holding my pug, Stinky, when she was crowned "perfect piglet" at the local farmers' market.

Outside the audition room, there was a long line of professional actors. It seemed to spiral up a nearby staircase, so I headed that way. A minute later, I faced a set of double doors leading to the stage itself. But first, there was a guard at the gate. The audition monitor— some middle-aged gal wearing all black with a bloodred "don't I look French?" beret.

She stood for a moment to gather her "sides," then suddenly

cupped her hand over her mouth. Her face turned first red then a little green around the gills before she dropped the sheets and ran into the bathroom, a few feet away.

Saved by the runs, once again!

I grabbed a sheet of dialogue and took off running for the double doors. This was my shot and I was gonna take it.

Inside, the room was all black except for a huge spotlight pointed at the stage. My tummy was tied in knots at this point, and my heart sat firmly in my throat. I didn't know what else to do, so I climbed the stairs and jumped in front of the massive light.

"Who's this?" a disembodied voice shouted.

"Um . . . hey," I said. "I'm . . ."

"You have a wonderful voice."

". . . Thanks. What do I . . ."

"And the hair. We *looove* the hair."

"Thanks. Should I . . ."

"Just start. Miss Byron will be reading with you."

And then Miss Byron, a red-headed transvestite with huge fake eyelashes, appeared by my side. She smiled and extended a hairy paw for me to shake. I blinked, shook it. Then I wrenched my eyes away from her Adam's apple and back down at my "sides."

Miss Byron had the first line. When I opened my mouth to respond . . . nothing came out. So, I cleared my throat and tried again, mumbling so softly that the director shouted out, "*Speak up, would ya?!*"

This made Miss Byron giggle, which made her red wig flop from side to side. I felt like I was doing a scene with Bozo the Clown's kid sister.

Finally, on the third try, my nerves quieted down enough for me to finish my lines. Then I just sort of stopped, not sure what I was supposed to do next.

As it turns out, not much.

The director's face appeared out of the darkened seats below. Then she stood up, climbed onstage and started moving toward me. I expected the worst. The kind of "No wire hangers *ever!*" reaction Joan Crawford would've offered a newbie actress standing before her. Instead, she reached out her hand. By now, I could see her whole body in the spotlight beside me. Miss Byron moved away respectfully, and suddenly, there she was: my first professional director. Just another lily-white gal with a fat ass. Just like me.

"I think we've found our Catherine," she said.

And just like that, the young'un who'd snuck in while the monitor tinkled next door was now the star of an Off-Broadway production. She was now getting her union card, something that took most actresses years to accomplish. She was now a "professional," all in one stroke of dumb luck . . . with a scoop of fate on the side.

Proof ran for about six weeks, and just about kicked my butt. First of all, I had no idea how to handle being the leading lady among a cast of thirty- to fortysomething actors. The play was about a crazy, dysfunctional family, and that's basically what we were, too. Two of them hated each other so much that one ended up nearly twisting the other's arm off in one scene. What's worse, the theater was so cheap it wouldn't pay for decent stagehands, so our props were missing most nights. It was so darn cold in the theater that I caught the flu and spent three of the six weeks hacking my guts out backstage. Then the girlfriend of the actor who played my onstage boyfriend got jealous of our kissing scenes and began ridiculing me behind my back. Finally, to top it all off, our director left to go direct something else. By the time she returned, the show had descended into complete chaos. The whole thing was a big ol' mess. But it taught me a lot about myself and a lot more about patience.

It also got me seen by Dustin McQueeny, a casting director in Boston, who just happened to be auditioning girls for a movie being filmed nearby. *Mona Lisa Smile*, Dustin told me, was a story about Julia Roberts teaching in some old-fashioned girls' school, and how she'd rebelled against all the stereotypes and prejudices of her time.

So, basically, I was a Rebel Deb auditioning to be in a movie about a Rebel Deb. Go figure.

I spent the next three weeks or so freezing my tail off at Wellesley, a girls' college just outside Boston. The Wellesley girls pretty much matched the architecture of their school: frigid, gothic and a little too precious for my taste. Plus, every room was high-ceilinged and dusty and the chairs made my fanny hurt. They all felt like those old-timey deals your Granddaddy carved out of wood and your Granny now kept in her attic "to remember him by." They also reminded me of waiting parlors right by the front doors at Wellingham—two rooms full of stiff, gilded armchairs, polished furniture and huge painted portraits of Jefferson Davis and Dolley Madison.

Worst of all, McQueeny hadn't told me how boring moviemaking was gonna be.

I showed up at six every morning just so somebody with a headset could bark at me to "get over to makeup!" Then, I'd stand around for two more hours, waiting for a hairdresser from Kennebunkport, Maine, to turn my hippie hair into a 1950s beehive and my makeup-free face into something Bettie Page would've hankered after.

On set, everybody hemmed and hawed while the lighting and camera folks set up their equipment. Then ... we waited. And waited. And waited some more.

Just as I was about to fall asleep, somebody pushed me into a golf cart and whizzed me off to the far side of a big green hill.

The whole school was covered in old-fashioned tents and what looked like my Granny's crystal. I watched as the gal from Kennebunkport, Maine, ooohed and awwwed over Maggie Gyllenhaal's perfectly coiffed curls.

"She's so beautiful!" she said.

To me, Maggie looked just like every other girl standing around that day, only skinnier and with bigger bags under her eyes. In fact, she reminded me of one of the raccoon-eyed Alpha Chis from URI.

When Mike Newell, the director, finally called Maggie to start the scene, the Maine lady moved on to "ooooh!" and "ahhhh!" over Julia Stiles. Julia wasn't in this one, it seemed.

Maine lady spent the next fifteen minutes powdering Julia's snobby, turned-up nose. Then, somebody else came over to pat down her hairline with buff brushes till she looked like a ghost-white geisha. I looked away from the buffing for a moment and saw Maggie holding Kirsten Dunst as she fought with some old lady. Apparently, the old lady was playing Kirsten's uptight Momma, and in this scene she had to cry.

Before every take, Kirsten would ask for a second alone so she could run off behind a tent. There, she'd pace back and forth, huffing and puffing until her cheeks blew out and her nose ran. After running back to spill her guts on camera, Kirsten and Maggie joined hands and harrumphed off together in a postadolescent, rebellious exodus.

Toward the end of Kirsten's crying fit, the great Julia Roberts emerged from her own, much more camouflaged, golf cart. She held up a hand to shield her eyes from paparazzi—of which there were none, but I guess old habits die hard—and then descended upon all us mere mortals. When I finally got a good look at her, she seemed taller than I'd imagined. She was also a brunette, which struck me as odd. I must've seen *Pretty Woman* too many times to be having such a strong reaction to hair color.

The first day on set, Julia was pretty subdued. The next day was a different story.

By midmorning, she was skipping up and down the green hill, chasing a '50s-era Cadillac. By afternoon, she'd started hugging and kissing on Maggie and Kirsten like little girls. She and Danny Moder had just gotten married, so I guess she had that lovin' feeling.

Up close, Danny Moder didn't look like I'd imagined, either. He was a short, skinny cameraman with floppy, blondish hair, who somebody told me was *married* before Julia came along. Still, she seemed totally in love and kept running off set to kiss him every time Mike Newell yelled, "Cut!"

Then, there was Marcia Gay Harden—the only "name" actress within earshot who actually bothered to smile at us lowly stand-ins. She seemed like one of those mothering women who, unlike some, looked at all of us as equals. Julia Stiles, on the other hand, walked around like God's gift to movies, shooting stink-eyes like somebody had pooped on her Cheerios.

Every day when we broke for lunch, Princess Stiles sat at her own separate table apart from the rest of us. While we crowded around the buffet and scrounged for seats at picnic tables, waiters brought her food over on covered plates. But at least she deigned to sit within sight. Julia Roberts, Maggie and Kirsten were nowhere to be found. A-list celebrities don't often hunker down by the food trough with the commoners, I guess.

Funny how much you pick up as a minor character in a big-ass movie.

For example, I overheard folks talking about the fella who played Julia Roberts's driver. Apparently, he'd been picked out of some big-ass national casting call, and though his part was tiny and he maybe didn't have any lines, he was treated like he'd hit the jackpot in five states.

Then I heard all about Maggie Gyllenhaal's chain-smoking. Lord knows she had the biggest raccoon eyes I'd ever seen. Plus, she was so thin, her hips stuck out like walker handles. She'd hobble around with them pushed forward in this stooping, awkward way that made her look sickly and old lady–like most of the time. But she also seemed the smartest actress of them all. She was constantly pulling Mike aside, asking questions about everything. You could tell she was talented, if maybe a bit odd-looking.

Most of the gossip I heard from Julia Roberts's full-time "stand-in," Marquette du Conquistador.

According to Marquette, Julia's fairy-tale movie-star life didn't sound like any fairy tale I'd ever heard. The media was mostly to blame for this, she said. Don't get me wrong. We all like scanning *People* and *Us Weekly* in line at the supermarket. But, apparently, when the Pretty Woman first hit tabloids back in the early 1990s, the tabloids hit back. Back when she and Richard Gere were an on-screen couple, Julia could barely walk down the street without getting mobbed. Marquette went into detail about the huge crowds outside the premiere. Folks had started lining up outside the theater a whole two nights before the performance, she said. Some gals even sent letters. A few even wanted to name their babies Vivian, to commemorate JR's role as the hooker with a heart of gold.

Marquette had obviously known Julia for a long time. And she didn't mind saying so. She was about five-foot-nine, with perfect, sleek hair like only movie stars (or, apparently, their stand-ins) have, and spent her days pretending to be the famous lady herself.

So, when you thought you recognized Julia Roberts in the drugstore, but were too shy to ask for an autograph . . . or when you finally got up the courage and watched closely as she signed her initials—JR— but something told you they weren't quite . . . *real?*

Sometimes your suspicions were correct.

Marquette's job was to try to convince you. This meant that the whole time I was standing around, beehived and makeupped and whatever else . . . well, she was, too. Marquette stood, sat, walked and ran around in Julia's costumes all day long. It took hours for the lighting and cameramen to set up each shot and make everything in the frame look perfect. Then Marquette was carted away so the real JR could take her place.

I couldn't believe my eyes. Only in Hollywood would your boss actually pay somebody to stand in for you at work so you could skip all the boring stuff, then get out of the way as soon as everything's up and running so you could take all the credit. It seemed really unfair that poor Marquette had to run around, getting all hot and sweaty, while JR relaxed in her air-conditioned trailer, munching on gourmet salad. In fact, the whole situation reminded me of my Uncle Stu's teaser horse, Dingleberry.

Dingleberry lived out on the family farm in Caswell County with about three hundred cows. His only purpose in the world was to get up real early in the morning and trot over to the "gettin' barn."

The "gettin' barn" was where all the horses "got some," as Uncle Stu put it.

All of them except Dingleberry, of course. After arriving at the barn, he'd trot into his stall to await the mare. And her stud.

Now, just so you know, the "teaser" is different from the "stud" in one really big way:

One teases and one . . . well . . . his name says everything.

Picture three stalls lined up one by one. Poor Dingleberry waits in the first one. After a while, the mare's led into the second, middle stall. Then a farmhand opens the window between the two stalls just wide enough for ol' Dingleberry to stick his head through. So he does. And promptly bites the mare on her neck.

Most girls I know would complain, but neck-biting drives female horses crazy. To them, it's the same as some really hot dude running his hand up the small of your back or Richard Gere giving a big fat diamond necklace to JR before they jet off to the opera.

Long story short, this gets the mare in the mood. Now, she's ready for action. And that's when another farmhand leads the stud into the third stall and starts "priming" him for his . . . well . . . studly duties. Once the stud's all hot and bothered, somebody leads him into the mare's stall. Then, the window is promptly shut on poor ol' Dingleberry. He's just spent the last several minutes "teasing" his lady, and now *wham!* The window's slammed shut and Dingleberry's led back to his pasture. Nothing but cows and cow patties stretching for 280 acres on each side. And here you thought *yours* was a sucky job.

Dingleberry, like Marquette, had one of the suckiest jobs *ever*: Professional Stand-In.

Both got stuck with all the work, all the early morning hours, all the anticipation infact of being *thisclose* to their hearts' desires—whether they be fame and fortune for Marquette, or just a roll in the hay with the mare whose neck meat you're gumming—but *none* of the glory.

At the end of the day, both of them were promptly led away once the studhorse—the star of the show—was ready for "Action!"

Like Alma used to say, "Sometimes life is just a big shit sandwich."

After I finished my part in *Mona Lisa Smile*, I ran right back into the theater. I was done with all the "hurry up and wait" Hollyweird had to offer . . . or, at least, that's what I thought at the time.

I spent the next summer as a lowly apprentice at the Williamstown Theatre Festival in Williamstown, Massa-*tu*-setts. I'd applied, but never thought I'd get in. Only snobs in black eyeliner who smoked a lot were supposed to get into Williamstown. I knew one kid from Brown who'd applied three times and never been invited anywhere near the place.

See, Williamstown was the place big-time movie stars did something called "summer stock." It was basically their excuse to get together in the woods and sleep around. I wouldn't be surprised if a dozen or so Suris and Apples and other celebrity babies were conceived right there. Needless to say, this was the big time, and I felt happy as a hog in shit. Till, of course, that very same shit hit the fan. And then I found out how very shady big-time movie stars could be.

Let me explain . . .

The movie stars and the rest of us wannabes were divided into four "companies" of actors: Equity, Non-Equity, Act I and Apprentices.

The Apprentices were the grunts. They were mostly nonunion, unknown youngsters, who came to Williamstown hoping to act but ended up building sets and cleaning up dressing rooms for the movie stars. Even though I was in the union, I was still an unknown, so I got stuck in this bunch.

The Non-Equity and Act I companies were student actors who went to schools like NYU, Yale and Juilliard. They were talented and hardworking, and some of them were even good-looking. But once you scratched the surface, some of them were just as rotten as the movie stars they yearned to be.

One of the worst was a fella named Chris Pine, but we all called him Actor Boy. Years later, I'd watch him make eyes at Lindsay Lohan and then pretend to surf outer space as Captain Kirk in a remake of *Star Trek*. Back in 2003, however, he was just another tall, skinny guy with bad skin and a worse haircut. He had one of those ducktail deals that made his scalp move up and down whenever he lifted his eyebrows. He also had a reputation for chasing anything in a skirt. I knocked on my girlfriend Margaret's door to walk with her to breakfast. When she didn't answer, I tried her doorknob . . . and though I guess it was a bad decision, I stepped inside.

And there was Chris Pine and Margaret lying together, costumes and stage makeup strewn all around them.

The next day, poor Margaret was old news to Chris. He'd loved her, left her and moved on to his next conquest quicker than she could say "rascal." Over the next six weeks, he slept with at least two more Apprentices that I knew about. No doubt, there were many more that I didn't.

Finally, above the student actors, was the renowned Equity Company.

This level was full of famous and almost famous folk, plus a few up-and-coming teenagers. One of these was named Hayden Panettiere (later a series regular on NBC's *Heroes*), but we called her "Lolita."

Long before she became a prime-time star, Hayden was a fourteen-year-old flirt who used to run around in cutoff blue jeans so short they bordered on gynecological. She also had a habit of flirting with older men, including the festival director's son, whether he liked it or not. One time, Hayden showed up to a company dinner with her whole family in tow. Watching them interact, her Momma and little brothers seemed oblivious to her behavior. That made me wonder if Hayden was really a Hero, or just a piggy bank they were grooming for stardom.

Even more notorious was redheaded Kate Mara, another up-and-comer. By 2005, she would play the sweet, downtrodden daughter of Heath Ledger in *Brokeback Mountain*. But that summer, she was the exact opposite—a teenage Cruella de Vil.

For example, I'd been told by other apprentices that Kate used to purposefully destroy her dressing room. At first, I was confused. Why would anybody want to destroy her own dressing room? Then I got to talking with the Apprentices forced to clean up her mess. Apparently, Kate got off on this kind of torture. I even overheard her belittling these same Apprentices by pointing out how she was at Williamstown to "you know . . . actually *act*. I'm here for a show, not to build stages and crap."

Another level of the Equity Company, above the up-and-comings, were the "professionals." Or so they were introduced.

First, there was Mandy Patinkin, who used to scream bloody murder at himself before, during and after every rehearsal. "*Fuck you, Mandy! Fuck you!*" we'd all hear echoing through the halls. Then, Estelle Parsons, who once told the festival director that I'd been "stalking her for an autograph." She even went so far as to have me fired from her dressing room staff.

"Who the hell is Estelle Parsons?" was my reaction.

"Remember that show, *Roseanne*? She was the mom," he said.

Apparently, back when I was in the fourth grade, she'd played a neurotic drunk on TV. Years later, at Williamstown, she played a neurotic drunk onstage. And, apparently, I was now "stalking" her.

Except for Jenny Gersten, the firm but fair right hand to the festival director, Sherie René Scott, the delightfully charming Broadway star who once said I looked just like her little sister (minus her huge boobs, of course); and Jesse L. Martin, the *Law & Order* star who proved a true gentleman through and through, and who made an enormous effort to attend each and every Apprentice performance over the entire summer, most everybody seemed like just another typical Hollyweird actor type. You know, totally selfish, self-absorbed and—most of all—crazy. So far, Williamstown seemed less like a famous theater festival and more like a funny farm.

Maybe everybody was going stir-crazy inside the tiny, cubicle-like dorm rooms we all shared. Or maybe the sticky, humid climate was seeping into our brains. Or maybe the long hours stuck in a theater were finally turning regular people into arrogant lunatics. Who knows? All's I could tell was, these big-time movie stars were big-time crazy. And—for the most part—mean, bipolar and hornier than toads. And they weren't the only ones.

Oh, no.

The festival director's kids were headed in the same direction. Only they were too young to be crazy. Instead, they were some of the most demanding, spoiled kids I'd ever met. And that included Diana Ross's brood of prima donnas, which I'll get to in a bit.

Billy and his younger sister, Charlotte, were the Prince and Princess of Williamstown. At the age of four, Charlotte loved to remind everyone within earshot that her Daddy was "the boss!" When Billy wasn't being chased by Hayden and her Daisy Duke shorts, he was pulling pranks. The one that sticks out the most was his end-of-summer send-off.

During his father's closing speech on the main stage in front of the entire festival, Billy suddenly appeared. He sat down in an office chair and slid across the stage while flipping the bird to the entire audience.

Guess some apples fall a bit farther from the tree.

Despite all the soap opera–like melodrama swirling around me, my summer at Williamstown was rewarding. I did a lot of great work and actually starred in three different productions over six weeks— which, in case you didn't know, is a *lot* of acting for one Rebel Deb in just one summer. By the time I left, I'd learned a lot about "professional" actors and the politics behind Hollywood.

So much, in fact, that I decided to move there.

About a week before my twenty-third birthday, I loaded up Connie, long since repaired after Alma's tragic accident, and drove straight from Carolina to California. The trip took three days. And at the end, when I stuck my feet in the Pacific Ocean and squooshed its sand between my toes, I knew I was on the verge of something big. Something better. Something Wellingham and Brown and all the craziness in between had prepared me for:

My future.

As I drove away, I stopped at a traffic light, where something inside me screamed, "Look left!" She was idling beside me in her high-end SUV. Through the open window, I saw her turn to me and offer an affectionate smile . . . the real Julia Roberts.

This time, she looked less like the Pretty Woman and more like a regular, down-to-earth Southern girl just like me. I'd always heard rumors about her upbringing—how she'd left Georgia to follow her dreams and make a bigger life in Los Angeles. And maybe, I thought, that made JR a Rebel Debutante, too.

I smiled back and hoped that was true . . . for both of our sakes.

I swear, at some point Hell and Ancient Rome got together and did the nasty.

The result?

. . . Rodeo Drive.

The first time I walked around Beverly Hills was August 15, 2004—two days after my twenty-third birthday. I was amazed. Everything was so pristine. So light and airy and manicured and . . . well . . . *clean*. Rodeo Drive was bright white, covered in stone and marble and glass with this big ol' statue of a half-naked body right there in the middle of the street. There was so much sun in my eyes I couldn't tell whether the genital-less figure was supposed to be a Barbie or a Ken. In the end, it looked more like an albino version of the Batman suit.

My first "apartment" in L.A. was the floor of my friend Adrien's one-bedroom. It stood on the very last street in Beverly Hills, where this neighborhood meets the Miracle Mile. He was away on vacation for a month, so I got to crash at his pad.

Adrien had warned me about his landlady, Celeste. We finally met while she was walking her herd of cats, which kind of reminded me of my Granny Ruth and gave me a bitter pang of homesickness.

"This is it," she said. Then she pointed down to the sidewalk beneath our feet.

"It . . . what?"

"*It*. The end of the run."

"There's a *run?*"

I looked down at my panty hose. Then I remembered: I wasn't wearing panty hose. So, what the hell was she talking about?

"It" was the end of the line, Celeste explained: The last street inside the 90210 zip code.

"It" was the street middle-class parents literally fought over. They'd line up to rent studio apartments here because they were the cheapest in Beverly Hills. Which, at about twelve hundred a pop isn't saying much.

Once they'd signed the lease, these parents would then force their teenagers to live there. Schools officials would visit on a regular basis, Celeste went on, to make sure whoever rented the place was actually occupying it. And since each apartment couldn't have been more than three hundred square feet, the poor kids had to basically sleep there *alone*. The rest of the family just wouldn't fit.

"Why 'school officials'?" I asked.

"Guidance counselors from Beverly Hills High School. It's the best public school in L.A. You can't go without proof that you have the right code."

"Like a locker combination?"

"Like, the *zip code*: 90210."

Now, don't get me wrong, I'm all about folks getting educated. But I grew up in the '90s, which means the last time I heard those particular numbers was back in sixth grade when me and every other preteen girl in the world watched *Beverly Hills, 90210*. After the first few episodes, I'd seen more drug overdoses, date rapes and shot-in-the-head teens than any wannabe Scarlett should. I was pretty sure anywhere within ten miles of Beverly Hills High was a kill zone for kids. When Adrien came back, I was a little relieved. I moved out the next day with nothing more than Connie, the clothes on my back and Celeste's blessing.

My next apartment was the second bedroom of my friend Nick's condo. He lived in West L.A.—a neighborhood known for being a little less "90210" and a lot less expensive.

Still, I paid more rent for that second bedroom than some folks paid for an entire house. Gas was also more than two dollars a gallon, which could buy a gallon of milk and a loaf of bread back home.

My roommate, Nick, was part "Goth kid" and part "Son of a Preacher Man." We met in Starbucks on the corner of Olympic and Pico, where he was serving up lattes with a smile and a head full of Kool-Aid colored highlights. When he wasn't strumming his guitar, sharpening his collection of Japanese steak knives or showing off his tongue ring, Nick was a pretty cool dude. At first, we were totally buddy-buddy . . . until I moved in.

That's when I met Nick's über-religious girlfriend, Shelly. She wasn't too fond of my sleeping just across the hall from her man. After a few weeks of her jealous tirades, I'd had enough. I found a few "Room-mate Wanted" ads on Craigslist.com and went surfing for a new pad.

First, there was the creepy Hispanic lady who had a room for rent in her house in Los Feliz. She wore thick, greasy makeup and a teased wig. Her entire house (including the room she was trying to rent) was covered floor to ceiling in porcelain Jesus figurines. Then, there was Cherie, whose definition of "roommate" was "willing to pay $600/ month to sleep on an old air mattress in my living room."

After three days, my standards had dropped. By now, all I wanted was a safe bed to sleep in, preferably *nowhere* near Jesus figurines or the 405 freeway. I scraped together some money and bought a futon, adding one stick of furniture to my name.

Too bad the stupid screws fell out and the whole contraption fell apart the minute it landed in my new locale . . .

Culver City, California.

I normally wouldn't be so specific or dramatic about my nomadic travels across L.A., but this place took the cake—drama-wise, of course.

Culver City was my very first foray into the world of crazy landladies. This trend would continue into my New York days, but here's where it all started.

When I first read her ad, I didn't know much about the Internet. Folks back home got out the newspaper when they needed a job or a car or a new home. But I was following my dreams and building a bigger life in L.A., right?

S he sounded nice on the phone. Famous last words.

We planned to meet outside her building. When I stepped onto the sidewalk, I saw a little old lady hobbling toward me.

Or . . . at least I thought she was a little old lady.

As she got closer, I saw that my new landlady was actually in her mid-forties but wearing about four pounds of makeup. Her eyebrows were shaved off and redrawn with big, black lines. Her mouth was painted fire engine red. Erma Finch's walk was kinda hobbly that day because she was carrying a huge load of what looked like accounting ledgers and a cash-counting machine.

As she got closer, I waved. Erma didn't say a word. She just held out her hand to shake. And when I took it, her fingers gripped mine so hard that I almost drew back a nub.

This was my second clue that maybe my little old landlady wasn't so little, old or ladylike.

She took me inside a huge apartment full of furniture. My new roommate would be Wanda, a thirtysomething modeling agent from Santa Monica. Once I moved in, I heard all about Wanda's sex life. Not because she told me, but because the walls were awful thin and her biker boyfriend, Howie, sure liked to holler awful loud.

Wanda also had a weird obsession with keeping her living room furniture clean. Even when she bought a new couch that covered the entire room, she insisted I never *ever* sit down. I had to gingerly tiptoe around the massive thing, instead, while trying to avoid her lamps and coffee tables and standing plants that only ever got watered when she'd invite her friends over to watch *I Love the '90s!* on VH1. I used to call them the ugly-sweater get-togethers. I was only comforted by the sight of all of them standing around like jackasses, too afraid to sit on the couch either.

I spent the next three months avoiding the living room. In fact, Wanda and Howie got so loud most nights that I tried to stay out of the apartment altogether.

Exhausted and virtually homeless, I dug out my trusty Brown Alumni Guide and started my initial attack on Hollywood. Some of these folks were helpful. Others, not so much.

When I got on the phone with Jonathan Groff, for example, he was nice enough to buy me lunch. That's when I first tried guacamole. It reminded me of the duck poop I'd find around Lamb's Lake back home. While we ate, Jonathan told me all about his switch from stand-up comedian to a writer at *Late Night with Conan O'Brien*. He was a great guy whose wife was from Arkansas, as I recall. That made me feel just a touch cozier inside.

Then there was Lucy Cashmere, a casting director at ABC, who'd been an Apprentice at Williamstown way back when. She made it a point to meet me just because of that, and it was nice to see a fellow former-grunt-worker making good.

Some of these folks, like Lucy and Jon, pointed me in good directions. Others tried to get my pants off the minute they heard me say

"Ya'll." But worst of all were the actresses. Theirs were the kinds of footsteps I'd never want to follow.

There was Katherine Plumpknuckle, whom I met for the first time at some trendy restaurant in Beverly Hills that served lemonade and French fries together with a straight face.

"Katie," as she insisted I call her, was about twenty-four, but sounded like a forty-five-year-old smoker. She spent the entire lunch avoiding her French fries, adding Sweet'n Low to her lemonade, telling me all about her girlhood in Marietta, Georgia, and bragging about the fourteen-year-old girls who "stalked" her online. "It's so sad!" she said. "These little dahlings think I'm some kind of role model or somethin'!"

Apparently, Estelle Parsons's egocentric delusions were spreading.

Even though she was blond and Southern, Katie was no lady. And though she'd left Georgia to follow her dreams, she wasn't a Rebel Debutante, either.

Oh, no.

A Rebel Debutante is easily recognized by a few key pieces of "insider" knowledge:

She knows tea is served sweet unless some fool specifically asks for unsweetened. She knows "y'all" isn't just a cute expression; it actually means something. She knows that Pepsi originated in New Bern, Cheerwine in Salisbury, and that Mountain Dew was invented in Fayetteville. She also knows that buttermilk is a sacred drink best served with barbecue and peach cobbler. That Krispy Kreme doughnuts are the best doughnuts ever. That Bojangles' beats Church's Chicken any day of the week, Cook Out has the best hamburgers and milk shakes known to man, and that hearing a fella say "hush puppies" doesn't mean he's ordering his dog to be quiet.

Katie Plumpknuckle was decidedly *not* a Rebel Deb. Hell, she couldn't even point out Swampsville, Mississippi, on a map. And, believe you me, I asked her to.

After our lunch, I spent the next few weeks pounding the pavement in search of opportunity. I read all kinds of shiny, intimidating "Industry" magazines. I even asked around on the street.

On the basis of the tip I got from some skinny actress in need of a sandwich, standing in line at a West Hollywood Coffee Bean, I finally found it:

That mysterious L.A. event called the "open call."

One morning, I took my brand-new Equity card and lined up at six a.m.—*sharp!*—for an audition at the Mark Taper Forum in downtown L.A. There was already a line out the door and down the street. This was enough to intimidate most mortal women, but the Rebel Deb was undaunted. I'd come a long way from Worcester, Massa-*tu*-setts, baby. I had no intention of sneaking in this time.

Oh, no.

This time, I walked in wearing a professional actor's uniform: black pants, black shoes, black shirt and hair swept up and away from my face.

The point of all this was to make the director feel my emotions. I, on the other hand, ended up feeling like a street mime.

When you walk into an audition, you're supposed to have two two-minute monologues ready to perform. Monologues are basically just long pieces of text from a play or movie or whatever, where you talk to somebody in front of you. Who's not there. Who you have to imagine is having some kinda relationship with you.

I chose to be one of the biggest Rebel Debs *ever*: Christina of Sweden from Ruth Wolff's play *The Abdication*.

Christina was a Protestant queen who gave up her crown after falling head over high heels for a Catholic priest. In my monologue,

I pretended to be Christina. At the beginning of my speech, I was supposed to be super-duper pissed off at the priest, but by the end, I was supposed to be totally in love with him again. It was a pretty wild ride. And I totally nailed it on my first try.

A couple minutes later, I landed my first gig at the Taper.

Here I was, brand-new to Hollywood, and already cast in a major Off-Broadway theater. I was half drunk on the thrill of waking up, driving to work and spending the next eight hours of each day playing make-believe so that I almost forgot the one snag in my underdrawers. . . .

Albie Von Tussel. The director.

Albie was a young fella from New York who reminded me of Ryan Seacrest. He'd finally hit the big time landing this show at the Taper, and when he showed up one morning in a pink buttoned-down shirt, tapered jeans and wingtips, a little voice inside my head started humming the tune to My Fair Lady.

He'd been absent for the first few weeks of rehearsal because he thought "Morocco would be the *puuuurrrfect* place to gather material for our little production" (pronounced "pro-duck-she-*on*").

Once Albie took hold of things, everything changed.

First, he insisted we do "stage exercises," to "discover ourselves." Like leaping across cinder blocks or interviewing high school kids about whether they "smoked the marijuana" (pronounced "mara-jew-wanna"). Even worse, Albie had a habit of picking favorites. His favorite would change from week to week, but was always a boy. The rest of us girls he barely looked at, let alone directed.

And then, all of a sudden, we weren't just not-favorites. We'd been written out of the play entirely. So much for my shot at the big time. I spent one night commiserating at a bar above Sunset with one of the other girls. Between complaining about Albie's horrible directing and blatant chauvinism, she kept slipping in details about her sex life—how much she "loooooved anal!" and how she'd just "loooooooooooooove" to make out with me right then and there. A few years later, when she appeared on *Grey's Anatomy*, I just couldn't get her lovin' feelings out of my mind and it basically killed my interest in the show.

After I got canned, I turned to the "dark side" for a little while: A temp agency.

Frankie at Apple Personnel Services had a face tattoo, purple highlights and four-inch boots laced all the way up to her thighs. Even she thought my job prospects were pretty slim. The only openings she had were an assistant at ICM—one of the biggest talent agencies in town—or the front desk at Advance Auto Parts. She also said my Southern Belle look—blond hair and blue eyes—was a little . . . well, typical. In L.A., everybody and I mean everybody was blond. So if I wanted to stand out from the crowd, I needed a makeover—*fast*. Otherwise, I could take the gig at Advance Auto.

I just sat there for a minute, weighing my options, asking myself . . . What would Scarlett do?

*Y*ou know how, in old romance novels, the heroine always dyes her hair red when she's ready to make a big life change? When she's getting ready to take a walk on the wild side?

Well, not once in any of those books did I ever read about the dye turning her blond locks purple and then pink before finally settling into something resembling Tang. Apparently, Clairol didn't think I was all that worth it.

When I walked into ICM the next day with a head full of Tang-colored highlights, I was sure I'd wasted my time. I had an appointment to see Toyota Carrel (pronounced "Car-*el*"), a "TV packaging agent" (whatever that meant) on the top floor.

The minute I walked inside, I knew I was in trouble.

Absolutely everybody in the place looked miserable. They kept their heads down, staring into their computer screens with dilated pupils. Nobody was talking. Phones were ringing off the hook. All in all, just about what I'd expected.

About five minutes into my interview with Toyota, I was hired. Twenty seconds after that, I was escorted to my new desk by a bristly young girl in a three-piece suit who told me, in no uncertain terms, that I had just gotten the job *she* wanted and was *destined* for.

She also warned me that a "*million billion trillion*" other girls would kill their Mommas to land my job. So, I'd better start memorizing the client list *right now*.

She then threw what looked like a phone book into my lap.

"Get started!" she barked, then marched away. "Oh, and you have a meeting with Team J-Lo in five minutes," she called over her shoulder.

Team J-Lo was Jennifer Lopez's "support team."

This meant a group of about five agents and their first, second and third assistants, all ready and waiting to do Her Highness's bidding.

Like any true diva, J-Lo had a habit of hiring, then firing, then rehiring Team J-Lo about every six months. Half of the year we were all supposed to run around like chickens with our heads cut off, making sure *Gigli*—or whatever film she was making at the time—didn't go too far over budget. The other half of the year, we were supposed to scorn all things J-Lo because she'd dumped us for another agency. Then, of course, she'd come back to us again, and the cycle would repeat.

For three exhausting weeks, I was at my desk by eight a.m. and left well after eight p.m. Working at ICM was like joining the Witness Protection Program of Hollywood: You went in and were never heard from again.

My main duties included opening Toyota's office every morning and placing every current issue of every entertainment magazine at a 10 and 2 position on her desk. On top of that went her daily schedule (hand-typed on company stationery).

When she finally arrived, my orders were to hide the fact that Toyota was out of the office more than she was in. She'd leave at lunch, which turned into the rest of the day. Every few minutes, she'd call to ask if anyone had noticed. Sometimes, she'd expect me to drop whatever I was doing and give her directions to this or that meeting. Mostly, though, she'd just start screaming about how I'd put too much cream in her coffee or misspelled "Château Marmot" on her daily schedule.

In between her calls, I spent my days making my own. Only my phone calls were frantic because Toyota somehow expected me to handle payroll for Icon—Mel Gibson's production company—while simultaneously typing the next day's schedule, making doctor's appointments for her kids, logging every single call and voice mail throughout the entire day, and submitting all of her clients' headshots and résumés for whatever mega huge box-office hit happened to grace the cover of *Variety* magazine that morning.

All the other assistants would constantly ask me if I was from Texas, which was the only part of the South they were remotely familiar with, and only because they'd watched all those Pace picante sauce commercials. Most of the agents would try and pretend they could relate to the "little Southern Belle" in the office. "You're Southern? Oh, I've been there!"

To which I would reply, "Oh, yeah? Which airport?"

Sucking the hot air out of several high-powered agents' balloons didn't exactly make me Miss Popular. Like most Hollyweird types, they liked to pretend to know everything and everyone. But, I'm sorry—just because you spent your half-hour layover at the Raleigh-Durham airport doesn't mean you've "been to the South."

Still, snarky and un–"little Southern Belle" as I was, my accent and manners garnered tons of respect from superiors, coworkers—pretty much everyone except Toyota. My saying "God bless you" whenever somebody sneezed, holding the door open for my elders and always remembering my *Please*s and *Thank you*s went a *long* way. And for some folks—especially the clients—I think it was a comfort knowing at least one polite, well-mannered person in the whole building would actually *listen* while they talked, not just wait impatiently for her turn to speak.

Oh, Lord—and speak they did!

I got to chitchat with everyone from Calista Flockhart to Christina Ricci. They, of course, had no idea who I was—nor did they care—but they appreciated my listening so sincerely and carefully and, hey, I grabbed any perks that came my way. After my first week, I was so exhausted and lonely sitting outside Toyota's empty office all day that I wanted to quit. That's when I found out about Toyota's last assistant. Rumor had it that Toyota had trouble keeping assistants. The last one had walked out after only five days. I thought maybe he'd been a flake, until we were introduced. That girl from *The Devil Wears Prada* had nothing on him. Turns out the fella was a well-seasoned member of Team J-Lo who'd been with the company for over five years, and nobody blamed him for walking out on Toyota. The only thing that kept me from doing the same was Carly, another assistant who sat right in front of my desk. Carly was sweet, Midwestern and used to carry around little napkins full of hard candy in her pocket. Whenever she offered you one, she always promised it would "sweeten your day!" And, somehow, it did.

She lasted about two weeks.

I remember the day Toyota escorted Carly out of the building in tears, still clutching her last butterscotch. After another two weeks, I went from pitying her to jealous she'd gotten out so soon. Working for Toyota was just like being a waitress, only the menu was a huge phone book of clients that I couldn't memorize and, quite frankly, didn't want to. I kept e-mailing the wrong Calistas and faxing the wrong Christinas. The only silver lining was that, for the first time since Wellingham, I started to value my education.

While other assistants who hadn't struggled through diagramming sentences now struggled with commas, sentence structure, semicolons and basic grammar, I was beyond all that. And when most of the girls in my office gave in to the boys around them, kowtowed by male egos and their own low self-esteem, I didn't. I stood up for myself and didn't believe that just being a girl made me inferior to them. I was, for the first time, proud to be a Wellingham graduate. And though I'd endured hell for my diploma, at least I knew it was worth something.

Toward the end, sitting alone in my cubicle after another Team J-Lo meeting, I felt like day-old bread. I was hardened, crusty and calcifying on the outside. I had to get out of there or I'd end up bawling in the parking lot like Carly. After I finally—mercifully—got the boot, Frankie at Apple Personnel was none too pleased. The Advance Auto job was now filled, so I had no choice:

I took the interview with Ms. Diana Ross.

The first time I ever met "Ms. Ross," as I was required to call her, was in a little run-down office near Sunset Boulevard that I mistook for a house. I almost scratched my car trying to park in the tiny driveway to the right, and there was another car right in front of me blocking half the entrance. The minute I stepped inside her "office," I could tell Ms. Ross was gonna live up to her crazy-ass reputation. She appeared suddenly to my right, darting out of what looked like a small bathroom with no door. I couldn't help but notice the head-to-toe black robes and huge black sunglasses that hid most of her face. She sat down without a word. And I followed.

Eye to eye, I wasn't nervous. I wasn't intimidated. I wasn't . . . well, "starstruck" is I guess the right term. Maybe it's a generational thing, but up close "Ms. Ross" looked less like a famous diva and more like a skinny old lady with too much kink in her perm.

We chatted for about twenty minutes. She asked me where I was from; I told her about North Carolina. She started to warm up and told me all about Detroit, and how she'd never had a real childhood there because it was a rough place and she'd started singing so young. We eventually got down to business. She told me she needed someone who could use a computer because she had no earthly idea how to use any such thing. Oh, and she had pets. And children. Lots of both. And in addition to their personal drivers, chefs and tutors, they *all* now needed a part-time nanny.

She held my résumé in her hands the whole time but never bothered to look. I lied and told her I was great with a computer and didn't have a problem with all her dogs running around all the time. All of that was basically code for "If you don't give me a job, I'll go broke and have to go home and give up my dreams. You know how that feels, don't you?"

She looked at me funny, like I had something caught between my teeth. Then she smiled and stood up without a word and left.

And Scarlett just sat there, alone, unsure what to do next.

I just can't *read* this," she said. "It's so *tiny!*"

"My apologies, Ms. Ross. You see, we were just trying to . . ." Kimmy replied.

"I don't *understand*, honey," she whimpered, jutting out her thin, unnaturally shapely for a sixtysomething-year-old hips. "I just don't *understand* why I can't have things done right when I *ask*. The first time."

"I'm so sorry, Ms. Ross. I'll fix it right away. . . ."

"Yes. You will." She whispered. Everything was a whisper. Or a sigh. Or a girlish, feminine gesture disguising the angrier, unacceptable emotion she was feeling at the time.

I was standing inside her mansion somewhere near Doheny Drive, watching a very nervous estate manager try to calm "Ms. Ross" down over her daily schedule not being typed in large enough print.

I've never seen any woman run her business completely on a whim. Every decision was made immediately, without thought, without hesitation, and mostly without considering any consequences. My first week, she hired and then fired and then rehired the same gardener three times. She first cut and then raised my salary by nearly $10,000 the next week. One minute, she loved me. She'd ask me to accompany her on business trips with music producers and take notes on whatever laptop "spoke to her" that day.

The next minute, she hated me. Those days, she wouldn't even look me in the eye. My orders would come directly from the diva's lips to Kimmy, the estate planner—a nervous, fidgety woman who couldn't stop wringing her hands—and back to me. To make things worse, her orders were never certain. In fact, I was never really sure what my job entailed at all. I just sort of showed up every morning around nine a.m. and started cleaning her costume closets.

By the time I finished, I'd dusted and pressed every single outfit from both *Solid Gold* and *The Wiz*. And I'd never seen either.

Her stage ensembles were the most outrageous. Like Cher only with more pearls, more sequins, more feathers and lots more pastels. "Ms. Ross" was all about the florals and pastels. And girlfriend had an apple bottom to rival any rap video dancer *ever*. Coming from a former fat-ass, "apple bottom" is quite a compliment. Mine always looked rather like a pear.

After I'd finished vacuum-packing her dresses back into their thick, black astronaut suits and hanging them up on rows and rows and rows of metal hangers, I usually hung around, shooting the shit with her kitchen staff.

A few hours later, either Kimmy or "Ms. Ross"—depending on whether she was speaking to me that day—bothered to tell me her plans. Then I'd go to whatever desk wasn't covered in broken glass or ripped-out weave from the diva's latest temper tantrum and type up her itinerary for the day.

The rest of each day I spent exploring her house.

The whole place was jam-packed with stuff. It was like walking through a wax museum or the Music Hall of Fame. There were huge portraits of "Ms. Ross" and her half dozen kids. There were photos of her ex-husbands, too. Most of them were Jewish, as I understood, and either lawyers or music producers. There were old photos of Michael Jackson, Barry Gordy and all sorts of singers she'd worked with, most of whom I didn't recognize.

I thought of all my Daddy's favorite Motown albums and how

much he'd dig walking through those hallowed halls of fame. I smiled at the thought of him recognizing all the singers I didn't, mostly because they were before my time.

Upstairs, in her private quarters, were hallways decked with flowers and gilded furniture and peacock feathers and such. There had to be at least three desktop computers in "Ms. Ross's" office, none of which she ever used. Sometimes, when the housekeepers got tired of dusting them, they'd use them as doorstops. Kimmy once hung begonias over a few monitors. She said maybe they'd look like postmodern flowerpots that way.

On her good days, "Ms. Ross" and I got on just fine. She'd show up at some random moment just as I was typing up the schedule. I'd hand it to her. She'd squint, tell me the font was still too small and ask me to redo it. So I did. And then she'd go away and forget I was there for the rest of the afternoon. Those days, she'd giggle at my jokes, or look at me like I was the sweetest thing on earth. Sometimes, she'd give me this strained, too-much-plastic-surgery bug-eyed smile, which was nice. In a demented bag lady kind of way.

More than the mood swings, her pets were the worst part of the job. Whenever one of her kids got a new puppy, the rest of us would have to take care of it. That meant I had to make sure it was potty-trained before "Ms. Ross" caught on to the pee smell and threw another screaming fit. Living with those puppies was like living with a crazy homeless guy. I would show up in the morning and the place was a wreck. Then the puppy would look at me with this shifty, pitiful, poor-me look that said, "I ate all the toilet paper, so I wiped my butt with the couch. Oh, and look! There's my erection—for no reason at all!"

Eventually, I got used to the uncertainty. I just showed up, kept my mouth shut and changed the font on her daily schedule from 12 point to 24 point. That way "Ms. Ross" couldn't complain. Hell, she could read the thing from space.

But no matter how eager to please her servants were, there was always something wrong. Something that would send "Ms. Ross" into angry diva mode, or racing toward a conniption fit. It happened so often I started to sense the calm before the storm. Kimmy and I came up with a code word to warn each other about her impending doom:

"The dragon is hungry."

And then both of us knew to flee to the safety of our computers, which were her kryptonite. She'd avoid anyone within ten feet of one.

Puppy pee, schedules and the dragon's appetite for drama I could handle. But whenever Kimmy couldn't reach a computer and the dragon fed on her, she'd respond with terrified stammering and hand-wringing.

I was the exact opposite. Whenever "Ms. Ross" blew up at me, I just stood there quietly like I was back in front of the Inquisition and not about to give in. I refused to believe my very existence hung in the balance around a creator named "Ms. Ross." I was a Rebel Deb, after all. I didn't like other people's rules, and never paid too much attention to the self-importance of self-important people. Even on her worst days, I didn't cower. Didn't stammer. Didn't go home and memorize her Top Ten hits just to sound impressive and quell her anger the next day. Hell, I wasn't even born when she recorded most of them.

To me, she'd always be just that little old lady with freaky hair and too-tiny hips. And, in all honesty, a sixty-year-old has no business prancing around in halter tops, skintight Capri pants and Spanx sized for teenagers. I saw her as a person—not the diva, not "Ms. Ross," not even the dragon, really.

To me, she was just Diana.

That's probably why she hired me. And in the end, that's probably why she fired me, too.

One day, things changed. Diana's mood had shifted, yet again, and the joke was now on me. I was working late that week getting things ready for Diana to catch a plane. She was supposed to appear at some honoree banquet in New York and I was typing up her itinerary for the whole trip . . . or, at least, I was trying to. She kept changing her mind about where she was going to eat lunch on what day and with whom. And like always, I was keeping my mouth shut and banging away on my keyboard to get everything done.

I was right in the middle of ". . . send flowers to Chaka Khan . . ." when guess who plops herself right down beside me? To chat.

I looked at my desk. There it was: my laptop computer. Why wasn't the kryptonite working?!

"Anna. Darling child. I was wondering if you'd do me a favor."

Well, butter my butt and call me a biscuit because the dragon was *starving* today.

"Um, sure, Ms. Ross. What is it?"

"My son's applying to colleges this year. I was wondering, seeing as you're such a smart girl, if you'd help him."

"Help him do what? Fill out his applications?"

"Well, something like that. Whatever he needs, really. I think he's having some trouble with his personal statement or some nonsense. . . ."

When I took a look at Prince Ross's partially filled-out application to USC, the reason for Diana's frustration became clear. No wonder she'd broken through the computer kryptonite. Essentially, Diana was "asking" (aka ordering) me to "help" her son write his college essay (aka write it for him).

And, it was also clear, my job depended on it.

Hmm. I can't say this one didn't make me queasy inside. More so than Katie or Albie or any of the other Hollyweird folks I'd encountered so far. I just couldn't bring myself to justify writing somebody else's college essay, job or no job. So I stuffed his application deep inside my desk and tried to pretend nothing ever happened . . .

Until the next day, when things got worse.

I dragged in that morning, nervous as a long-tailed polecat in a room full of rocking chairs. I hadn't slept all night. I was too worried about what to do with this damn fool essay. Don't get me wrong, I still wasn't buying the whole "Ms. Ross is the Boss" hype. On the other hand, I didn't want to lose my job. So I tossed and I turned and I wracked my brain for a compromise. Around three a.m., the Rebel Deb won out.

I finally decided to tell Diana the ugly truth. I wasn't writing that essay, no matter the consequences. Take it or leave it. End of story. All I could do now was grit my teeth, swallow my pride and prepare for the ultimate dragon-feeding-slash-diva-meltdown.

As a Rebel Deb, I'd always been on the "outspoken" side. Some folks called me brave. Others, foolish. But like my Uncle Stu always said, a man (or woman) ain't judged by his britches but by the size of his beans.

Working for Diana Ross, I'd had to put away my beans for a time. Each time the dragon reared her ugly head, I prayed for the strength to keep my mouth shut. And I felt lucky to have kept quiet as often as I did in the middle of Diana's craziness. Like I said, after a while, I got used to the uncertainty and, thus, used to shutting up.

But at that moment, looking into her crazy eyes, I was tempted to tell the truth to her face. Maybe more truth than she'd heard in a long, long time. Somewhere in the back of my mind, Uncle Stu was daring me. I could hear him egging me on . . . *Come on, Anna Lee! Ya got any hair on yer peaches er what? She's a big gal—she can take it! Lay it on her!*

So I did.

The next day, Frankie told me "Ms. Ross" had let me go.

"It just didn't work out," he said.

But I knew Diana better than that. I never found out where Prince Ross wound up, but essentially it didn't matter. Especially not to his Momma. To me it seemed like she didn't actually care whether I wrote his essay. All I felt she'd really wanted was for me to lie to her face like everybody else.

And, in the end, that's something this Scarlett just wouldn't do.

After my gig with Diana ended, I took a job as a hostess at Blowfish Sushi. Anybody who's ever watched MTV's *The Hills* knows that Blowfish is one of those trendy, upscale places where celebrities are always getting mauled by paparazzi and the chef's special is always something totally unappetizing. Like tiger penis. Or frog leg soup.

Man, do I hate frog leg soup.

The first (and last) time I ever ate frog legs was at Billy the Kid's seafood restaurant in Cherry Grove, South Carolina.

Billy the Kid's serves seafood up right. It's always battered and deep-fried with a healthy side of hush puppies, French fries and coleslaw. On the back of the menu you can read all about Billy the Kid's career as a bandit and his eventual shooting. It's all right there, just below "Frog Legs. Beer battered and fried: $12.99 per pound."

During one family dinner, I convinced Daddy to let me order the frog leg soup. Momma was against it—she knew I liked to try new things and then quit them, just like sleepaway camp. But Daddy finally agreed, so I gave the waitress my order.

When the steaming bowl of amphibian meat arrived, I was intrigued. I grabbed a spoon, ladled some out and stuck it in my mouth. And swallowed . . . or tried to.

Lord help me, I had a webbed foot stuck in my throat.

After a few hard pounds on the back, I finally coughed the thing up. Then I tried fishing the frog feet out and cutting them into smaller bites with my fork and knife. But no such luck. Even Daddy tried and couldn't manage it, either. Momma was steaming mad at me for ordering such a silly, frivolous dinner that she wouldn't let me send it all back. I was going to eat my soup, webbed feet and all.

After a while, I gave up and munched on salad the rest of the night. That at least I could chew and swallow.

Anywho.

Blowfish served frog leg soup on special occasions. I didn't bother to try a bowl, but I did taste the rest of the menu. I'd never eaten so much sushi in my life—and at Blowfish, this wasn't just your run-of-the-mill fish on rice.

Oh, no.

Blowfish was a *celebrity* sushi bar that served *celebrity* sushi. This meant I had to make sure everybody in the whole place was ecstatically happy at all times . . . with *everything*.

The food, the service, the tablecloths—even the weird sink in the bathroom that didn't have a faucet—all had to be perfect. The first time I used that sink, water just sort of spouted up from the flat stone countertop. The thing felt like a huge Wet-Nap waiting to soak my hands free of fish guts and rice.

Being a hostess at Blowfish also meant catering to all the celebutantes that came through its doors.

One night, for example, a little man with doll hair appeared by my hostess stand. He looked just like the troll-doll pens Alma used in biology class.

He stomped toward me, surrounded by tall, gorgeous, vapid-looking women, and stopped to examine the blowfish maki—our signature dish. When he stopped, we stood eyeball to eyeball. I tried to see his face but couldn't quite make it out through the perfectly coiffed bangs that adorned his forehead. He was also very thin and had a hound dog's face with big, sad, droopy eyes and a downturned mouth.

Suddenly, an even tinier fella emerged from beneath the hound dog's armpit. He was clean shaven, nearly bald and missing a few teeth.

Together, the pair reminded me of one of the bluegrass duos back home: the "Soggy Bottom Boys" or "Baldy McGregor and Two Cents McGee." Only this time, Two Cents was wearing a very well-styled mop on his head.

They ordered the blowfish and the prawns for appetizers. For their main course, frog leg soup, octopus testicles and two orders of tiger penis. By the time Baldy, Two Cents and their entourage left, the bill was over two grand. That's a whole lotta raw fish and rice, folks. They paid it, then got up—Two Cents first, then Baldy—and started toward the door. That's when some kid with spiked hair and covered in so many tattoos I thought he was wearing a hunting jacket got up and shouted across the room:

"Hey, Kiedis! You *rock*!"

And the whole place erupted into hoots, hollers and clapping. Almost like a *celebrity* had just finished eating his *celebrity* sushi in our *celebrity* sushi bar.

Meanwhile, I was dumbfounded. I'd had no idea Anthony Kiedis resembled a combination of hound dog, Two Cents McGee and a malnourished Raggedy Ann.

Anthony Kiedis wasn't the only celebutante who graced my hostess stand.

Bebe Neuwirth came in once with a whole bunch of German actors that looked like they'd just walked right out of *Cabaret*. I kept looking around for Liza the whole time.

Then there was Rebecca Gayheart, who I recognized as yet another victim from *90210*. She ordered all-veggie sushi because she'd just started a "raw diet" that made her face look green and shimmery from certain angles. She was friendly until I made a joke about her slender figure. Then her face puckered up like a rainbow trout. For a second, I thought her lips were gonna fall off and carrot juice was gonna spurt out her mouth from too many undigested vegetables.

She was sitting beside a good-looking fella with a soul patch. At the time, I mistook him for one of the Backstreet Boys. I later learned his name—Eric Dane—once he became Dr. McSteamy on *Grey's Anatomy*. I also learned he was trout-face's hubby-to-be. They were a real cute couple, as far as toothpicks go. Afterward, I felt bad for hurting Rebecca's feelings. But I still say she could've used a pork chop sandwich now and then to complement her veggies.

Some not-so-celebutantes also visited the Blowfish.

These not-so-celebrated *celebrities* were some of the kookiest folks I'd ever seen. There was one married European couple who dressed up in the same outfits. This would've been cute if it weren't for the shaved heads and clown makeup. Raw fish, rice and face paint don't look too appetizing smeared all over your face. My manager finally asked them to leave. All that smear made other customers wanna upchuck their two-hundred-dollar tiger penises.

Blowfish paid pretty well, but for extra money I'd take occasional gigs at private parties in Calabasas, where all the other celebrities (who weren't already at Blowfish) dined.

The whole event was supposed to last four hours. In return, they offered me a whopping four hundred dollars, so I jumped at the chance. Little did I know I'd be walking into a celebutante beehive. I showed up outside the palatial Spanish mansion at a quarter to six. The instructions read seven p.m., but I knew showing up early meant better tips at the end of the night.

First thing I noticed were all the Persian rugs, white statues and gold curtain rods. Second thing I noticed were all the girls: three sisters, all in various states of undress . . . or close enough to make a preacher blush. They all had long hair, thick eyebrows, thicker eye makeup and donned the absolute minimum required to hide their girly parts. The oldest sister, Barbie, was teeny-tiny like a little Greek figurine with huge flotation devices attached to her chest. The second sister, Suzie, was tall, plump, loudmouthed and obviously jealous of her older sister.

Suzie was definitely the Rebel Deb of the bunch. I watched her down a bottle of Krystal in one long pull—just like Alma used to do a long-necked Budweiser.

Then there was the youngest sister, Fluyztie. Pronounced "floozy." Fluyztie was the kinda gal every man wanted, every woman envied and I tried not to gawk at whenever she stopped flirting long enough to pick a sky-high wedgie out of her way-up-yonder. The first time I saw Fluyztie, I was standing in the kitchen, chatting with the regular staff about what limes to serve with which beers and whatnot . . . when all of sudden, a Shakira impersonator waltzed in.

Shakira was wearing a belly shirt and skintight hip-huggers and suede boots laced up to her hoo-ha. I noticed the shirt, pants and boots first, and her camel toe second. She picked a wedgie, then demanded the chef put shrimp lo mein on tonight's menu. I was just grateful it wasn't frog legs or tiger penis.

Fluyztie was clearly the queen bee of this hive. She had the munchies, she said, but strolled past the tray of whore-da-vores and went straight for the cocktail cherries. She grabbed a handful and shoved them into her mouth.

That's when I noticed the nails. Or were they talons?

All ten were bright red and decorated with slightly smudgy henna tattoos. For a second, I wondered if I'd stepped into a Californian gypsy camp. Or maybe these folks were just holding a belly-dancing party, and here I was making silent fun of their required costumes. I tried to bury my thoughts, hide my smiles. About an hour later, Fluyztie's boyfriend showed up with his entourage. They were all rich, greasy playboy types that reminded me of Marky Mark and the Funky Bunch. At any moment, I expected them to sing "Good Vibrations."

I spent the next hour or so slicing fruit for apple-tinis, a favorite among this crowd. Then an especially tipsy fella with a hair lip and too much cologne started bugging me for orange juice. He was just *dying* for orange juice and couldn't get enough. So, in the middle of slicing fruit and checking on dinner, I had to start pouring half glasses of orange juice. I gave him just enough to shut him up but not enough to spill all over the carpet, which I'd no doubt have to clean.

Barbie, Suzie, Fluyztie and the drunken Funky Bunch finally sat down for dinner. And that's when the real trouble started.

I could barely serve all the food without keeling over from juice boy's cologne. I didn't know if it was sunny in there or what, but nobody wanted to take off his Gucci sunglasses, even at the table. All the gold chains kept reflecting whatever dim light was hurting everybody's eyes and flashing it back into mine. I nearly poured a whole glass of Krystal into Fluyztie's lap. Good thing she'd already grabbed it out of my hands and downed it like a pro.

Eventually, the Funky Bunch started asking me if I "had a Jewish husband." I was immediately confused. Was it funny to have a Jewish husband? Was it some kind of inside joke told only amongst Funky folks? If so, I didn't get it. And by that point, all the orange juice, apple-tinis and shrimp lo mein were making this bunch smell pretty funky, too.

By the end of the night, I was exhausted. The whole house was now filled with the kind of smoke only Woody Harrelson would appreciate. Even worse, Fluyztie's boyfriend was threatening to not pay me at all if I didn't clean up all the bong water. Something deep inside told me get out and get out *now*. Obeying my Rebel Deb instincts, I forgot about the cash and just bolted.

A couple days later, word got around at Blowfish: The FBI busted "Marky," his "Funky Bunch" and everybody else within fifty yards of that house.

And for the rest of my days, I'll remember that as the best four hundred dollars I ever lost.

Next day, I was back in Frankie's office, asking for a "reg-ler" desk job. I was done with *celebrities* for a while.

Only I think Frankie's idea of "reg-ler" was a bit different.

I spent the next seven months as a book slave for Borders in West Hollywood. There, I sold a Star Wars sword to Jonathan Rhys Meyers. I even helped a slew of folks from Andy Dick to Sir Ben Kingsley find cookbooks, memoirs and those little pocket travel guides that always get you lost at truck stops. Borders barely paid me enough to buy the gas to get to work, so I switched over to the dark side for a while.

While most folks think "industry" people are the dark side of Hollyweird, it's actually lawyers who do most of the dirty work. Frankie got me an interview with a lawyer who had an office in Malibu, and I spent the next six months listening to my alcoholic boss squabble with one of Liza Minnelli's many ex-husbands. Another six months I spent in Westwood filing paternity lawsuits against a former boy band member, whose pants-dropping routine was apparently costing him millions in illegitimate babies. Then, it was back to Beverly Hills, where I spent another month tying bows around Christmas party invitations at one of L.A.'s biggest and most prestigious firms.

By now, L.A. seemed like a whole bunch of people fighting and arguing and ruining each other's lives over nothing. My Rebel Deb spirit was slowly being vacuum-sucked into a corporate nightmare. I needed release. So once my bow-tying was finished, I flew South for a well-needed break.

My first day back, Uncle Stu showed me his new hunting-dog belt buckle: the bronzed figure of May Bud pointing the way to a dying bird. Behind her, the Smoky Mountains.

"Got this made special at Dollywood. You been so many places, seen so many things . . . you wouldn't like it," he said. Then he squinted like he expected me to laugh at his country taste.

"Actually, yeah. I would."

Then his eyes opened up and he smiled instead—the slow, crooked smile of a Southerner at ease.

That's when I knew I was home. Maybe not for good, but at least for now. Because even though I'd spent the last eight years running away from my roots, I was relieved to slow down.

And I'm pretty sure Scarlett was, too.

Chapter Seven

My Momma Says Hummus Looks Like Cat Sick:

A Rebel Deb Finds
Her Home in New York

Like Lewis Grizzard, Jr., a great American, once said: "If I ever get back to Georgia, I'm gonna nail my feet to the ground."

Good thing I never learned to use a hammer. I would've never made it to New York.

In January of 2006, I was home in Carolina for a visit when I came across a website for New York University's Graduate Department of Dramatic Writing. It looked interesting, and though I didn't know much about what writers did, I was sure there'd be good things to eat at their parties. So, I filled out an application and sent it in. Only problem was, I needed to write something "dramatic" to send in along with it.

I was flat stumped. I'd spent the last year working for artists (and their crazy agents and lawyers)—how could I suddenly become one? I racked my brain—what in the world could I possibly write about that anybody would want to read?

That same night, Momma and I sat down to watch one of our favorite movies—an old Technicolor from the '60s called *This Property Is Condemned*. Besides *Pride and Prejudice*, this was probably our favorite. Maybe we loved the old scenes of great romance and unspoken torment. Maybe we just loved Natalie Wood's impersonation of a sassy Southerner. Either way, watching her climb out of a swimming hole just to give a soaking-wet Robert Redford a piece of her mind was so inspiring that, afterward, I sat down and wrote my first play. It was a classic three-act deal called *Where's My Alva Starr?* I had less than a week to pull something together for my NYU application, so it was rough and unedited, but after six and a half days—done. So, I popped it in an envelope and sent it along, express mail, straight to NYU. It was the last day they were taking applications, and I had no choice but to pay extra to get it there on time. They'd also asked for recommendation letters and transcripts and all that stuff, but I didn't have time—so I just sent what I had: my name and my play.

About a week later, I was back in L.A. when somebody from NYU called me to ask for letters of recommendation. So, I rustled up a few friends and faxed in a few notes here and there—just enough to satisfy the requirements—and went back to working days at yet another hellish law firm in Westwood, a ritzy suburban community in West L.A. By March, I'd forgotten about the whole thing. Until I got a fat envelope in the mail, that is.

I was standing by my kitchen sink when I first opened it. At first, I just assumed the folks at NYU had been nice enough to return my play along with their rejection letter . . . but then those first few words flashed across my eyes. . . .

"Congratulations on your acceptance to the Master of Fine Arts Program at the Department of Dramatic Writing. . . ."

And then a whole page full of details I couldn't pull myself together enough to read. The next page was even more shocking. . . .

"Dean Mary Schmidt Campbell is please to award you a full-tuition fellowship, renewable for all four semesters of your two-year MFA program. . . ."

Well, hot damn, was all I could think in response. By the second page of my acceptance letter, detailing how I'd been chosen out of thousands of applicants to enter an exclusive graduate program of only twenty writers—for *free*, no less—my brain was too stunned to do anything but wonder. . . .

Was Scarlett ready to jump from the Hollywood Hills to "the City"?

That August, I spent my twenty-fifth birthday looking up at the Empire State Building for the very first time. Like most folks, I'd only ever seen it on TV: scenes from *Sex and the City* that made New York look like a place where a Rebel Deb could walk around in four-inch heels all day long because it never rains and the subway doesn't exist.

Only—wait a minute—they'd never even heard of a Rebel Deb.

And why not?

Because until I arrived in August 2006, "the City"—New York, that is—had never seen a Rebel Deb before. Gals like me didn't exist. New Yorkers didn't go to girls' boarding schools or learn how to curtsy and ride ladies' sidesaddle. Every single one of them was skinny and fashionable and made varsity cheerleader on her very first tryout.

Right?

Welcome to my first impression upon landing at LaGuardia Airport. All the New Yorkers around me looked so cool and upscale and rich and, most of all, *busy* that I couldn't relate to any of them at all. None of them looked or sounded anything like me whatsoever. And so, I entered New York much like I entered middle school: the lone fat girl in a city full of varsity cheerleaders.

As I headed outside, I tried to hail a cab to the Empire State. That's when some airport official ran up to me and started waving in my face.

"There! You have to wait *in line*. Over *there!*" he screamed.

I followed his waving hand to a taxicab stand, where a fella in an orange prison jumpsuit handed me a flyer. When a cab finally pulled up at the curb, he pointed me inside.

Since it was getting toward fall and I'd always heard that the "frozen North" would be cold, I'd worn fleece underdrawers and an overcoat on the plane. This meant that by the time we landed, my fanny was mighty sweaty. All my life, I'd been told only the South was humid while the North was crisp and cool and the dirt was brown so it wouldn't stick to your shoes. This is all a huge whopper. Not even Alma would make up something like that. Most Southerners either overestimate or underestimate Northern weather like this. We either ignore the old wives' tales and pack like we're going to the beach or we wear our fleece underdrawers on the plane.

In L.A., it only ever got cold in January—and only a few degrees at a time. You could only tell the seasons apart out West when it rained and when it got windy. The entire place felt kind of like a casino. Like somebody had taken control of the light switches and kept changing things around. Your system eventually got so confused that you couldn't tell day from night and you never knew when it was time to go home.

- ♡ The North is different. It's either extreme winter or extreme summer. Either baking hot or freezing cold. Some folks, like me, shouldn't be caught in this kinda extreme weather. We shouldn't be sloshing around outside the airport like wet poodles with ripped-open suitcases.
- ♡ And Lord knows, once we catch a cab, we're horrible customers. We're all frenzied and riled up, our hair-dos are ruined, and our etiquette goes right out the window.
- ♡ No, sir.
- ♡ Rebel Debs, in general, shouldn't hail taxicabs. And some people, I soon found out, shouldn't drive them.
- ♡ Heading away from LaGuardia in my very first taxi-cab, I leaned down to hug my broken, Japanese beetle of a suitcase. And that's when I saw the handwritten note stuck to the driver's seat.

Dear Customer:
Please try to follow these rules of my cab . . .

1. Keep shoes off backseat.
2. Exit curbside only.
3. Take all your belongings, except my tips and fare!!
4. Do not slam door. . . . My ears!

I had no idea there were so many rules involved in catching a ride. My driver got lost on the way into Manhattan because he couldn't read the road signs. He finally pulled over to ask for directions and we were on our way. I spent the rest of the ride trying not to pee my pants as the cabbie came *thisclose* to hitting every other cab on the road. I would've asked him to slow down but he was too busy screaming in Farsi at someone on his cell phone.

Every time I looked out the window, I saw things that sent me straight into Southern culture shock. First of all, New York, unlike the South, is almost empty of trees. Folks can't just see foliage from their windows and doorsteps. Oh, no. They have to go to specially designated parks to find a single oak to sit under and rest awhile. Also, unlike their Southern counterparts, New York men don't usually open doors for women on their way into or out of buildings. I found this lack of chivalry—or even basic courtesy—truly disturbing. Then again, these women weren't exactly the "won't you please open this big ol' heavy door for little ol' me?" types. These New York women were dressed in power suits and six-inch stilettos. They wore thick makeup with lots of eye shadow and lip liner, and sported the kinds of slick, crispy hairdos and long, red nails I'd only ever seen on Michelle Pfeiffer in *Married to the Mob*. They galloped down the sidewalks, ignoring red lights and speeding taxis, stopping only to pull out their BlackBerrys or kick a rat into the gutter. Cab drivers and delivery men cursed at one another over parking spaces, and a couple of them actually got out of their cars and started fighting in the middle of the street. The whole city was loud and busy and scary and stressful for a small-town girl. Even though I'd lived in L.A., New York didn't compare. Everything was taller and made me so small inside. Everyone looked and sounded so different and, most of all, *angry*. Absolutely nothing about New York or New Yorkers seemed even remotely familiar—not even to my days at Brown in Providence. And sure, I suspected sleepy New England towns weren't any closer to New York than Burlington—but how was I supposed to know for sure, fresh off the plane?

Once I stepped out of the cab, my first stop was Midtown Manhattan . . . only the map I'd bought in the airport tourist shop would not open, and I didn't yet know my "uptown" from "downtown." In the South—like most places in America—"downtown" pretty much means the center of everything citified. And, thus, any place outside "downtown" was the suburbs, or in the South, the "country."

I finally got up my nerve to ask for directions and stopped an angry-looking fella drinking from a paper bag outside a deli—perhaps not the best choice, but I was desperate at the time. I asked him nicely where I could find the Empire State Building, but before I could finish, he scoffed at me and told me to "go home to Dixie." Undeterred, I asked two more people—neither of whom spoke a word of English—which direction was "uptown." You'd be amazed how hard it is to find someone who speaks English in New York. The first of them just shook her head and pointed to the second, who smiled at me like one of Uncle Stu's deer in the headlights and said only, "You have nice hat."

Finally, I went inside the deli and tried to ask the salesman behind the counter. I smiled and tried to be nice, but he didn't even look at me—just pointed to a sign that read: NO BUY, NO SERVICE. Apparently, folks in New York were so greedy that they wouldn't even make change or give directions unless there was something in it for them. And since the store didn't take credit cards and I didn't have any cash on me, I had to pay a two-dollar fee at a local ATM, simply so I could buy a pack of gum—for four dollars!—and then, finally, ask for directions.

This time, the crotchety old salesman actually met my gaze. That's when I learned that "uptown" meant north and "downtown" meant south. And, apparently, I was only three blocks away from my destination. So off I went, map, coffee and battered Southern Belle pride in hand.

Walking those short three blocks, I witnessed more shocking things. For example, cabdrivers couldn't turn right on red. In the South, you could turn right pretty much anywhere you damn well pleased, as long as you checked the road for migrating ducks or the occasional slow-moving farmer on a John Deere tractor. Also, in the South, folks had lots of land. The whole island of Manhattan, on the other hand, is only about fourteen miles long, so folks are crammed into tiny little apartments and stacked on top of one another like sardines. In Carolina, this kind of living wouldn't be tolerated—and neither would the rats and cockroaches so common to New York City. Rodents and insects—with the exception of field mice, bunnies, silverfish, Japanese beetles and the occasional possum—are pretty much never found in or around any respectable Southern home. Folks just don't put up with dirty streets and overflowing gutters. And most folks are too polite to leave their food sitting out long enough to attract unwanted guests.

Even more shocking to me was the sales tax in New York—almost 10 percent! In Carolina, it never broke 4.2 percent—and only because the state started taxing places that broke blue laws and sold whiskey and tobacco on Sundays. But at least we could use credit and debit cards to buy most everything we needed. In New York, most of the stores and restaurants wouldn't accept anything but cash—which is a money racket if I ever saw one. They all have their handy-dandy ATM machines lurking nearby so they basically screw over their customers, if you'll pardon my language. These stores are so greedy that they don't mind saying, "Well, we won't accept your cards because we don't want to have pay correct taxes or fees to the credit card companies. We'd much rather just charge you an extra two dollars to withdraw cash, and get paid twice." Sounds like something a slick salesman would try and pull down at your local used-car dealership.

Whenever I was bumped out of the way by yet another thin, busy New York woman power-walking down the street like my Granny Ruth taking exercise at the mall, I couldn't help but wonder—why do these gals walk so fast? Why does *everybody* walk so fast? And how do they make so much money? Are they all bankers? Lawyers? Doctors? What?

See, in the South, folks have this same kind of money—they just don't flash it around like a kid with a new toy. Maybe this is because so much of it's old and inherited, whereas in New York, most wealthy people are first- or second-generation riches. These power-walking women had only just recently come into some cash. They were all young and flashy—showing off their diamond rings, pashmina scarves, designer stilettos and huge hoop earrings, even while using the ATM in a deli—whereas Southern ladies had had their money for many generations, over many years. Southern Debutantes were taught to be modest and considerate and, most of all, humble in front of others. Plus, wealthy Debutantes knew each other so well that, besides their annual Balls, they didn't feel the need to flash their cash. But in New York, it seemed, women worked for what they had, and often gave up marriage and children for it. So, they wanted to show all their hard-earned stuff—and, if I'd been in their same position, I'd have done the same. Only some of them seemed so eager to show anyone and everyone that they now had enough money to buy class that, ultimately, all their jewelry and stilettos and designer outfits just made them look lonely and insecure.

Just in a few blocks, I'd come up with a nickname for these Northern wannabe Debs: the *real* housewives of New York City. You know, like the ones you'd see on Bravo Network, parading around in their brownstone condos or in their Hamptons beach houses . . . only, outside of a TV set and in the real light of day. Here, finding my way to the Empire State Building, I could see a few of their true colors. These gals with new money, some of it earned, some of it married through older husbands. The gals who pretended to be just like the Astors and Vanderbilts of yore . . . yet had none of the same class. Any Rebel Deb could see that. These housewives of New York, I was noticing, were just the Northern versions of Wellingham's Debutantes, only *way* more eager for their M.R.S. degrees and Coming-Out Balls. Worst of all, none of these gals wore any panty hose! And the men they were with never bothered to take off their hats—even *inside*.

Plus, they were all carrying some kind of food, no doubt bought from another rip-off deli. From a short distance, whatever they were eating looked yucky—the kind of health food that probably kept these "Yankee" women looking skinny as rails. Stuff like gefilte fish sandwiches and hummus on crackers. Hummus, just so you know, is thick gunk that my Momma always said looked just like cat sick and that sticks to your mouth worse than peanut butter. Only hummus is a poor man's substitute for peanut butter. Instead of being sweet and filling, it's salty and bitter. Plus, it leaves an oily residue on your tongue that only toothpaste will wash off. I discovered all this when somebody offered it to me atop a Ritz cracker outside a restaurant on my way to the Empire State Building. Who knew New York restaurants served whore-da-vores to strangers on the street? I gave it a try, thinking "When in Rome" . . . until *bleh!* It stuck to my throat like quicksand and I coughed up the yucky mess, lesson learned.

You'd think I'd react better, considering my Granny Ruth lived with more than a dozen cats and, by default, lots of hairballs and cat sick. Her house was the perfect haven for these animals. Stuck out on Loop Road in a little remote part of town called Glen Raven, where the post office only stays open till noon and folks buy fried chicken gizzards by the pound at the local Love of Jesus flea market.

Outside of Dollywood, Loop Road is and always will be one of the prettiest places in the world. My Granny Ruth's house—surrounded by an acre of flowers, ferns and throw up—included.

When her two boys grew up and left home, she started taking in strays. Granny Ruth must've taken in every stray cat in town. After a few months, Granny Ruth had developed a herd of them wandering around her property. They'd eat out of my hand and howl at the moon, but mostly they'd be busy making more cats.

I had my favorites, of course.

There was Maple, who had one green eye and one blue eye. At the age of seven, I took that to mean she was deaf.

Maple also had a tender stomach. Every time I shared my chicken-fried steak, she'd throw up at my feet. That big puddle of chunky cat sick would stink up the whole house for the next three days. Sometimes, when she got sick, Maple would hide out behind Granny Ruth's rosebushes. Granny Ruth loved her roses. She'd take me out there to water and inspect each new bud for Japanese beetles. There's nothing a Japanese beetle likes more than a tasty new rosebud. But if Granny Ruth found him, the poor sucker would wind up drowned in a fruit jar full of gasoline. I'm guessing all this is where my strong dislike of hummus comes from. Back then, I couldn't stand the sight or smell of it. Or of gasoline, for that matter.

Anywho, thank goodness nobody was serving hummus 'n' Ritz whore-da-vores inside the Empire State Building. Otherwise, I would've never made the trip. Only by the time I got to the elevator, a guard stopped me. I had to pay the toll.

"I'm so sorry, sir. How much is it?" I asked.

"Thirty-five bucks. Pay up," he replied.

Thirty-five dollars to ride up an elevator? Did these folks not know the meaning of the words "grad student"? Guess not, by the look on his face—steely-eyed, with an open fist waiting to be paid. But since I'd spent all my money on the cab ride from the airport and then using the ATM for directions, I didn't have a choice—my mission to the top of the Empire State Building was, at least for today, abruptly over.

I turned around and trudged out, rejected yet again. As a child, I was too chubby, as a teenager, too rebellious, and now as an adult, too broke.

My first few months in New York were rough. I felt like a fish out of water. This was mostly because I was the first person in my entire family—or all of Wellingham, for that matter—who'd ever dared strike out on her own and travel so far away from home. My parents had *hated* the fact that I moved to L.A. Whenever I ran out of money, Momma would tell me, "If you can't afford to live there, come home!" like that was really an option. Like coming back to North Carolina, marrying a local car salesman and having babies for the rest of my life was some kind of golden ticket to fulfillment.

Now that I'd left L.A. and was in New York, they felt a tiny bit better—at least I was on the same coast. But I was still in the "frozen, heartless" North, and they still didn't approve. And, quite frankly, I couldn't blame them. Almost every rumor I'd ever heard about New York was about to come true. And with each one, I learned a new and different lesson—the kinds of things a Rebel Deb should know when she moves up North, and the kinds of lessons Wellingham's Cotillion classes didn't teach:

For example:

♡ Don't be greedy.

Besides the real housewives, some other types of New Yorkers really are as greedy as they're rumored to be. Especially apartment brokers. Almost everyone looking for an apartment in New York, I soon learned, is forced to hire a broker to find a suitable place to live. If you don't, you're liable to wind up with cockroaches in your bed or hypodermic needles in your toilet. And the broker's fee is 12 to 15 percent of your *entire year's rent*. And on top of that, you have to pay the landlord first and last month's rent *plus* a security deposit— another whole month's worth of rent—*up front*.

After leaving the Empire State Building, since I couldn't afford the cab fare all the way to my new apartment, I discovered the subway— and for a Southern Rebel Deb used to burning up the road in her own car, this was my own personal version of hell.

Since my first apartment was all the way out in Midwood, Brooklyn, my commute to and from Manhattan was long and painful. Just so you know, Midwood is all the way out on the B/Q subway line, about forty minutes from "downtown" Manhattan.

The apartment was a tiny, four-hundred-square-foot dungeon with a view of a Hasidic rabbinical school. My landlord's name was Merv Levinson. Standing at about five foot five on a good day, Merv was a hairy gnome of a man with the angriest, most neurotic personality I'd ever encountered. From the first moment I met him, he bragged about how "his" apartments "rented in minutes." This, he said, was because he was such an amazing landlord, who'd once worked on Wall Street. At first, I was impressed by all this. But when I found out that Merv wasn't actually my landlord, but instead had quit Wall Street to work for his Momma managing *her* apartment complexes, I was more impressed by the size of his current Napoleonic complex than by his former job.

The first time I saw my new place was a full two weeks after I'd signed the lease and paid a full month's rent, security deposit plus $1,100 to Merv because, he claimed, he was not only the landlord but also the broker for his own building. This sounded fishy, but as a newbie, I didn't know any better, and so I believed him. Plus, he went on, I couldn't move in yet, because he hadn't finished "renovating" my apartment. Then he went on and on again about what a great landlord he was, how everyone knew this and how, as a result, his apartments "rented in a minute!"

Napoleon indeed. As soon as I moved in, I understood why the French had banished him.

First of all, there was the neighborhood. New York, like folks always warned me but I never listened, really isn't all that safe. Sure, it's not the pre–Mayor Giuliani, rough-and-tumble, *Taxi Driver* New York of the '70s and '80s, where hookers service customers out in the open and drug dealers hustle at every corner, but it's still pretty dangerous out there—especially after midnight. This fact is made even more apparent by the landlords and brokers themselves, because when you finally sign the lease, they give you three different keys—the outside door lock, the inside door lock and the lock on your mailbox. Why would any "safe" city need *three* different barriers for basic protection? By the time I got to my front door, I felt lucky to be alive. My new neighborhood was so unsafe that my apartment had *five*: one for the razor-wire fence outside the building, a second for the iron gate protecting the main outside door, a third for the main door itself, a fourth for my apartment door and a fifth to the trash bin outside. Folks are so unsafe in New York that they have to lock up their *trash*. And in case you're wondering: There wasn't a mail key. And why? Because nobody got any mail. The postman's oath promised delivery regardless of wind, sleet or hail, but he damn sure wasn't about to brave this part of town.

Outside my building, homeless people gathered to sleep by the front door, which was so old and rusty that every time I turned the lock, my key would get stuck, leaving me trapped out in the cold. Plus, there was no doorman, no buzzer and, much like the postman, UPS wasn't too keen on delivering to my neck of the wood. The UPS fella wouldn't leave anything on my doorstep without a personal signature—and since there was no buzzer to let me know when he arrived, I basically had to wait and watch by the window till his truck approached, praying I could run outside and catch him before he drove away again with my undelivered packages.

Inside my apartment, there were so many problems it took me all of first semester to sort them out. First, there was the heat . . . or, should I say, the lack of. As part of his being a "great landlord," Merv covered heat and water costs—all I had to pay was the rent and power bill. To a penniless grad student, this sounded great! Only problem was, during his "remodeling," Merv had done such a quick, sloppy job of fixing up the place that he'd painted over the entire radiator—including the heat release valve. As a result, absolutely nothing was coming out of that baby anytime soon. In August, this wasn't a problem, but once October rolled around, I found myself putting on all of my clothes to go to bed. I felt like a bag lady. Or like I was suddenly back in the Great Depression and had to bundle up to keep from freezing to death in my sleep. What's worse, every time I asked Merv about it, he laughed in my face. He said I must be just another stupid Southerner who didn't know how to operate a radiator properly. Then, when I demonstrated my ability to turn the thing on and still nothing came out, he switched tactics. His story changed, and he started insisting that the heater for the whole building only came on when the weather outside dropped below 40 degrees.

You don't put off a Rebel Deb that easy. After shivering through an early snowstorm, I finally caught a nasty cold. This time, instead of dealing with Napoleon, I called the building super, Robert.

Robert was a nice Puerto Rican man who lived next door. Since he wasn't a fellow Southerner, Merv apparently gave him the benefit of the doubt and assumed he had a brain in his head. When Robert discovered the painted-over heat valve, he immediately started scraping away, and about three minutes later, my apartment switched from hell frozen over back to just regular hell.

I say this because there were *way* more problems than just the heat. Next, there was the shower. Or, as I liked to call it: the Exorcist.

Just so you know, the building was over a hundred years old—which, apparently, also meant that neither Merv nor any of the other Levinsons had bothered to change the plumbing in all that time. The whole bathroom was a mess to begin with. In his rush to remodel my apartment so he could up the rent, Merv had forgotten to install any towel or toilet paper racks, or even an electrical outlet, which meant I had to blow-dry my hair over the sink in the tiny kitchenette. But the shower was the worst of all. Mostly because it seemed to have its own personality that, like Merv's, was highly neurotic and suffered from violent mood swings. Plus, it seemed to have a personal vendetta against Southerners—or, at least, against me.

Whenever I turned on the water, I had to wait a good five to seven minutes for any pressure. Then, another two to three minutes for the water heater to switch on. Then, suddenly and without warning, the ice-cold shower would *blast* steam out of its spout and spit scalding hot water all over its naked, burning victim—just like Linda whatsherface in *The Exorcist* did with her split-pea soup. By the time I finished showering, my skin was so cooked and pink that I looked like one of my Granny Blanche's homemade salmon cakes. And every time I'd ask Merv to fix it, he'd blame it on my being "a Southern Belle," who just didn't understand New York. Then, for the thousandth time, he'd start bragging about how his apartments "rented in minutes!" and how I shouldn't expect a working shower or working heat or even working locks because "this ain't Park Avenue, honey."

The rest of the apartment was almost as bad. Only a single drawer in the kitchen, holes in the closets, and cracks in the bedroom ceiling big enough for mice to crawl through. When I woke up one morning to find a dead one on my bedroom floor, I almost burst into tears. I didn't know what to do—in the South, like I said, folks don't live in places crawling with rodents—so I wrapped it up in a paper towel, put it in a Ziploc bag, and called Merv to let him know I'd found a rat in my apartment.

Hearing that finally put his greedy ass in gear, let me tell ya. He rushed over and asked to see the rat.

"It's in the refrigerator," I said.

That's when he started laughing at me. "Are you serious?" Which, of course, made my Rebel Deb blood boil. I'd put up with a scalding/freezing shower, getting locked out of my apartment because he was too cheap to install a working lock, holes in my floors and ceilings—and now *this*. How dare he laugh at me? Only, when I took the Ziploc bag out of the freezer and showed it to him, Merv's behavior went from bad to worse.

"This isn't a rat," he said. "Don't you know the difference between a rat and a mouse? You call me and tell me there's a rat in the apartment—that means I have a problem—but one little mouse?" Then he chuckled again—that snorting, obnoxious, carpetbagger character from *Gone With the Wind* chuckle. "Just deal with it, honey. This ain't Park Avenue, ya know. I'm sure, if you had a boyfriend, he'd be able to tell the difference between a rat and a mouse."

And with that, I'd had enough. No more Miss Nice Girl. Wellingham had taught me to be kind, considerate, dignified and ever the ladylike Debutante . . . but it also taught me to stand up for myself. Especially to sexist pigs.

"Listen, I've never been sarcastic or impolite to you in any way— but you're being extremely unprofessional right now," I said. "I've already put up with faulty plumbing, faulty heat and faulty locks, and now I've just found a dead *whatever* in my apartment. And whether I'm a man or a woman, whether this is a rat or a mouse, or whether I live on Park Avenue or not, quite frankly doesn't matter. What does matter is that I shouldn't have to be scalded in the shower every morning, frozen in my own bed at night or waking up with rodents *ever.* So you can either fix this, or I can call the Board of Health—which will it be?"

I'd never had to get so Rebel Deb on anybody before—something about my upbringing just wouldn't let me go there. In the South, respectable people settled their differences calmly and privately. They didn't slur hurtful, sarcastic comments at each other, or argue where others—like Robert, who had come up to fix the cracks in the ceiling and caught me chewing out Merv—could hear them. To upper-class Southerners, that kind of behavior just wasn't appropriate. So when I found out that, like Merv, a lot of New Yorkers believed all Southerners to be the kinds of folks suing their Mommas on *Judge Judy* or arguing over their baby-daddies on *Jerry Springer*, I was stunned and appalled. Folks on *Jerry* don't exactly graduate from high-class boarding schools or attend Debutante Balls. And as sweet as Southern women can be, when pushed, the Rebel Debs inside all of us command just as much respect as the Northern ones. But, till he pulled the sexist card, Merv didn't know this. He'd assumed I was the kind of girl he'd seen on TV, and since he'd never encountered a Rebel Deb before, he didn't realize how strong one could be when forced to defend her own honor.

Needless to say, my Rebel Deb rant shut Merv up. Once he'd crossed the line from just another greedy landlord to an outright sexist, I couldn't put up with it anymore. I'd left the South to escape sexism, but clearly, the North was just as full of it. He immediately started backtracking and apologizing, and told me how "seriously" he took his tenants finding any kind of rodent in his building. I found that kinda ironic considering how, about five minutes ago, he'd stood in my kitchen, laughing in my face for being unable to tolerate "one little mouse," and now he was suddenly "taking this rodent problem very seriously." But I'd learned another post-Wellingham lesson that I wasn't about to forget:

♡ Choose your battles.

At that point, I just wanted him—and the other rats—out of my apartment *now*. And after shattering at least one New Yorker's notion of the ignorant, sweet, easily-pushed-around Southern Belle, I was proud when he finally left.

Meanwhile, during all this landlord drama, I was starting my first semester as a graduate writing student at NYU. This, as it turned out, would be as full of peril and prejudice as any of my encounters with Merv.

My first day of school, as soon as I stepped off the subway in front of the Tisch School of the Arts, I was almost flattened by a dry-cleaning truck. This was surprising considering that, in the grand tradition of most Southern ladies, I was wearing bright pastels and, surrounded by a sea of depressed-looking NYU students in all black, stuck out like a sore thumb. I'm surprised the driver of the truck couldn't see me a mile away. At NYU, I was now—like Alma used to call lesbians at Wellingham so butch you could spot them across a football field—a "hundred-footer."

Even in summertime, almost everybody wears black. Some folks partially, others totally, but you can bet your bottom that *everyone* in New York is wearing at least *one* article of solid-black clothing at all times. After I spent my first few weeks at Tisch dressed in a Rebel Deb's typical uniform of cheery attitude and colorful wardrobe, it was painfully clear that the Ball was certainly not out of the Belle.

I also found this to be true back in Brooklyn when trying to interact with my new Hasidic neighbors. Since my apartment stood right beside an all-boys' rabbinical school, I almost never saw any Hasidic women, and the men wouldn't even look at me—not exactly a friendly neighborhood for a newbie in need of friends and community. I soon found out that staring at women was considered a mortal sin, but I still suspected they were just appalled by my outfits. And though I hated the idea of walking around looking like a funeral director, if I was gonna fit in with the "Yankees," I was gonna have to choose my battles carefully—and that meant investing in a new, all-black wardrobe.

After buying a few items from the local thrift shop, I settled down one night in my newly rodent-free apartment. Only, all the shopping had left me mighty thirsty. About two a.m., I got up to fetch a glass of juice. Only I was still so hot and sweaty from the shopping trip that I'd only worn my skivvies to bed that night. So when I made it to the kitchen, opened the refrigerator and the light shined on my near-naked behind, I barely noticed . . . until I heard a sudden *gasp* through the window to my left.

I glanced and saw, over the two feet separating my window from his, a young rabbi. He was staring at me and holding his chest like his heart was gonna explode. His eyes were bugging clean out of his head and, after a few shocked seconds, he started grabbing at his shutters—finally *slamming* them shut with a bang!

So much for fitting in with my neighbors. Apparently, I was sending them straight to hell instead.

Over that first semester, I'd wake up every morning at about six a.m., take off all the clothes I'd worn to bed and then step into yet another scalding hot shower before starting my long commute to NYU. At first, riding the B/Q during early-morning rush hour was another firestorm of culture shock. I'd walk the six blocks or so to the train, and once it came, just sit there staring at my lap, trying not to stare at all the depressed-looking commuters eating breakfast. As a New York newbie, I found eating on the subway totally gross—especially when folks ate things that required them to use their hands, like hummus on Ritz crackers.

Once I got to NYU, more shock came hurling my way. Most of my fellow grad students had dirty hair and nails and looked like they hadn't slept in a week, but wore their pajamas to class just in case they got the chance. Others wore uncomfortable-looking high-heeled shoes, which always made me wonder how they survived in a city that required so much walking every day. Plus, everything they wore looked faded and worn out. And, in turn, that made them look old and worn out. On the other hand, some of the other grad students came from rich Manhattan socialite families. Since they hadn't left home for the "heartless North," their parents would actually pay for them to rent apartments close to NYU—thus, saving them from freezing, rodent-infested apartments or long commutes. These places would be tasteful lofts in the West Village, two blocks from campus, or one-bedrooms on Astor Place. Then, there were still others who'd moved to New York from far-off places like Utah, or whose parents resented their becoming artists instead of doctors and lawyers. These folks were poor like me and forced to schlep into Manhattan from Brooklyn every single day. Otherwise, they shared single beds in studio apartments and rotated sleep schedules with two or even three roommates at a time.

The rich ones with their own West Village pads were wealthy types who'd spend two hundred bucks on a T-shirt that looked like it came from Goodwill. In the South, folks with money don't buy dingy rags that make them look just like rednecks. In the North, however, looking poor was cool—which, at first, was hard for me to understand.

Why would anyone work really hard to achieve a certain economic status, just to act and dress like someone who worked at McDonald's?

On the other hand, the other out-of-towners, like me, bought *real* Goodwill clothes—in all black, of course, so we wouldn't stand out so much. Some of the more artistic ones would then take their new, cheap clothes home, tear them apart and remake them into the kinds of funky, artistic outfits you'd see on *Project Runway*.

This actually wasn't as shocking. In fact, this sounded like what a lot of Southern folks—of all classes—would do. Reusing things, avoiding wastefulness and being generally grateful for what little you had was a common theme amongst most Southerners I grew up with. I always wondered whether this trait came from the Civil War, when the South was left penniless, or the Great Depression, when most of the country was in the same boat. Regardless, I do remember my Granny Ruth remaking my clothes the same way these NYU students would— when she wasn't killing beetles or taking in cats, that is.

My Granny Ruth was the most resourceful woman I'd ever met. Growing up poor in the rural South, she'd had to be—if she wanted to make anything of herself someday. Granny Ruth was at any given time a realtor, landlord, contractor and the best self-taught seam- stress in all Alamance County. If I ever wanted new sneakers, for example, and she couldn't afford to buy them, she'd decorate a pair of old tennis shoes in glitter and puff paint. Or if I was craving a trendy new outfit from the JCPenney catalog, she'd sew patches onto a jean jacket, pair it with some stirrup pants and, voilà, I was the new fash- ionista of Burlington. And if I frowned or sighed or showed any sign of resistance, she was ready with her age-old defense.

"Well, if you don't like it, suit yourself! Give it back to me—won't hurt my feelings." Which, of course, it would. She'd poured all her heart and soul into making riches from rags, and who could blame her for being hurt if her only grandbaby in the whole world didn't like her Granny Ruth's creations?

Anywho, every morning, as I put on one of my new, all-black mortuary ensembles and jumped on the train, I thought of how my Granny Ruth might redesign my wardrobe. I thought about it all the way from Midwood to NYU, and right into my first playwriting class.

The routine was always the same: We'd pull our chairs together into a "circle of sharing," then break apart to start "giving notes" on each other's latest writing—which was basically code for "ripping each other to shreds."

Our teacher, Vince LaRue, was what I like to call the "angry ex-pat from the South." He loved to "share"—especially the details of his horrible childhood in Texas, his abusive homophobic family and his rough years as a gay actor in New York. He was the kind of man who loved to pretend he hated the South—and then, of course, put on the drawl whenever it would earn him some extra sympathy or attention. He was bald as a jaybird and wearing a pair of jeans so tight I wondered if his zipper might explode. That kind of sharing I could've done without. Our first class, Vince smiled, introduced himself and asked us all to explain why we'd all come to NYU. In ten words or less.

I was so nervous that first day that I almost choked. But when it was my turn, I got an idea: Why not tell a joke to lighten the mood?

"I'm Anna, and I'm an alcoholic . . ." I started.

I didn't get any farther than that. In the South, this would've garnered at least a smile or a mild chuckle. At NYU? Nothing. Not a peep from the stone-cold faces surrounding me.

"I'm Juanita," the girl next to me suddenly interjected, taking the lead. "I was a theater critic in Scotland, and now I'm here."

Juanita definitely looked like some kind of critic. Her face was so puckered up I thought maybe she'd smelled something nasty beneath her seat. Like a leftover Ritz cracker with hummus still on it.

Next came Farrouk. He was a hairy, intense fella with big bushy eyebrows. When he got angry, he reminded me of an arms dealer from some scary country I couldn't pronounce.

Despite his appearance, Farrouk was nice enough. He once sent me something called "the Man Code" that taught me a lot more about boys than I'd ever wanted to know. The Code was a whole list of rules and regulations for how fellas deal with one another when girls aren't looking.

His rules were basically a male version of the "Rules of the Rebel Debutantes," only a bit rougher around the edges. They mostly forbade any man from ever sharing his umbrella, bringing a camera to a bachelor party, dating a buddy's sister, complaining about the brand of free beer at a Super Bowl party, buying birthday presents worth more than twenty dollars, dating a buddy's ex without permission, staring at another man's open zipper or ever owning a cat. The Code was, apparently, something of a religion to fellas like Farrouk.

As we went around the circle and more folks introduced themselves, I got to know Sammy, who turned out to be one of the sweetest guys I ever met. He was an ex-Mormon from Utah whose wife and kids used to visit the class. Then I met Linda Lee, who couldn't stick to the ten-words-or-less limit and at four-foot-eight and two hundred pounds was about as wide as she was tall. Beside her was Richie, a bike messenger delivering packages anywhere his twiggy legs would take him. Then Stewie from Philly, who wore thick bookworm glasses and once took a job fetching frozen yogurt for Lindsay Lohan. He especially enjoyed my stories about working for Diana Ross.

Last but not least was Pinto.

Pinto was a pudgy youngster from San Francisco, who showed up to every class hugging a bag of McDonald's and never met a bottle of vodka he didn't like.

Sometimes Pinto, aka "the Bean," would get so tipsy he'd walk into traffic. On more than one occasion, I grabbed his shoulder before a taxi took it off. I once hired a cab and drove Pinto straight to his doorstep after a near-fatal collision, which he didn't remember the next day and which I never mentioned again. I hated to further embarrass anybody named after a magical bean.

By the time first semester ended, I knew I was in trouble.

I didn't fit in with the rest of my classmates—especially with Juanita. She heard my accent and immediately labeled me "just another hick racist like all the rest." I was done already, labeled and categorized, just in those first few minutes, and she quickly lumped me into her assumptions about all Southerners.

As I quickly learned at NYU, a lot of New Yorkers actually believe everyone from the South is a white supremacist, a former slave-owner, an inbred hick, a tobacco and/or cotton farmer, a homophobe, an alcoholic welfare mother who lives in a trailer park, a die-hard Republican, a country music lover or some combination of these. Oh, and we all fly Confederate flags in our front yards and own season tickets to NASCAR. To these folks, my small town of Burlington seemed laughable at best. And according to most of the people in the Writing department, all Southerners who weren't gay, atheist or openly scorning the South somehow became bigots—simply by default. Oh, and of course, we all worshipped the ground Bill O'Reilly, Rush Limbaugh and Jesse Helms walked on . . . simply because of our having grown up below the Mason-Dixon. Because, apparently, that's how all "those people" in the South were.

By the time January rolled around, most of my classmates had labeled me "the hick." This made my second semester even worse than my first.

All of this was partially my fault. I'd naively decided to expand my horizons—like NYU encouraged new writers to do—and write about something new. So, I came up with the idea for a play based around an African-American preacher's family back in 1964. This idea mostly came from some of the stories I'd heard Hattie and June telling as I grew up, and I wanted to write something accurate about the South—something that might work against my classmates' stereotypes of "all Southerners"—and something that would honor my memories of Hattie and June. But when my classmates read the material, all hell broke loose. Juanita got all riled up and demanded to know why I would dare broach such a topic.

"You're not black. You don't have any right to write about black people. It shouldn't be allowed."

"Does that mean no black writers should be allowed to write about white people? Or that none of the guys in this class should be allowed to write about women?"

She didn't have an answer to that. And, I guess, neither did I.

After that, folks started gossiping even more about me. Instead of just "the hick," I soon became known as "the racist." I'll admit: This hurt my feelings—a lot. It also made me wonder if NYU was any less passive-aggressive and hypocritical than Wellingham.

At Wellingham, folks called me "bad" because they thought I was too liberal. But now, at NYU, folks called me "racist" because they thought I wasn't liberal enough. It was all very confusing and frustrating, and yet somehow familiar—like I was reliving my freshman year at Brown all over again. It seemed, for all my culture shock and all the surface-level differences between North, South, East and West, that everywhere I'd traveled was actually exactly the same little town with the same small-minded gossip and the same knee-jerk reactions to anyone who was in the slightest bit different or unfamiliar. As accepting of diversity as NYU claimed to be, it sure seemed that my classmates hadn't gotten the memo. Or maybe they only accepted certain kinds of diversity—not including Rebel Debs.

At least in high school, if folks hadn't liked me, they'd be kind enough to keep it to themselves and smile anyways. They wouldn't openly mock me in class or snicker loud enough for me to overhear. The only girls who did that, like Diane, were well-known bullies. Certainly not the majority of the pack.

And so, by second semester, it started to feel like all the rumors I'd heard about open, in-your-face, brutally honest New Yorkers were half fact and half fiction. While folks here certainly were rougher, they weren't necessarily acting for honesty's sake, but for their own self-preservation. And so, through those first few playwriting classes, I finally learned another important post-Wellingham lesson:

♡ The only real difference between North and South is the weather.

I was quickly learning that, as rebellious a Debutante as I'd been growing up, I didn't seem to fit in at NYU any better than at Wellingham. And so, that first year at NYU's Department of Dramatic Writing was just like suffering through high school all over again. Or, worse, like entering that room full of KAT House sorority girls back at Brown, who took one look at me then snubbed their noses at the unwanted shiksa.

Every day at NYU, I put up with my classmates' gossiping in the halls and snickering during class, and let them go on believing their stereotypes about "all Southerners." What else could I do? And after all, I couldn't blame them for misunderstanding me. I was the first Rebel Debutante they'd ever seen, and so I didn't exactly fit in. I wasn't gay or atheist or poly-amorous (which just sounds like a fancy word for loose). I didn't try to dig up dirt about my classmates or Google them after class so I could spread gossip. I also didn't openly criticize straight people, Christians, the federal government, the war in Iraq, or most of all, George W. Bush—all of which they expected me to make fun of just like any "real artist" would. But I just didn't think all that was necessary. Spending time making up rumors, competing for teachers' attention and getting all riled up and jealous over nothing seemed like a waste of my time. And, quite frankly, I didn't have any. I was too busy tutoring, interning, writing and trying to survive in New York.

On top of everything, I was still dead broke. I'd been given a scholarship that paid for my tuition—you know Granny Blanche wasn't about to fund my traitorous trip above the Mason-Dixon—but provided nothing for my basic survival. I still had to find some way to pay for housing, food and subway cards to get back and forth from home to classes. So, to stave off starvation, Scarlett went looking for a job.

First, I went back to my tried-and-true dark side: temp agencies.

Marla at Legal Personnel services thought I'd make a perfect paralegal. But when she found out I could only work third shift, I became perfectly unemployable. Then, I tried pounding the pavement for waitressing gigs, which taught me even more Rebel Deb lessons:

♡ You'll never make a better purchase than a pair of comfortable shoes.

♡ Everything you buy will cost approximately three to four times more than it's worth. I first confirmed this at Katz's Deli, where about four ounces of pastrami on rye with a little side of mustard will run you about fifteen dollars.

♡ Even a fella you can't stand might give you really good advice.

♡ Everywhere's a small town if you live there long enough.

♡ Always be suspicious of a salesman who's wearing nicer clothes than his customer.

And, finally . . .

♡ Riding the subway will make you miss sitting in traffic.

I figured this out after a few months on the B/Q commute to NYU, then again traveling to my first interview at As the World Turns. I was applying as an intern in the writing department. Only once I landed the job, I now had an even longer commute, and now up to four times each day: once in the morning from my apartment in Midwood to NYU, then again in the afternoon between classes to the ATWT studios, again in the evening from ATWT back to NYU for evening classes, and then finally back home each night.

It took over forty minutes each way, but I had to do it. My internship was only a semester long. Plus, this was my shot at working on a real, honest-to-goodness TV show! And though they only paid me a few bucks per hour, at least it was something—enough to survive the rest of my first year at NYU.

*A*s the World Turns was a funny place.

First, there were the writers. There were usually about ten to twelve of them and they were separated into two camps: breakdown and script.

The breakdown writers were responsible for outlining the plotline of the show. Every Tuesday, Lincoln Town Cars would pick all of them up from wherever they lived and bring them to Midwood. Then they'd gather together around the big table in the lounge, where I usually watched SOAPnet, and order big feasts of food.

Once that arrived, they'd start discussing who was going to live, die or come back from the dead that week. I'd pick a spot in the back of the room and try to absorb their process. It was fascinating watching a whole week's worth of episodes being written, shot and aired on TV. And since the show had been on for fifty or more years, it was quite a task keeping up with who'd been married to whom and who'd pushed whom off a cliff. These folks were amazing to watch—not only because they were brilliant but because they really cared about the world they'd created. I was grateful to the head writer, Jean Passanante, and a creative executive, Amy Handlesman—two dear souls and gracious women—for being kind enough to let me stay.

They usually planned five episodes, Monday through Friday, about two months in advance. During their Tuesday meetings, each breakdown writer would be assigned a different weekday. So, for example, once the meeting ended and the Town Car dropped her off at home, Ms. Monday was responsible for writing a twenty-plus-page outline for that day's episode and delivering it back to Jean and the executive producer. Once approved, the interns—that's me!—would then e-mail each outline to the scriptwriter assigned to Monday's episode.

I never met any of the scriptwriters face-to-face. This was mostly because they never came into the studio. A lot of them didn't even live in New York. Their job was to take their day's outline and turn it into an eighty-plus–page script full of dialogue. The basic point of all this was to connect all the plot points to match what the break-down writers had intended their audience to see. But there was a good amount of room for each scriptwriter to be as funny or romantic or serious as she wanted, and to make each episode her own. To me, this sounded like the best job in the whole wide world.

Think about it: You get to sit at home making up funny stories to tell folks at parties, only the party's aired on national television every afternoon at two p.m. Not even Sissy Pickins, beer pong champion of all Alamance County, could say that many people watched her shake her stuff.

Second, we were out in the middle of *nowhere*. The neighborhoods around the studio were home to many Hasidic synagogues, schools and temples. The people there were quiet and neighborly and didn't leave Midwood too often. That meant a lot of them had never seen a Rebel Deb before.

Then again, I hadn't seen too many of them, either.

The only ultra-Orthodox Jewish girl I knew was an Episcopalian now. She converted when she got married and opened a Christian bookstore in Yanceyville, Louisiana. Then she went on some kind of missionary trip to the jungles of Peru and was never heard from again. That meant I had nobody to call whenever I had questions about Judaism.

The first time I walked into the studio, heads turned. Like I said, not too many blue-eyed, blond-headed, big-butted Rebel Debs around here.

If I were really paying attention at *As the World Turns*, I would've remembered to be careful. It's pretty much a rule of thumb for daytime soaps: Whenever a vulnerable outsider moves into town, you know she's headed for trouble.

One morning, for example, about halfway through my internship, I had to mail a big package. So, I took a moment away from my usual duties—getting coffee, making copies and watching SOAPnet—to look up the nearest post office. As it turned out, the dern thing was an entire mile away.

Ugh . . . exercise.

Not one to get my underdrawers in a bunch over nothing, I headed down Avenue M toward Coney Island Avenue. Slowly but surely, a few Jewish men in tall, black hats started popping their heads out of windows. Their wives and daughters soon stuck their heads out, too. They were all blatantly staring at me as I made my way down the street. I tried to ignore it, hugged my package tight and kept moving.

By the time I arrived at the post office, my stomach was growling like a tomcat in heat. The trip had taken much longer than expected, and now my belly was screaming "Feed me!"

I dropped my package in the mail and went outside looking for food. That's when I spotted the pizza parlor just a few blocks away. Cute place, family atmosphere, and when I stepped inside, wide-eyed children's faces peered up at me, still munching on their slices of pizza. The man behind the counter smiled warmly at me. Finally, I thought, I'm a person and not an outsider!

Only a true idiot could mess up this next part. But, in true Rebel Deb style, I opened my big mouth and unloaded my small brain.

"Got any pepperoni?"

Apparently, my time with Ms. Ross had taught me nothing.

The man behind the counter blinked, stuck in his tracks. He looked shocked and not exactly sure what to say next.

Slowly, his smile faded . . . then his whole face dropped, and he muttered . . .

"We don't carry any pork products, actually."

He proceeded to stand there, motionless, staring at me like I'd just pointed a gun at his chest and pulled the trigger. I didn't blame him, that's for sure. I'd completely insulted his entire culture without any intention of doing so.

I didn't know how to respond, either. I just stood there feeling like a complete and utter tail-licker, as Uncle Stu used to call folks who stuck their noses where noses shouldn't go.

Once I got my mouth working, I ordered a plain slice and left quickly.

On my way out, an old woman in all black with a shawl over her head spit at me to erase the *kinna hurra* I'd put on the pizza.

Unfortunately, by the next day, my luck hadn't gotten any better.

I was watching *Beverly Hills, 90210* on SOAPnet in the writer's room as usual. This was an especially juicy rerun. Just when Brenda was about to confront Luke for cheating with her best friend, Kelly, one of the other interns rushes in and disrupts my fun. He tells me there's some big issue downstairs and he needs to run out for a disposable camera—*stat*. But who's going to grab lunch?

At that, my stomach starts growling again. I hadn't eaten break-fast and, somehow, I'd already forgotten yesterday's pizza curse.

"Honey," I say sweetly, "why don't I go grab us some lunch instead?"

Oh, that I had never spoken!

"Sure," he replies. "Good idea!" And then he hands me some cash for sandwiches from the local deli.

That's another thing people don't tell you about the city: choose your deli carefully.

Almost all of New York is covered with them. They sell every-thing from pastrami-on-rye sandwiches to Scotch tape. They're real expensive but handy in a pinch.

He gives me his order: whitefish on a bagel. For me: pastrami on rye.

I took the cash and sauntered on down to wee ol' deli to order our grub. This time, I was careful. I took a look around for any immediate warning signs. I checked the corners for little old ladies who might hock a loogie my way if I said the wrong thing.

Coast was clear, so I paid for the sandwiches and headed out the door. Twenty minutes later, I'd finished a quick, working lunch.

There was only one tiny hiccup . . . my head was hurting.

Half an hour later, my forehead was pounding and I was seriously nauseous. I headed home early, and by the time I arrived, I was sweaty and exhausted. So, I lay down for a nap and drifted off to sleep. A little catnap would cure everything, right?

Wrong.

An hour into napping, I awoke with a jolt. I was sweating. My heart was racing. My eyes couldn't focus and, when I tried to get up, I stumbled around like a drunken sailor. I staggered toward the bathroom, where I tried running a hot bath to relax . . . and promptly puked what looked like my *entire* intestinal system into the toilet. . . .

All because I'd bought a sandwich from this *evil* Midwood deli.

My mind started racing. . . .

Maybe the pizza parlor and the deli are in cahoots! You can't kill somebody just because she asked for pepperoni . . . can you?

I proceeded to "worship the porcelain goddess," as Alma would say, for the next *five hours.* I felt like I was in labor. Every thirty to forty-five minutes I would literally give oral birth to a huge pastrami-on-rye baby. My abs got a workout that left me breathless. I finally passed out and slept for hours while my body recuperated.

Once I awoke, I had yet another problem: My place was slowly being overrun by bedbugs. New York rodents are aggressive about getting into your underdrawers. And unless you live in some fancy-pants loft on Park Avenue, prepare to live with them—and their bug friends. I awoke from my food-poisoned stupor, looked in the mirror and found red bites all over my arms and legs. Even the back of my neck was swollen, itchy and eaten up.

Don't get me wrong, I expected New York would be a rough place. One day, when I was walking a friend's dog through Central Park, a guy came up to me and had the balls to ask, "I didn't think women could do anything unsupervised?" That downright boiled my Rebel Deb blood. I turned on my heel and told him, "I can kick your ass unsupervised." After that, he ran away, and I went back to my walk, grateful for Alma's long-ago influence that was now helping me adjust to such a rude, rough city. Another time, I saw a homeless lady curtsy on a bench and do what the folks down at Farmers Market dance normally take care of behind a haystack or the VA Truck Stop. But through it all, I couldn't have anticipated how many of the rumors

I'd heard about "the City" would turn out to be true—especially the ones about creepy-crawly bugs stealing into your bed at night and turning your mattress into an anthill.

Thank goodness I was still a confirmed Rebel Debutante and not your typical good girl from the South. Good girls studied elementary education, taught vacation Bible school, watched old Westerns where Eastwood (aka the Outlaw Josey Wales) got chased around by the redlegs and wore secondhand Winnie-the-Pooh sweatshirts on first dates. They sure as sugar didn't go all the way up to New York to wake up with their whole bodies covered in mite bites. I was definitely, one hundred percent *not* a good girl—and that's the only reason I was tough enough to survive the rest of that first year in New York.

When my semester ended, so did my internship at ATWT. By now, I'd decided enough was enough. I'd spent my whole first year of grad school riding the subway back and forth from Brooklyn to NYU, just so I could go to classes with folks who laughed at my Southern accent and called me names behind my back. This was worse than cheerleading tryouts! Plus, I was still being occasionally hassled by Merv—"little Napoleon," as I now called him—who, despite my Rebel Deb outburst over the dead mouse in my bedroom, still occasionally told me to "go back to the big house, Scarlett."

So, I did . . . in a manner of speaking. I went out searching for a new job and a newer, bigger and hopefully better place to live. Like Scarlett, this Rebel Deb was gonna make sure she never went hungry again.

My first appointment was with a local broker in Midwood, though he claimed to have apartments in much nicer neighborhoods. Anything, I told him, was better than bedbugs. Walking to his office, I was bright-eyed and bushy-tailed that first day . . . until I saw the sign:

KING DAVID REALTY, it read, in broken, rusted letters. The dilapidated building behind it looked like a shanty straight out of the Great Depression. I questioned whether I should even go inside.

It kinda reminded me of Neely Ray Privat, the only male beautician in town. Momma refused to let me visit Neely Ray because his sideburns were too short. "He doesn't bother to keep his *own* hair looking nice, Anna Lee. How's he supposed to treat *yours?*"

I must admit, Momma had a point. This broker didn't seem capable of finding himself a decent place, so what was I expecting him to do for me? Still, I'd woken up that morning and dragged myself out of bed—bugs and all—to find a decent place. And I was determined to get it. I took one step inside when two Hasidic Jewish men immediately pulled me into the center of the room. The older of the two had huge goiters on his neck, and his teeth looked rotten and yellowed. He leaned close to my face and started rattling off questions.

What's your price range? Do you have the funds available to sign a lease today? How's your credit? What is your annual income? Do you need a cosigner? How do you feel about pesticides?

Their questions went on and on. I tried to answer—I had no choice. I was sick of listening to gunshots all night long and waking up every morning covered in big, red sores. I felt like a leper. There were so many I'd started wearing long pants and turtlenecks to hide them.

After the interrogation, we all piled into a sweat-stained 1976 minivan that smelled like a pair of Russell hunting boots. The older guy got behind the wheel and took off for Lorimer Street, deep in the heart of Bed-Stuy, Brooklyn: one of the roughest neighborhoods in town.

Anna Fields

Bed-Stuy was off the G train, which is one subway in New York I wanted to avoid. The G is constantly late and runs through neighborhoods where folks carry switchblades in case they lose a bet. When I got out of the van, the older broker led me up two flights of stairs to a tiny door covered by a huge sign:

"Warning: Pit Bull with AIDS Inside. Beware."

He unlocked the door with a *creeeaaakkkk* and we stepped inside . . .

A dirty old shoe box.

Looking at this new apartment, I suddenly understood why New Yorkers kept themselves so skinny. It was about four hundred square feet—just about the size of my Granny Blanche's laundry room back home—and smelled exactly like the lint trap after Hattie emptied the dryer. Not everything, as it turned out, was better than bedbugs.

I took a few steps further into the room, when my coat got caught on a closet door. As if on cue, an enormous pile of dirty dishes, laundry, bicycle equipment and baby food spilled onto the floor. After it, a huge washer/dryer combo then rolled unceremoniously out into the middle of the room with its lids popping open like some freaky jack-in-the-box.

When I pointed out to the broker that his ad had described a "palatial" apartment with "indoor washing equipment," he responded:

"Yes! Palatial, right? Like palace! It is *heaven*, no?"

Which forced me to give him the same face Momma always made each time I'd quit another after-school activity. Something between "Bless your heart" and "You've gotta be shitting me, right?" By his reaction, I could tell he got the point. Scarlett wasn't about to be fooled into thinking this trash was anybody's treasure. And since I apparently wasn't the dumb, inbred yokel he'd expected, willing to hand over my life's savings for a hole in a wall, he quickly snorted, turned on his heel and led me out of the place. Outside, we jumped back into his minivan and about two minutes later, he was dumping me about a block from his office with a quick, "Call me when you change your mind!"

This kind of apartment-hunting went on for months, by which point I'd learned that New York real estate was intended for two groups only: wealthy tycoons and suckers. By now, I was almost ready to give up and go home. Things weren't going any better at NYU, I was still dead broke and, as I hadn't yet escaped the bedbugs, itchy as a leper. I realized that if I didn't make some serious dough—FAST— I'd never be able to afford to move out of Midwood. And that meant living in the mite farm forever.

And then, as it happened, Scarlett's luck suddenly changed.

As I was stepping off the B/Q train and heading to class, something caught my eye—a copy of the *Village Voice*. It was new, marked "Free," and on page 3, I spotted an old-fashioned "Want Ads" section, just like the kind folks back home used to find a job or a home—or both. Up to now, I'd considered going back to Carolina and learning to use that hammer when, about halfway down page 3, I came across a "Tutor Wanted" ad.

It was short and deceptively sweet:

> Seeking young, responsible tutor for my 14-year-old daughter. She needs help with English, Math, essay-writing and French. If this sounds like you, please send a résumé and brief description of your experience to . . .

Plus, it listed a name and a number, so I took a chance and dialed. The woman who picked up had the heaviest Long Island accent I've ever heard. Listening to her, I started to wonder whether her nose got achy with all that air blasting straight through it. She asked me a few questions—my name, where I was from—but just like Beth Paragon back in Providence, once she heard my first "ya'll," she was hooked. She asked me to come in for an interview—immediately!—and I agreed. I suppose I should've taken longer to think it over, but the hunger pains and bug bites screamed—Go on! *Take a chance! How hard could a teaching job be?*

And besides, she sounded so nice on the phone.

*F*ill Zarin's high-rise on 90th Street and First Avenue was lavishly decorated. The floors were a mix of hardwoods and marble and covered in fur rugs and pricey antique furniture. Scarlett had definitely reached the Big House this time. I'm not sure how they acted before or after I worked for them, but this is what I saw and heard.

Ally was Jill's only daughter from her first marriage. It seemed to me that Jill gave her daughter free rein to act however she wanted, whenever she wanted, to apparently whomever she wanted.

Ally's room was a teenage girl's dream. Her bed was covered in stuffed animals, furry pink pillows and purple sateen bedding. Floor-to-ceiling windows gave her a perfect view of the city, and almost every inch of her walls was decorated with pictures of fashion models. Not exactly Jill's choice marble and hardwoods, but then again, what fourteen-year-old girl shares her fortysomething Momma's taste?

When I came by to interview, Jill showed me around the house.

Ally's and Jill's rooms were both littered with shoes. All together, they probably had about two hundred pairs. The kitchen was modern and looked like something from *Top Chef*, but nobody seemed to like cooking.

"That's what Matilda's for," Jill said.

When we sat down to talk about Ally's tutoring, Jill's breasts kept finding ways to peep out of her clothes. I tried not to stare at them while she told me about how involved she wanted to be in Ally's education. She then rattled off the list of subjects Ally needed help with—everything from French to algebra. She didn't stop until she heard the words "Brown University" come out of my mouth.

This brought me to my next Rebel Deb lesson:

♡ Money doesn't buy class.

That's another thing folks don't tell you about the city: Women who marry into money always seem to think they've also married into class. And, for some reason, their kids usually fall into one of two categories: the ones who loaf around the house, half doing their homework and never displaying even the tiniest bit of ambition or work ethic, or the ones who are desperate to prove themselves worthy of their family's money and their parents' approval, and fly around the world, trying to save everyone in it, all to quell their rich-kid guilt. Worst of all, their wealthy housewife mothers all seem to think they buy their kids into joining the second group. And so they go about hiring a tutor with an Ivy League degree, because—voilà!—that will somehow save their kids from becoming indigent, upper-class fops.

That being said, Jill hired me immediately. Whether Ally really needed a tutor, or whether Jill just needed a babysitter, remained to be seen. But, either way, Jill wanted to make sure I'd stay for a while. This was mostly because Matilda, their current housekeeper and babysitter, was soon retiring.

After two weeks in that house, I could see why.

Everything started out fine, if a little awkward. Jill's second husband, Bobby—an aging furniture salesman with grown children of his own—apparently owned the place and stayed as far away as possible. From what I could tell, he only seemed to appear at dinnertime or whenever Jill needed money.

The situation between Bobby and Ally was uncomfortable at best. I had the impression from the beginning that Ally didn't especially like her step-Daddy, and vice versa. At home, Ally mostly seemed to interact with her mom, me, and Matilda. I once heard her ask Matilda to rearrange her entire sweater collection. I don't know about ya'll, but at fourteen I could rearrange my own sweaters. I wondered how such a little girl could be so spoiled.

Then Jill showed me the photos of Ally's Bat Mitzvah. They looked like the cover of *Rolling Stone*. Any moment I was expecting to find Annie Leibovitz's signature on the corner of Ally's portrait. Jill spent $30,000 on the thing. Or, should I say, Bobby did.

I probably would've hid in the bedroom, too.

In the beginning it was a pretty good deal. Jill was generous to me. She introduced me to her friends—or, at least, to the ones she wanted to impress with her new Ivy League tutor. She complimented me and we struck a bargain: I would tutor Ally for six hours each week—in return, Jill would pay me forty dollars an hour. It wasn't a fortune by any means, but it was enough to eat on. She even gifted me with one of her many pairs of high-heeled shoes—already used, of course. They were silver high heels that, just like all those stilettos galloping the sidewalks outside the Empire State Building, looked like they'd come straight out of Michelle Pfeiffer's closet in *Married to the Mob*. Plus, Jill said they gave her blisters. Then, she went so far as to send an article I'd written to Haley Binn, the wife of some big-shot magazine owner. Jill said Haley and her husband, Jason, pretty much owned everything in print. Then, she went on to show me pictures of their house in the Hamptons. I was "invited there anytime," she insisted. Turning each photo, she shook the massive diamond ring on her hand, which she claimed was worth more than most folks earn in a lifetime.

"Anything bad happens, you take this thing to South America and buy yourself a house," she said.

The way she was trying to impress me with all her houses and jewels and rich friends, you'd think she was making it all up.

Anywho, Haley never responded to my article—big surprise. Still, I was grateful for an employer kind enough to cast some of her socialite glow onto a poor Rebel Deb. . . . And then, like in any good story, disaster struck.

Jill started getting greedy with my time. She started demanding more and more hours each week, and every time she went into her bedroom with Bobby to ask him for money to pay me, I thought he resented paying for his new stepdaughter's education. As I'd soon learn, wealthy New Yorkers didn't really care whether you've actually learned anything in college. Instead, I got the feeling Jill was primarily concerned with whether I would become a future somebody she could brag about. I suspected she was secretly hoping that I'd stored away a secret degree in Economics and was just tutoring Ally before moving on to a consulting job at Goldman Sachs with a six-figure salary. That way, she could brag about how she once had a future so-and-so for a servant. And, as I was slowly coming to realize, she was a bit of what my Granny Blanche would call an "Indian giver." She'd make a big gesture, offer me something she knew I'd want, something that would make her seem the beneficent employer, and then once I took it—*snap!*—the trap was sprung. Because once I'd taken the bait, she could use her "generous" gift to force me into tutoring Ally more and more often, later and later into the night, and even asking me to leave class early so I could help Ally struggle through even a single-paragraph essay. Plus, Jill would constantly brag to me about being an involved mother . . . and yet, she often seemed to be away—forever going out with her socialite friends or flying off to Miami with Bobby on yet another vacation.

Then again, if I was married to a wealthy business owner like Bobby Zarin, I'd probably spend his money like water, too. Bobby had already been married a couple times and already raised his own kids, and now he wanted to indulge himself and his much younger wife . . . up to a point, of course. Like many of her friends, Jill was on an allowance. And that meant that despite being pretentious, uptight and fake, she was—most of all—*cheap*. When she saw how broke I was all the time, as if I didn't have enough on my plate, Jill suggested I work for her friend, Ramona, tutoring her daughter in addition to Ally. When Ramona called me, however, she was even more aggressive and pushy and, though she was as loaded as Jill, claimed she couldn't afford my prices and tried to haggle me into settling for minimum wage.

These New York housewives' whole preoccupation with money and status wasn't any different from that of all the rich Southern ladies I'd known back home—only, like most demanding, spoiled rich folks, Ramona's and Jill's entitled attitudes were way more exaggerated. After I refused Ramona's prices and she abruptly hung up, I felt lucky to have just one housewife on my hands.

Back home, rich people immediately respected you because of your past—your family lineage, religion, ladylike behavior and/or military service. In New York, rich people respected you for your present—for landing that corner-office, nine-to-five job that allowed you to invest, buy a brownstone, travel to France three months out of the year and fill your closet with your own uncomfortable silver high heels, which you'd eventually give away to your own poor Ivy League tutor.

In New York, these kinds of people were either absentee parents, who hired nannies to raise their kids, or workaholics who had none and bought pets to compensate. And there was an entire industry of doggie day cares to cater to their crazy, impulsive needs.

Businesses like Happy Paws in the East Village provided pick-up and delivery service for doggie day care, where they'd drive up to your door, pick up your pet and, after six to eight hours, deliver him like a pizza straight back to your door at night. That way, you could be an absentee pet-parent, too. Some guilt-ridden "parents" would spend thousands of dollars on facial scrubs, grooming, baths, massages and even acupuncture for their pets. They'd even rent out the whole place for doggie weddings and Valentine's Day dances, all out of guilt for working ninety-hour weeks and not spending any actual time with their pets. And if they don't send their pets to places like Happy Paws, they'll often hire doggie nannies to spend time with the pooch in its owner's absence. Everyone and everything is a potential baby- or dog-sitter to these kinds of people—and, as opposed to the South, New Yorkers spend money like water on these kinds of luxuries. Even the wealthiest Southern Debutante families will throw a ball around with their family dog in the backyard—but, in New York, even this kind of quality time can be bought and sold.

That being said, the Zarins were as complicated as my job was simple: Show up, teach Ally some basic skills and go home. Getting her to string a sentence together, let alone write a school essay, took hours at a time. Like Momma always said, "You can't pump blood from a turnip." Trying to get Ally to comprehend even basic writing skills seemed just as hard.

What's worse, though I wasn't starving, I still couldn't afford to move out of Midwood and away from the mites. And since Jill lived all the way on the Upper East Side, traveling from my place to NYU for classes, then to her place for Ally's tutoring, then back home all the way to Brooklyn was grueling. Another forty extra minutes on the subway, one way. I might as well have been going all the way to ATWT again.

All of it added up to what felt like my whole life spent underground. After only a couple weeks of tutoring Ally, I was still broke, even more exhausted and on the point of a nervous breakdown. I just couldn't take it anymore. This supposed dream job was turning into a soul-sucking nightmare . . . and then, wonder of wonders, Jill noticed. She asked why I looked so tired all the time, and God help me, I told her.

"I'm spending my whole life riding the subway. I'm covered in bug bites. My classmates hate me and I can't do this anymore."

I thought she'd take pity and maybe give me a raise. I thought maybe she'd remember back when she was a poor, struggling twentysomething and give me a break. . . .

But oh, no. She was way too smart for that.

Oh, if only I'd already learned all my lessons and kept my mouth shut like I'd been taught back at Wellingham. If only I'd stayed in Brooklyn where I belonged!

But how could I have known that, once I'd spilled my guts, Jill would come up with a better solution (for her, at least)? How could I have known she'd say those six magic words and seal my doom. . . .

"Why don't you just move in?"

The next day, Scarlett moved into the Big House.

Except by "Big House," I mean a two-bedroom apartment shared with Joe, Jill's immigrant handyman-slash-driver.

Joe was a short, stocky man in his thirties who sported the kind of sparse mustache that looked less like facial hair and more like a dirty upper lip. He'd immigrated to the United States several years before—supposedly to work for Bobby Zarin—and never stopped complaining about Jill.

Since he basically did everything for Bobby, he probably had a right to. When Bobby first "hired" Joe, he'd been given the same offer: free labor in exchange for a free place to live. And to someone as new to New York as me, I'm sure Joe jumped at the chance. So, he went to work in Zarin Fabrics, Bobby's family business. The store was just a few blocks down from the two-bedroom apartment we now shared, and Joe literally spent twelve hours there every single day. He picked up upholstery, moved carpets, fixed leaks in the plumbing and even drove a van all the way to Brooklyn to pick up my things and bring them to the Lower East Side of Manhattan.

At first, I thought Joe was just really hardworking. Then I realized Jill was basically treating him the same as me—like her personal, on-call slave.

When Bobby and Jill married, Joe went from dealing with a quiet, semi-elderly man who needed help around his store, to putting up with the elderly man's new wife, a housewife who'd hit the jackpot marrying an older, wealthy man, and who'd decided Joe should be so *grateful* to even be in America that he should be automatically willing to work whenever, wherever and however she wanted.

Meanwhile, of course, Joe's complaining to me about his Boss's "crazy wife" night and day. And as much as I hate to say it—misery loves company. Hearing I wasn't the only one feeling Jill's wrath was, sad to say, comforting.

Don't get me wrong, it was nerve-wracking at first, living with a complete—and *male*—stranger, but Jill insisted. Once I complained about the lengthy commute from Brooklyn, she'd offered me a bargain: six hours of tutoring every week for Ally in exchange for a free place to stay living with Joe in the apartment Bobby owned on the Lower East Side. The place was situated just a few blocks north of the fish market in Chinatown and across the street from one of the noisiest clubs known to man.

Plus, I would have to move in immediately, and buy my own furniture for the near-empty place. Since all Joe owned was a few sticks of his own bedroom furniture, an old TV set and a broken-down armchair, this was gonna cost a bundle. Plus, since Jill was now no longer paying me a dime out of the allowance Bobby gave her, I would have to find some way to buy food and subway tickets to get back and forth from home to Jill's high-rise to tutor Ally three afternoons a week. In the end, though, I didn't have a choice. I was stuck between a rock and a hard place: Since I couldn't afford the moving costs to Manhattan and Joe couldn't fit all my old stuff in his van, I could either spend everything I'd saved working for Jill so far buying new furniture and having it delivered, or refuse Jill's "generous" offer and be fired on the spot.

What would a Rebel Deb do? In the end, between living with Merv in Midwood or Joe in Manhattan, I chose the lesser of two evils. I would keep my job and move to the Lower East Side. Ulti-mately, needing a job and a way out of my frozen, bug-infested apart-ment outweighed my suspicions about Jill and Ally.

When I first moved in, I was guarded around Joe. He seemed nice, but this Rebel Deb wasn't stupid—he was still a man. I installed a dead bolt on my door right away and kept to myself most of the time. After a few weeks of living together, though, I started to loosen up. Joe's complaining about Jill got more and more understandable, once I saw him leaving for the store at around eight a.m. and coming home past eleven p.m. Eventually, he started telling me—in English so broken that it was like forming words out of alphabet soup—about his family back home. He even went down to the furniture store with me and helped me haggle the Chinatown merchants for a better deal. In return, I helped him with his English. If I was tutoring someone as spoiled as Ally, why couldn't I also help out someone as deserving as Joe?

And so, as it happened, I'd found my first real friend in New York. Just like Alma back in her day, Joe was considered an outsider—and treated as a lesser-than by both Jill and Ally, who demanded he do pretty much anything they wanted at the drop of a hat. All because they were rich and he was poor.

Still, Joe and I tried to make the best of things and turn our lem-ons to lemonade, as my Granny Ruth would say.

He kept his mouth shut about Bobby's crazy new wife—in front of her and the rest of the family, of course. I did my best to pump every ounce of intellectual blood out of Ally. After morning classes, I spent the rest of every Monday through Thursday in Ally's room teaching her how to write. Thursday through Sunday I spent either in the library studying for my NYU classes, or buying earplugs so I could sleep through all the House music bumping and grinding through my bedroom walls all night. Not that I really needed them. I was so dead exhausted from dealing with my classmates' snickers, then riding the subway back and forth to Jill's house, then forcing Ally to learn basic grammar, then doing my own homework that I slept like the dead.

But, like I said, I needed to keep my new home and job—I couldn't survive or graduate from NYU without them, in fact—and so I couldn't quit no matter how much I wanted to.

I was stuck putting up with it all.

It was either this or the bugs—or, worst of all, giving up and going home to all my "I told ya so" relatives, who all hated the North and wouldn't have moved there for all King Solomon's gold.

And after all, I rationalized, I felt sorry for Ally. Beyond all the issues with her friends and teachers, she had a boatload of emotional holes left over from early childhood to fill.

The sour icing on this sad cake was Ginger, the Zarin family dog.

Ginger was the kind of tiny, yapping Chihuahua old ladies keep around the house. Even after several months on the job, Ginger still didn't recognize me whenever I came through the door. She'd bark and howl and bite my toes till they bled. So, every day, as soon as I got inside, I'd have to run to Ally's bedroom and slam the door in the toe-monster's face—and if I ever left Ally's room to get some water or go to the bathroom, there Ginger would be: ready to chomp my feet with her tiny doggie teeth of death.

All this tutoring-slash-slavery went on for months, and I was so exhausted juggling Jill's ever-changing demands that I could barely finish my own homework, let alone Ally's. One week, I'd work the six hours we'd agreed upon; then Jill would call to complain about how much Ally needed my "help," so for the next two I'd be there every night till eleven. And that didn't include the travel time from the Lower East Side to the Upper East Side—far less than it had been coming from Brooklyn, but there was only one bus line that went straight from my door to Jill's, no subway lines came close. And since buses in Manhattan take twice as long as the subway, I still spent a good forty minutes to an hour—one way—just to get to work each day. Once I was home, I'd call my Momma, as most good Southern girls are apt to. And every night, she'd worry about the strain in my voice. By December, she'd gotten so worried that she decided to do what few Southern Mommas would—travel all the way up to NYC for a visit.

When I told her about Momma's coming, Jill was reluctant, but I finally talked her into giving me a few days off. When I picked Momma up at LaGuardia Airport, I could see the same telltale sign of Southern culture shock in her eyes: nervous glances at all the dirty-looking people wearing head-to-toe black. But even sweaty from too many layers of wool underclothes and exhausted from her hour-long flight, we both knew I looked way worse. Her jet lag was nothing compared to the bags under my eyes.

Naturally, as soon as we got back to my place with Joe, Momma did a double take. What was I doing, living with a grown man? She was shocked, but after meeting him, she calmed down and started to realize that, like a lot of New Yorkers, her little girl was now forced to live in shared, cramped quarters simply to survive in such an expensive city. After calming her nerves, she did what any good mother would and put me straight to bed. Then, she started cooking. Since my refrigerator was absolutely empty except for take-out pizza and Joe's canned papaya and coconut juice, this proved difficult.

In New York, Momma soon found out, you can't just go grocery shopping. And especially not in my neighborhood. On the Lower East Side, you had to huff it all the way to Whole Foods on Houston Street. There, you could spend fifty bucks on a couple boxes of cereal and a gallon of milk, so you had to make your purchases carefully. And then, since Momma was used to the South where folks drive everywhere they go, she had to find some way to get all her bags back to my apartment and up the stairs all by herself.

Poor thing, by the time she got done shopping, Momma was even sweatier than when she stepped off the plane. Nice Southern ladies weren't accustomed to doing this much legwork, and I was grateful to have the kind of Momma who'd put all that away and roll up her sleeves to help her baby girl. Then again, she'd always been the kind of mother to put me first—staying home with me as a child before I went to Wellingham, reading me books and helping me with my homework through my childhood.

Before I knew it, Momma had the crockpot going, filled up with the usual fixin's and trimmin's—no ifs, ands or buts. For those of you who may not be from the proud South, there are several basic Southern get-together-for-baby-Jesus'-sake foods. Gather and mix the following for any small-town Carolina holiday:

Butter beans

Sweet potatoes

Beef stew *(mixed in with cream of mushroom soup and roasted in a crockpot for approximately six hours)*

Black-eyed peas

Candied ham

Chicken pie

Boiled corn cobs

String beans

Cornbread *(not that sweet, yellow stuff that comes in a blue-and-white-box. No. I'm referring to flat, salty, fried corn cakes)*

Whole milk

Butter

Barbecued, sliced pork loin

Fried okra

Fried squash / Squash casserole

Sliced tomatoes *(with salt to taste)*

. . . and, last but not least, for dessert—

Deep-fried cheesecake

This was the kind of pure, down-home cuisine I grew up with. The food that turned Paula Dean into the next Julia Child and my Momma into one of the best cooks in Burlington.

As if sensing my thoughts, Jill started calling. Ally needed extra help with her upcoming midterm exams *stat*. Jill said she needed me back to work right away—and working overtime this week— to make sure Ally was prepared. When I explained to her that my mother was in town, she threw down her ultimatum: I hadn't worked as many hours as she'd hoped before Ally's exams, and so I needed to make them up. *Now.* Before I could respond, she said a quick good-bye and hung up.

When I explained that I needed to go back to work, Momma was furious—in her own ladylike, mothering way, of course. I was already skinny as a beanpole with raccoon rings for eyes. How dare Jill demand I come back to work in my condition? I was the ghost of the child she'd raised—and now I couldn't even enjoy the Christmas dinner she slaved over? Why was I still working for Jill, anyway, Momma wanted to know. Wasn't NYU aware that one of their students was killing herself, just to graduate?

I have to admit: She had a point. Some of my classmates at NYU were still making my life a living hell, and though the administration knew about it, they essentially ignored it. When I tried to talk to the head of my department about all the snickering and gossip inside and out of classes, he told me to stop complaining and focus on my writing. But by my second year of juggling their emotional abuse, all my homework, plus working for Jill to keep a roof over my head, I started showing up late for classes . . . which made folks gossip even more. Finally, Vince LaRue called me into his office and told me I was "messing up" at NYU. And when I burst into tears—all the pent-up stress and strain flowing out of me and onto his desk—he basically just sat there and told me to stop tutoring Ally. But when I told him I had no choice—that if I gave up my tutoring job, I'd lose my room with Joe, and have to quit school and go home . . . he just told me to "work it out." But when I asked NYU for a job on campus, and even interviewed for a few positions in my department with Vince himself, I was denied. They weren't going to give me a job, so quitting Ally wasn't an option.

After Jill's phone call, I explained all this to Momma. It was either obey Jill's ultimatum or be fired, which meant quitting school and going home. After a whole childhood spent quitting everything I set out to accomplish—first Brownies, then dance classes, and finally even Cotillion—I wasn't about to give up. I was a Rebel Deb now, and like Scarlett, I wasn't about to go hungry.

So, despite Momma's protests, I got my butt back on the bus and, about an hour later, past Ginger the toe-monster straight to Ally's room.

I spent the next two days reviewing history and English till I was about to drop. Anywho, on the second day, my tutoring was interrupted when Jill showed her "special guest"—a producer from

Bravo—into Ally's bedroom during his tour of the house. She was going on and on about her *fabulous* house in the Hamptons—which, of course, he was welcome to visit anytime (yeah, right!) and how much she loved chatting with her *fabulous* Ivy League tutor, Anna, about her *fabulous* daughter's education. Apparently, Bravo was interested in putting her on the TV show, which, she said, she was only mildly interested in doing—"If it works out, it works out," she said. All she really wanted was publicity for Zarin Fabrics. "It'll be good for the store. And who knows what else could happen?"

Finally, at about midnight, Jill gave me twenty dollars and I caught a cab back to the Lower East Side. By then, however, Momma was already half asleep and it was my turn to put her straight into bed. All the food was in Tupperware, stuck in the freezer behind Joe's plantains. I'd missed practically her whole visit, and she was leaving the next morning.

I rode with her in the cab all the way to LaGuardia—hailing one herself was a little too nerve-racking for a delicate lady like Momma. And once she waved good-bye and got on her plane, I almost burst into tears again. It felt like I'd never fit in anywhere again—not back home, not in L.A. and certainly not here in New York.

For the next week, while Ally took her exams, I spent a lot of time in Jill's kitchen with her housekeeper, Matilda. I learned that she was the daughter of a furniture maker from Swale (pronounced "Swa-*lee*"), North Carolina. That name always reminded me of Granny Ruth calling her cats in at night.

Swale was just a stone's throw away from Burlington. Matilda's Daddy, Rector, made the finest coffee tables in the South. Every year, he'd load up his truck and haul them over to market in Kernersville over forty miles away. Before all his business moved to Mexico, Rector made a good enough living to feed his family.

Matilda went on about her family and all sorts of things, but what I especially enjoyed were her stories about New York. Even though Matilda hadn't grown up here, either, she seemed to know everything there was to know. For example, she knew the names and rundowns on all the different cliques in the greater tristate area.

First, you had your consultants.

These were the button-down-shirt types Jill hoped I'd become—or preferably marry—one day. The guys and gals who worked ninety hours a week and snorted their Ritalin to stay awake. They moved in herds and spent hours gelling their hair into faux hawks or spraying themselves down with bottles of cologne shaped like some nekkid torso from the middle of Rodeo Drive.

Consultants went to bars most nights, where they ordered shots and head butted each other for fun. Then they'd hit on chubby girls they'd normally ignore in public.

Next, you had your Goths.

Goths were the folks who walked around town, wearing all black with white face paint. They usually talked about how stupid and pointless life was.

Then, you had your computer geeks.

These were the fellas who shaved their heads to keep their bald spots from showing. They usually traveled in pairs, wearing two-sizes-too-small T-shirts. They'd go to bars, too, just like the consultants, where they'd spend the whole night bragging about playing drums in garage bands before trudging back to their IT jobs the next morning.

Then, you had the "Little Bit Marrieds."

These were the late-twenty to thirtysomething folks who'd been dating the same person for years but just couldn't seem to tie the knot. Each Little Bit Married—LBM—couple usually lived together and they usually shared a cat. The LBM cat was their attempt at co-parenting. They just couldn't help themselves—LBMs could only seem to commit to the creature, but not to the one sharing their bed. Still, LBMs talked about their cat till they were blue in the face. A fun-loving, carefree, yet aggressively hot-tempered creature, the cat had its own furniture—the cat hotel—and preferred to drink from the toilet. Yet the LBM cat would deign to lap casually from water bowls—provided they were well-kept and located next to a small plate of Fancy Feast.

On special occasions, LBMs would show up in single-sex groups. On these nights, LBM gals would rush into Midtown sports bars hootin' and hollerin' and having a grand ol' time. A few apple-tinis later and they'd be crying their eyes out. It was always the same thing. . . .

I'm getting older, but am I getting wiser? When is he ever gonna propose? How old's too old to start having babies?

Other nights, LBM fellas would show up at the same bars. They'd crowd around the TVs to argue over football while secretly agonizing over their shrinking hairlines and widening bellies.

Sometimes, a LBM fella would bring along the same best friend he'd had for years. The friend who he grew up playing video games and rolling neighbors' houses with, but who never seemed to grow up. This friend had never gotten anywhere close to the "Little Bit Married" stage.

Matilda liked to call this type of friend "Mr. Boston."

Yessir, Mr. Boston. A bar-crawling creature of New York, he enjoyed pale ale, hair gel and any reference to "poon-tang." With his uncanny ability to fart, burp and/or vomit on cue, Mr. Boston was a welcome addition to any group of LBM fellas. Although with his slant-eyed, leering grin toward the LBM ladies' bosoms, he wasn't likely to get anywhere with them.

Whenever an LBM fella got cross with his own lady, Mr. Boston was right there with a shoulder ready to lean on. Like any good wingman, he'd be sure to tell Mr. LBM how "bad-ass" and "right on" and "mature, dude!" he was, and how "slutty" and "crazy" Ms. LBM had become to their video-game-playing schedule.

Last but not least on Matilda's list were the Cat People.

Cat People were just like Little Bit Marrieds only they preferred two-dollar PBR beers to apple-tinis, and instead of sharing a cat with their mates, their cats usually were their mates.

Matilda would give me the rundown on all these folks. She had all kinds of helpful advice about living in New York. After our long talk, she'd make fried Spam sandwiches or ambrosia with cottage cheese. Sometimes, she'd even slice tomatoes and fan them out on my plate, just like Momma would do back home. It was comforting. She made me feel like I was a kid again and sitting back behind the lunch counter at Woolworth's.

I was on my way home after our last late-night chat when my cell phone rang. It was Jill. When I picked up, she didn't say anything at first, then finally asked a quick "How ya doing?" before spitting out "You're fired."

She told me that Ally's teachers had just called. Apparently, Ally was getting C's or below in all her classes, even with the exam grades we'd just studied so hard for. When I asked Jill why Ally's grades were so low, she finally told me what I'd been suspecting for weeks but thought she wouldn't believe: Besides the English assignments she'd told me about, Ally hadn't actually done much of her other homework in weeks. Naturally, in Jill's eyes, I was to blame for Ally's grades. She gave me a week to move out, which in Manhattan apartment-hunting time is next to nothing. Otherwise, Jill said, I could start paying her $2,800 a month in rent.

When I hung up, I hardly knew I'd been fired. Maybe this was because I'd been working so hard for so long for, ultimately, so little that I was too dazed to notice. Maybe this was because she'd sounded so nice over the phone. Or maybe, despite my suspicions all along, I'd been so surprised when Jill finally showed her true colors that I hadn't realized I'd just discovered the *real* truth behind at least one housewife of New York.

A few days later, Joe helped me moved the last of my bags and boxes back to Brooklyn. I don't know what I would've done without him, and during our quick good-bye, he told me to remember that none of what happened with Jill was my fault. He told me I was smart and capable and, in as many words as he knew, one of the nicest New Yorkers he'd met.

Which made me wonder, was I a New Yorker now? Was there at least *one* person in this whole city who was thankful for my being here, and wanted me to stay?

I started thinking about the new lessons I'd learned since Wellingham and all the things I now knew about the North—and especially New York. Like how cold it gets in December. Or how, when you move back to Brooklyn, your new apartment will smell like mothballs and chicken stew and sweat. And how there's a catch to all that money you're saving. Nobody tells you that even though your rent includes heat and hot water, you won't be getting much of either. That you'll end up taking steaming baths at friends' houses just to keep warm. Friends who, at twenty-five, are just waiting to take that six-figure job at Goldman Sachs.

Nobody tells you how hard the simplest tasks can be in a city without cars. Carrying more than two bags out of the grocery store and then getting them onto the subway seems daunting. Finding a cab in the rain seems impossible. And then, when you're finally home, nobody tells you how to get those bags all the way up your five-story walkup because that's all most people your age can afford. On the bright side, this means you'll never need StairMaster. When you go back out again, nobody tells you to donate your fancy shoes to Goodwill because walking around the city will ruin them. Nobody tells you to check over your shoulder before you open your door at night.

And they especially don't tell you how, the farther south you go, the more New York is a labyrinth of twisty, winding streets. Nobody tells you to lean forward when you're walking along them after it's snowed because that's the only way to keep from falling. Or how you can get lost in the West Village and wind up in one of a hundred different sex shops with mannequins wearing vegetables where their naughty parts should be. Or how nobody below Houston Street pays his taxes. But when you're at a restaurant on the Lower East Side and the waiter only accepts cash, you'll figure out his scheme mighty quick. Nobody tells you how expensive the food is, whether you've paid cash or not, or that you'll get so hungry sometimes you'll eat leftover crusts from other people's sandwiches.

Right about then, I started to get mighty grateful. For Momma and Joe and Matilda. For Wellingham, and Alma, who first taught me to speak up and stand on my own. For Granny Ruth and all her jean jackets puff-painted with love that made me sweaty and uncomfortable down South, but now kept me from freezing to death up North.

By now, I was in the home stretch of my classes at NYU and doing all kinds of random odd jobs writers are forced into to survive. None of which had much of anything to do with my degree and all of which, somehow, threw me back into the paths of celebrities.

As a "talent scout" for a live show called Comedy Gone Wild, I was supposed to look for talented comics. That meant I had to show up at all kinds of late-night stand-up routines and sit through all the usual folks till somebody really great went onstage. One night, I watched Tracy Morgan do a stand-up routine about how awful white women were and how much he hated his wife, who he said was cheating on him at the time. After the show, he and Marc Maron came up and introduced themselves to me. By the way he shook my hand, I could tell Tracy was more than a little bit angry. When I asked him why, he said only that "information is worth more than gold. Remember that." Whatever that meant, it sounded like very good advice.

Another time, I took a job as a sex advice columnist for an online newspaper. They sent me to interview Dr. Ruth, which I was excited about. She wasn't too excited about me, however. She wasn't even friendly. I naively assumed that, standing at about four foot eleven, she'd be the bubbly, mothering old-lady type.

Oh, no.

I didn't realize that she'd been a freedom fighter for the Israeli army back in her day. So when I asked her what kind of porn she personally enjoyed and she ended the interview right then and there, I was a bit confused. Wasn't she supposed to be an expert in that kind of thing?

Guess not. Or maybe that's just how folks respond to questions in the Israeli army.

After a while, I started to get used to the sticky summers and freezing winters. I dressed in layers to keep warm. I packed my book bag full of everything I could need throughout the day and started to enjoy the crowded streets and subways. I memorized maps of the city so I'd never get lost again. After some trial and error, I found out which delis served safe sandwiches and which ones only accepted cash. I even tried hummus on pita bread instead of Ritz crackers. After six months, I loved the stuff. Couldn't eat a salad without it. Greek salad with hummus had now become one of my newfound New York loves.

One night around dinnertime, on my way to a local Brooklyn deli for one of my newfound loves, I passed by a newly built Starbucks. Having a coffee shop only four blocks away was a blessing in my new neighborhood, but I'll admit: I was still reluctant to go inside. Until I went to Brown, I'd never tried Starbucks. I didn't too much care for that little green and white building with the weird-looking mermaid lady on its side. Until 2006, Schlabach's was still Burlington's only coffee shop and my main source for java, and seeing corporate conglomerates invade my small little hometown made me sad. Starbucks moving in no doubt spelled the end for corner-store coffee shops.

On the bright side, there still weren't any Dunkin' Donuts. The only doughnut I ever tasted growing up was Krispy Kreme, and I hope that never changes. That warm, glazed, powdery goodness just can't be replaced.

Anyway, since this new Starbucks wasn't out of my way and I could already feel the temperature getting colder by the second, I went inside. I bought a regular "tall" coffee—no milk, no foam, no frills—and picked a lounge chair toward the back to nestle into. And eventually, once I'd relaxed my small-town guilt, I found myself people-watching.

Suddenly, a horde of sweet-sixteen-year-olds came tromping across my path on their way to a Cotillion dance. A couple of them sat down nearby, clearly invading my quiet space. They were laughing, cutting up and pushing tables together into a big clique. The girls sat on one side, boys on the other. I looked them over and spotted the telltale signs of all small-town kids, whether Northern or Southern:

For the girls: push-up bras, panty hose with opened-toed sandals, lined lips with no lipstick, blue eye shadow, white eyeliner, Wal-Mart perfume, poufy hair bows, butterfly-shaped necklaces and big carnation wrist corsages because their teenage dates just weren't coordinated enough to work the pin-on ones.

For the boys: pinstripes with cowboy boots, cigar-box rings, Wal-Mart cologne and belt buckles with images of T Boone, their favorite bird dog, holding a fresh trout between his teeth.

They were all headed to the Christmas Cotillion dance at the local country club. Since Granny Blanche was a longtime member of ours back home, I went to several of these myself.

I remember Alma dared me to wear this tiny black dress with slits cut into the back, and the tallest pair of stilettos I'd ever dared to slip into. I spent about two hours getting up the nerve to put everything on, then another hour waiting for Alma to finish curling her hair. Once I was in the dress with my hair shellacked with Aqua Net and my entire body sprayed with enough magnolia perfume to raise the dead, we were off to the party.

I kept my nerves at bay by chewing my Granny Blanche's violet gum the whole night. My date, as I remember, was this hotshot from Charlotte with bushy blond sideburns and dirty fingernails. When I saw them, I couldn't bring myself to dance with him. I ended up dancing hands on shoulders with Alma instead.

I remember we danced to "Danny Boy," with all the other Debs and their dates staring at us. Some of them called us "the Lesbos" because we went to a girls' school. Others called us "nasty" or "naughty" or "queer." A few even used bad words Debutantes weren't supposed to know.

To distract me from all this, Alma made up another story.

Till middle school, the worst word I knew was "busto." Whenever somebody made me mad, I'd call them "busto." I'm guessing I saw part of an old Buster Keaton movie and took it from there.

Alma, on the other hand, claimed she'd started cursing and raising hell by age four.

She'd listen to adults and memorize every dirty word they thought she wouldn't remember. She'd even retell their jokes. Or, at least, the parts that were funny. Sometimes, she'd even make up her own.

One day she got a wild hair up her butt and decided to tell her Momma the dirtiest joke her toddler mind could conjure.

"Why did the chicken cross the road?" she asked.

"I don't know, sugar. Why?" her Momma replied.

"To get five dollars from its baby-daddy. Duh!"

And true to form, Mrs. Claire promptly punished her little potty mouth. But instead of making Alma eat the usual bar of soap, she shoved a tiny sliver up Alma's rear end to, as she put it, "extricate her naughty."

The word "extricate," in my opinion, should be avoided when discussing a four-year-old's backside. Kinda sounds like you're digging for gold back there.

Anywho, the soap irritated Alma's bottom so much that she spent the next few hours on the toilet, ridding herself of every possible "naughty."

Years later, watching those same kinds of Debs and their dates stomp through my spot at Starbucks, I remembered how awful it felt being called "naughty" and "queer." But looking at their young faces, something inside let all that go.

These kids looked so frustrated. So trapped, forced into their suits and ties and crinoline dresses. They looked just as "naughty" as me and Alma, but not nearly as happy. They were living proof that growing up is hard no matter where you do it, and that any real differences between Northerners and Southerners fade away after that chapter on the Civil War in U.S. History—especially when it comes to Cotillion.

Somewhere around my second cup of coffee, I silently forgave the small-town kids from my youth. And right then and there, I learned my final post-Wellingham lesson:

♡ Remember who you are. And be proud of where you came from.

Until I moved to New York, I'd never truly learned this lesson. And as great as Momma, Daddy, Granny Blanche and Granny Ruth always were—no matter how well they raised me—I fell into the same trap that snares a lot of small-town kids: hating my roots.

It's easy to hate the tiny Podunk town you came from . . . until you leave it, that is. Then you start to realize how much you need those roots to survive, and how much they've helped you grow. You look back and finally remember how nice people were, how kind they were to strangers, how good it felt to smile at people you'd meet on the street, and how freeing it was to get by on minimum wage with enough left over for a cup of coffee.

With this in mind, I didn't go straight home that night. After my dinner of coffee, salad and hummus, I took a subway detour into Midtown Manhattan.

When I got off the train, I found myself, once again, standing at the foot of the Empire State Building. I milled around and bought more coffee to keep warm, but mostly I just stared up at its pointy phallic shape.

In Winston, Alma and I always sought out the Big Dick in the sky.

As horrible as the Inquisition, the snobbiness and backward prejudice got, we always looked for it. It pointed the way to Wellingham—the place that taught me an inner strength to carry me through the rest of my life. The place where I developed a self-confidence I never found in public school, where I wouldn't have to compete with boys for the teacher's attention, and where I defined myself by accomplishing, not by looking hot.

Whether coming back from Cotillion or sneaking through a first-floor window, spotting the Big Dick overhead was how Alma and I knew we were home.

Years later, staring up at New York City's favorite phallus in the sky, I felt the same way.

That little girl itching inside her Brownie uniform and washing the dirty sock smell off her nose was ready for bigger adventures. She was free and grown-up and ready to write her life story, full of facts and figures and inaccuracies and cloudy memories. Something wild. Something, some day, she could tell people at parties. A great story about how she became a Debutante as rebellious as Scarlett O'Hara . . .

And, okay, sure: She'd heard the old saying, "If I ever get back to Georgia, I'm gonna nail my feet to the ground." But there wasn't a hammer heavy enough to keep her there.

And just between us? Not even Scarlett could swing it.

Epilogue

I wrote *Confessions of a Rebel Debutante* to illustrate my own personal rags-to-riches, not-quite-Cinderella story. Mine is a firsthand look at what it's like to grow up a fat kid in a small town, picking mosquito bites and catfish guts off your overalls, be thrown into all-girls' school to "become a lady," rebel against your Southern upbringing enough to get yourself almost kicked out of school and absolutely rejected from Debutante society, and then wind up going to Brown and becoming a soap opera writer. Go figure.

Given all this, just so you know: I was always destined to write. I'd already memorized whole books of Bible stories when I was just three years old. By the time I was five, I'd started pulling random folks off the street into my house and forcing them to read to me. I wrote three or four novellas in middle school, and my first real "big girl" Christmas present was an electric typewriter—followed by a desktop computer by the age of fourteen. And in rural North Carolina in

1995, not too many folks even knew how to spell "computer." Years later, like any other small-town girl who moved to the big city with stars in her eyes, I had good times and bad. But also like so many people who leave their hometowns searching for something better, I ultimately learned to love the South so much more for having left it, and in New York, I finally learned that there's no place like home—even if it's not the home you grew up in.

By 2007, I'd started writing down all my crazy adventures, and by 2008, I had a book deal and a website (www.RebelDebutante.com). A few weeks later, I went back to Winston to visit and met the good ol' boy of my dreams—my very own Rhett Butler. Today, after penning episodes for two networks, ABC and CBS, I'm no longer working on soaps, but I'm happy, settled and above all more proud of my Southern roots than ever before. I'm in love with my present but I still cherish my past. And I'll always remember the bright, intelligent, talented women I went to high school with, all the teachers who opened my eyes to learning, and the Wellingham faculty who never gave up on the Rebel Deb in their charge—who, instead, taught me to respect myself and my ambitions above all else. I've always had these kinds of stories and people and places that I wanted to talk about and share. I just hope somebody—somewhere—gets a good laugh out of them. 'Cause let me tell you, every time I hear a Diana Ross song or turn on the TV and see Jill Zarin, *I* sure do. Life is funny. At this point, I've learned to laugh at all its jokes. I just hope milk doesn't come shooting out of my nose when I do.

Acknowledgments

I'm so grateful to have Putnam; my wonderful editor, Rachel Kahan; my friend and mentor, Amy Handlesman; my best friend/badass, Nikki Marterre; and my loyal agents, John Silbersack, Ricki Olshan, John Bauman, and Gayla Nethercott, to nurture and support both sides of me—the Rebel and the Deb.